BE PREPARED

ROBERT E. KIRSCH AND EMILY RAY

BE PREPARED

Doomsday Prepping in the United States

COLUMBIA UNIVERSITY PRESS

NEW YORK

Columbia University Press
Publishers Since 1893
New York   Chichester, West Sussex

Library of Congress Cataloging-in-Publication Data
Names: Kirsch, Robert E., author. | Ray, Emily
(Political scientist), author.
Title: Be prepared : doomsday prepping in the United States /
Robert E. Kirsch and Emily Ray.
Description: New York : Columbia University Press, 2025. |
Includes bibliographical references and index.
Identifiers: LCCN 2024021672 (print) | LCCN 2024021673 (ebook) |
ISBN 9780231204262 (hardback) | ISBN 9780231204279 (trade paperback) |
ISBN 9780231555456 (ebook)
Subjects: LCSH: Emergency management—United States—History. |
Survivalism—United States—History. | Preparedness—Social
aspects—United States—History. | Preparedness—Political
aspects—United States—History. | Self-reliance—United States. |
Democracy—United States. | Middle class—United States. |
Civil defense—United States. | Americans—Attitudes.
Classification: LCC HV551.3 .K63 2025 (print) |
LCC HV551.3 (ebook) | DDC 363.34/8—dc23/eng/20240624

Cover design: Chang Jae Lee
Cover image: © Shutterstock

CONTENTS

ACKNOWLEDGMENTS

THIS PROJECT began in 2018 when Emily sent Robert a short article on a doomsday-prepping start-up out of Silicon Valley. This
seemingly innocuous bit of digital effluvia turned into conference papers, reflections in web zines, and academic articles. It grew
larger still during the lockdowns of the coronavirus pandemic, when
it turned into a book proposal. Between then and now, we are fortunate to have many people to thank for their thoughtful and intense
engagement with this ongoing research project. We are humbled to
recognize them here; starting from the end seems appropriate in more
ways than one.

We were fortunate enough to receive a fellowship in residence from
the Käte Hamburger Centre for Apocalyptic and Post-Apocalyptic
Studies (CAPAS) at the University of Heidelberg in Germany during the
2022–2023 academic year. While we have worked together on many
projects going back to our years as graduate students, living in a cam-
pus community with scholars from around the world with the
express purpose of working on this project made it come together far
more completely than it would have otherwise. CAPAS is a truly
remarkable place, made possible by an exceptional core of people:
Robert Folger, Felicitas Loest, Laura Mendoza, Jenny Stuemer, Michael P.
Dunn, Theresa Meerwarth, Eva Bergdolt, Gregor Kohl, Ute Von Fig-
ura, and the student research assistants. The intellectual culture

they foster through working groups, workshops, and presentations encouraged us to be at our best and gave us the time and space to build our research projects. They facilitated opportunities in the broader university community, including Heidelberg's Centre for American Studies, and supported research presentations at the University of Frankfurt's Normative Orders group. Other fellows at the center provided constructive feedback even at our most stubborn: Florian Mussgnug, Patricia Murietta-Flores, Elke Schwarz, Amin Samman, Nina Boy, Brad Evans, Adolfo Mantilla, and Teresa Heffernan. They also generously invited us to collaborate or present research at their institutions, so we are also grateful to the Queen Mary University TheoryLAB, the Political Economy Research Centre at City College London, and the National Institute of Anthropology and History in Mexico City.

Before our time at CAPAS, we remain grateful for the intellectual communities that would have interdisciplinary critical political theorists like us. The Environmental Political Theory working group has long provided us with an intellectual home and serious engagement with any research project we have. The Caucus for a Critical Political Science encourages work by critically engaged scholars within the discipline of political science. Many members of these groups overlap, so in alphabetical order the present work owes gratitude to Ira Allen, Andrew Biro, Teena Gabrielson, John Hultgren, Jennifer Lawrence, Sean Parson, James Rowe, Andy Scerri, Cedar Welker, Sarah Wiebe, and Mary Witlacil. Chad Lavin was vital to our entrainment as scholars, and his work has always been so clear and compelling that we consciously aspire to do the same.

We were part of Holum Press, a writing collective that published essays when this project was in its proof-of-concept stage. Their feedback and encouragement were vital in developing this project into a manuscript, but even more importantly, it provided a community to workshop any and all ideas, make attempts at creative writing, learn how to use a Perfect Binder, and produce documents in LaTeX: Charlotte Ballard, Taylor Hines, Devin Howard, Andrew Dana Hudson, Benjamin Lobato, Samantha Poelstra, Susie Seal, and Joshua Vincent. The oasis remains on the horizon.

Emily would like to thank her dissertation committee members, who were foundational during her graduate school years and provided a supportive and challenging mentorship that she has come to understand is a very fortunate experience: Timothy Luke, Chad Lavin, Mark Barrow, and Eileen Crist. She thanks dear friends for support, co-thinking, and generally putting up with her while she thought out loud and wrung her hands (in alphabetical order and certainly not exhaustive): Julie Anderson, Sam Cohen, Kyla Doughty, Diana Robles, Alyssa Vincent, and colleagues in the Political Science Department at Sonoma State University. She thanks Robert Kirsch, who, beyond a coauthor, is a dear friend and, whether he likes it or not, a lifelong one at that. Finally, Emily thanks her parents and family, especially her small unit at home, for telling her to keep going, keep going.

Robert would like to thank the School of Applied Professional Studies at Arizona State University for ongoing support of his research, as well as the critically engaged scholars who have given feedback in some form or another on the present work: Taylor Hines, Nicole K. Mayberry, Benjamin Y. Fong, Craig Calhoun, Marie Wallace, David Corlett, and Erica Peters. Robert also thanks the International Herbert Marcuse Society for its support and critical engagement with various pieces or drafts of this manuscript: Terry Maley, Andrew Lamas, and Peter-Erwin Jansen. Thanks to William Viestenz and Brandon W. Kliewer for their thoughtful engagement at every stage of this project, even beyond the bounds of collegiality or reason, and to the countless friends and family who provided support even if he didn't deserve it.

We thank Columbia University Press, which has supported our work throughout. In particular, our editor, Stephen Wesley, has championed our project, facilitated helpful peer reviews, and maintained open communication throughout every step of the project. His attention and professionalism allowed us to focus on the manuscript. Rob Fellman copyedited the manuscript. Any remaining errors belong to us.

We want to acknowledge our longstanding intellectual collaborations, formal and informal, extending back to 2008, when we were graduate students sharing an office. We are lucky that arguments never lead to acrimony (they usually just lead to lunch) and that our collaborative work is more than the sum of its parts. Finally, we want to dedicate this manuscript to Tim Luke, our teacher, mentor, and friend.

BE PREPARED

INTRODUCTION

N A 2021 episode of *Keeping Up with the Kardashians*, Kim and Khloe Kardashian spent a short trial period inside an Atlas doomsday bunker to test out the conditions of hunkering down through a disaster, although with the expectation that they would be able to reemerge into the life they left outside of the shelter. Also in 2021, the design magazine *Dezeen* ran an online story about homes and kits that provided increased chances of surviving apocalypse, and in 2018 *Interview* magazine featured a list of quotes from notable doomsday preppers about their approach to anticipating apocalyptic conditions. While doomsday prepping is ordinarily thought of as a paranoid activity on the social fringes of everyday life, these instances of prepping instead show up in mainstream popular culture and in the output of cultural tastemakers. As prepping moves from the edge to the center of cultural consumption, what does this tell us about the state of politics in the United States and about what it means to anticipate the end of the world? This book seeks to address these questions through a political theorization of doomsday prepping in the United States and by drawing out the political possibilities of what it means to live in a society that bunkers. Yet this work moves beyond the bunker and the culture of prepping: this book is about the neoliberal foreclosure of the future, how prepping and bunkering structure the very possibilities of politics, how the prepping subject is produced, and what the future looks like with the prepping subject populating it. How does the bunker structure inform theorizing about statecraft, neoliberalism, and democracy?

A preoccupation with end times and preparedness exceeds the prepping household. In January 2023, the Bulletin of the Atomic Scientists updated their famous "doomsday clock" to be "90 seconds to midnight."[1] This is the closest yet to the "midnight" of nuclear annihilation, according to the agency. The furthest from midnight was seventeen minutes in 1991, thanks to the "new era" of the end of the Cold War—good enough to break the fifteen-minute scale envisioned for the clock because of the "consensus . . . that the world was changing in fundamental and positive ways."[2] The subsequent decades seem to indicate that those fundamental and positive ways did not materialize. While this book does not address all of the myriad risks, insecurities, and weak points manifesting in the global order in those years, it does ask, in the context of the United States, why there is such anxiety around preparing for doomsday. Perhaps the way to put the kinds of questions this book seeks to answer is why a clock set a mere fifteen minutes from nuclear annihilation was assumed to be the *best-case scenario.*

This is not to say that the threats, challenges, and insecurities facing American society are immaterial, the nuclear varieties not least among them. Surely the uneven, patchwork response to the coronavirus pandemic has demonstrated a justifiable skepticism in the ability of state and other institutional actors to provide a robust program to protect public health and ensure social cohesion. The threats to security are international, too. The musings over "tactical" nuclear deployment to hasten the end of the Russian invasion of Ukraine reanimate old fears about the prospects of all-out thermonuclear war.[3] In some sense, it might be prudent to prepare for a variety of contingencies. Yet not all preparative measures are the same, and not all preparers have the same access to resources. There is a very clear distinction between a well-coordinated public response managed by the state and functioning social institutions, on the one hand, and the idea of individuals "prepping" by accumulating, maintaining, and deploying a cache of consumer goods, on the other. This book argues that anxieties about catastrophic disintegration and the need to prepare for it are woven into the political fabric of American society, as well as the (perhaps justified) assumption that the state is not able to provide adequate security in the face of uncertainty under the regime of neoliberalism, thus leaving it up to individual volition to withstand the vicissitudes of an uncertain future. In this sense, the *worst-case scenario* is baked into everyday life as a distinctly American phenomenon; it is a mere fourteen minutes away from the best-case scenario. Out of this framework comes the idea of "prepping" as a mode of living that predates neoliberalism but merges easily into its political schema of responsibilized political subjects.

CONTAINING "PREPPING"

Prepping has become a mainstream activity in the United States. One does not need to look very far to see the increasing market for prepping materials, such as voluminous amounts of shelf-stable food at wholesalers, Silicon Valley start-ups producing bug-out bags, or the steady stream of reality television shows designed around prepping, going off-grid, or extreme survivalism. This mainstream version of prepping could easily be dismissed as a kind of extreme camping or as the peculiar behaviors of social outliers. However, doing so does not explain why prepping has become increasingly mainstream, and it ignores the question of why prepping has become the de facto response to myriad problems—apocalyptic or otherwise. This book takes up the phenomenon of prepping with an eye to just these broader questions, to see how prepping feeds into a certain kind of politics that is viable in contemporary America.

Prepping is seemingly simple to define: preparing for anticipated disruptions to the flow of everyday life. In this sense, prepping is a normal activity of well-regulated adults who might buy a few extra groceries ahead of a snowstorm or even anticipate some variation in the social and environmental status quo for which having a surplus of life's necessities—and maybe some pleasures—would be useful, even if the specific disrupting event is not yet known. Yet prepping also denotes stockpiling supplies for weeks, months, or years of living in isolation in a world that is so severely ruptured there is no guarantee of a stable state, society, or economy. A prepper might have extra cans of shelf-stable food on hand, or they might have a basement room dedicated to fabricating bullets from a 3-D printer. While we acknowledge the breadth and depth of what prepping can mean to different people in different circumstances, we deliberately avoid cataloguing different types of prepping and attempting to find arbitrary boundaries among "normal," "crisis," and "extreme" prepping. Rather, we argue that prepping is a set of practices fundamental to the American way of life, traceable from the rapid onset of industrialization at the turn of the twentieth century, evidenced in the Boy Scouts of America, through the atomic age of the mid-twentieth century, and in the new space race of the twenty-first century.

Preparation is an expansive concept, of course, and one could easily find fertile grounds for a whole career in the detailed history of statecraft, military preparedness, zoning laws, or religious movements preparing for an eschatological rupture. The plan of the present work, however, is to tightly bind the analysis to the mass consumption of industrial production, resulting in a hegemonic practice that is commonly referred to as "prepping." Prepping in this sense is defined as a manifestation of consumer society that, against the backdrop of skepticism of the state's ability to provide meaningful social support and the attendant anxiety about disintegrating social life, compels individuals to accumulate, hoard, and stockpile consumer goods in such quantities and in such places as to "ride out" events that disrupt, destroy, or derail the status quo of their everyday lives. Drivers of prepping behavior can take on apocalyptic dimensions such as anticipating the detonation of nuclear, neutron, or "dirty" bombs that render the surface of Earth inhospitable if not uninhabitable. They might also foresee a degraded electrical grid and telecommunications system, either from electromagnetic pulse attacks or an unlucky solar flare. They might anticipate a retreat from (real or imagined) civil unrest or extreme weather events. In any of these, the logic is similar: the social fabric is frayed and brittle, and any number of things can degrade it to the point of absolute dysfunction. The ideological thrust of the prepper's solution is to accumulate and wisely use a hoard of consumer goods to make it through to the other side. Prepping has little to do with the collective action and planning problems of social preparedness to deal with global climate change, mass migration patterns (which are also accelerating in the face of global climate change), or military hostilities. Rather, prepping takes the shape of "opt-out" politics where individuals attempt to remove and repurpose a parallel everyday life that runs alongside the mass production and mass politics of the current context; the origins of opt-out politics, the anxieties opting out seeks to assuage, and the extent to which such schemes are desirable or even possible will run through this book. It is also the contention of this book that such anxieties and the seductive appeal of opt-out politics are not recent but are in fact woven into the institutional fabric of American political society. Prepper culture in the way we outline it is a uniquely American phenomenon.

Thus, we begin with the institutional development of American politics, which we do not intend as a linear history. Instead, we look at various social movements that emerged during rapid industrialization in the United States in the early twentieth century in response to the rise of mass production and mass consumption and how Americans saw themselves in relation to these developments. We look at what kinds of self-conceptions persist, what kind of ideals were mythologized, and how these movements are part of the reordering of American life into a consumer society made possible by mass production. We also tie these movements to myths of national character such as self-reliance and the need to take personal responsibility, even during upheavals at a more social scale, so that by the time we take up the Cold War bunker, the American imaginary of responding to crises by bunkering and assuming personal responsibility for preparedness dovetails with the broader onset of neoliberalism. This pairing also helps us explain the space race, outer space sovereignty and resource extraction, and off-world colonization efforts.

PREPPING AND WHITE NATIONALISM

White supremacy and masculinity are often joined through an identity politics of their own, one formed through grievance, a sense of loss, nostalgia for a fantastical past, and a victimization narrative.[4] In the United States, white supremacy, particularly among men, has found an affinity with prepping and survivalist subcultures. From Ruby Ridge to Charlottesville, the sense of history being overtaken by modernity has prompted violence and bunkering behavior. Yet bunkering and prepping are not inherently a white masculinist project. We argue that bunkering and prepping have long been features of American politics. While many subcultures take up prepping and survivalism, the prepping and survivalism of bunker society are not reducible to these subcultural groups. Casey Ryan Kelly explains the preoccupation with white masculinity as an identity as one of mistaking absence for loss. Working through Freud and Marcuse, he argues that the powerful, virile white men who supposedly sat atop the social, economic, and political hierarchy never existed, but the movement of white male victimhood has reconstructed a mythic past of a powerful white man who is now threatened by the relocation of industrial jobs to other countries, waves of migration from the global south, and a feminist movement that has threatened the gender binary and the gendered/racial relations of power that favor white men: "Put differently, because one can never recover what one never had, conflating the historicity of loss with the transhistoricity of absence mistakes lack for a specific traumatic event or violent interruption of the psyche. Thus, the general precarity common to human existence can be reinterpreted as a discrete traumatic event that is more characteristic of loss than of lack."[5]

The white male identity hinges on a presumed past supremacy that emerged naturally, rather than as a consequence of structural violence from institutionalized racism, sexism, and imperialism. Many of those under the sway of this identity forecast a doomed future emerging from this runaway modernity of civil rights, feminism, and, in their estimation, overly porous borders. One way to fortify themselves against this future is to prepare for worsening conditions and bunker down to survive them: "Doomsday preppers, survivalists, mass shooters, men's rights activists, pro-gun activists, demagogues, and white supremacists alike cling to life in the name of death. Their apocalyptic fantasies are organized around compulsive repetition, masochism, and melancholia—they carry death with them every-where they go."[6]

Bolstering the attitudes and actions of people who fear this future, pop culture reinforces the message that there is good reason to be fearful, to be aggrieved, and to desire surviving to rebuild the world as it was always meant to be. "Postapocalyptic American television of this era arguably fetishizes these politics: the survival of the white het-erosexual nuclear family is conservative white wish fulfillment, as whatever catastrophe wipes out most of the human race also clears the way for the return of the unchallenged white patriarchy."[7] Doomsday prepping in this vector is less preoccupied with avoiding cataclysmic events than with preparing for race war, reasserting masculine domi-nance, and, in the wake of such massive social and political disrup-tions, reclaiming the rightful mantle of superiority. "The overarching lesson of American doomsday culture is that the future is indefinite but that hegemonic white masculinity—aggression, self-reliance, sto-icism, competitiveness—remains necessary."[8] This persistent myth reaches back into the scouting movements of the early twentieth cen-tury. These anxieties and myths are not new; bunkerization is a more contemporary iteration of the old Boy Scout motto: "Be Prepared."

While these observations make strong connections among race, gender, and prepping, Kelly contends that prepping was once a fringe activity that is now moving into the mainstream. We argue the oppo-site is true: prepping has always been a mainstream American activ-ity and indeed an institution. While reality television programs draw attention to subcultural acts of prepping, these programs are not pull-ing prepping out of the fringes. The pop cultural interest in prepping does reveal, however, the deep veins of white supremacy and sexism that characterize prepping in the United States as part of the effort to reclaim a world, now or in the postapocalyptic future, from those ruinous forces of modernity, including multiculturalism, gender par-ity, queerness, and shifting economic landscapes. Kelly joins mascu-linity and whiteness as an identity, one that propels some white men toward prepping and survivalism not just to survive a catastrophe or world-ending event but to prepare a postapocalyptic world in their own image:

Doomsday preppers argue that the feminine attributes that characterize modernity are ultimately unsustainable luxuries that will
inevitably collapse into barbarism. Simulating the apocalypse, then,
is an opportunity for white men to display masculine traits as a set
of survival tools—the antidote for a crumbling and emasculated
society. Longing to resuscitate a past that never existed, doomsday
preppers seek to domesticate the trauma of white masculinity's dis-
placement by promising a future in which white men are restored
to their proper place in both nature and the social order. In short,
the apocalypse serves as the ultimate resolution to the so-called crisis of masculinity.[9]

Just as some evangelical groups welcome end times and the second
coming of Christ, the white male prepper may happily anticipate the
end of a feminized culture that victimizes white men and their natural place in the social hierarchy so that they, the survivors of the apocalypse, can remake the world as it ought to be organized.

In Bring the War Home, Katherine Belew describes the American
white power movement as one that transcends national boundaries
to unite white people around the world and that may have some patriotic attachments but ultimately seeks to defend and build a white
supremacist world in the face of oppressive governments and states,
the United States among those that cannot be fully trusted.[10] Belew
traces this to the Vietnam War era, a period of white supremacy that
is related to but distinct from the eras that preceded it and firmly in
the Cold War period of bunkerization. Whereas early white power
movements in the United States were part of and supportive of the
state, movements that gained traction around the Vietnam War and
after were skeptical or antistate. The white power movement in the
1980s and 1990s increasingly embraced an apocalyptic evangelicalism
that required congregants to rid the world of the unworthy, a turn
from the evangelical movements and churches that readied themselves for rapture before the period of tribulation.

Instead, they held that the faithful would be tasked with ridding the
world of the unfaithful, the world's nonwhite and Jewish population,
before the return of Christ. At the very least, the faithful would have

to outlast the great tribulation, a period of bloodshed and strife. Many movement followers prepared by becoming survivalists: stocking food and learning to administer medical care. Other proponents of white cosmologies saw it as their personal responsibility to amass arms and train themselves to take part in a coming end-times battle that would take the shape of a race war.[11]

White supremacy, survivalism, and bracing for apocalyptic conditions form one version of prepping culture and what drives prepping behaviors. Many white supremacist groups suspect the government of interfering with white power through progressive social and political change: guaranteeing reproductive rights, extending some civil rights to the LGBTQIA+ communities, and, most critically, allegedly ceding power to the imaginary Zionist Occupational Government, a world order of Jews masterminding the demise of the white race through control of banks, media, and culture—the classic antisemitic trope of the wandering Jew upending traditional societies with modernity and progressivism. The failures of the Vietnam War and the ongoing fear of a communist takeover made inroads between prepping and broader cultural shifts during the middle of the twentieth century. Much like mainstream approaches to prepping, white power movements concerned themselves with the integrity of the nuclear family and protecting the free market. White power groups, as extremists, constitute a more violent, paranoid, and antigovernment version of prepping, but one with critical intersections in the everyday movements that characterize prepping as an institution. White supremacy after the Vietnam War, in Belew's account, organized around defeating militarized state power with a paramilitarized countermovement to bring an apocalyptic conclusion to the faltering state and usher in a white postapocalypse worth living in. While there is an unnerving overlap between prepping and white power movements, mainstream prepping is not characterized by overcoming the state to force a world-ending conflict. Prepping anticipates multiple apocalyptic conditions and multiple postapocalyptic fantasies and can be rooted in rational planning as well as in violent white nationalist movements, but it is not white supremacist by definition. To account for this variance, we approach prepping as a political institution rather than as a subcultural phenomenon, interest group constituency, or demographic development.

THE APPROACH

Prepping and responding to pending catastrophes can be taken up through many methodological and disciplinary lenses, including ontologizing what is or is not a bunker, what levels of preparation determine prepping, how public policy ordinances and zoning laws allow or restrict certain kinds of prepping behavior, and the role of states in prepping, militarily or otherwise, in their sovereign capacity. All of these are worthy objectives, although our project asks a set of questions that we believe precedes these considerations: What are the political conditions whereby prepping has become the normalized response to crisis? How did those conditions come about? And how do they shape our possible futures as a result? To get at this ideological question, our approach centers on interpreting the phenomenon of prepping in the United States through the lenses of critical political theory and the institutionalism of Thorstein Veblen, with the goal of producing a diagnosis and critique of neoliberalism as a political project and a series of cultural and economic relations. Synthesizing these bodies of theory allows us to build an analysis of prepping as part of the ideology of—and cultural dominance of—neoliberalism, which valorizes individual responsibility and discourages state action. It also allows us to see how prepping drives the institutional evolution of neoliberalism as an emergent set of economic relations. Doing so will contextualize the neoliberal project both historically and culturally.

VEBLEN'S INSTITUTIONALISM

Thorstein Veblen is one of the originators of the institutionalist approach in political economy. How he fits into the current landscape of institutional economics is a different project, but we marshal him here for his theory of institutional evolution, which suggests that economic developments were always already co-constitutive with the morass of cultural, political, and historical experiences of people. Veblen was not only an economist; he offered (often acerbic) social critique as well. The approach that we adopt from Veblen posits that political phenomena as well as the preconditions for possible social change are co-constituted by two factors: the mode of production (what Veblen called "the machine process") and the "habits of mind" that they impart to those who engage the relations of production. These are co-constitutive in Veblen's approach because they shape each other in an evolutionary fashion—the machine process that imparts habits of mind is also the machine process that is developed according to those same habits of mind. Veblen is adamant that there is no teleological register to this relationship; contra Hegel and Marx (at least as he read them), he insisted that without a mediating force, the "blind drift" between this codetermination could produce any variety of social forms, with no overarching sense of progress or direction that necessarily culminates in a more just society. The mediating force that guides these changes, Veblen posits, is institutions, which can outlast human life spans and direct human energies toward specific goals, although whether they can be directed for the good cannot be assumed.

This dynamic of various forces shaping one another is what Veblen has in mind when he analyzes America through institutions and how they are guided. In Veblen's framework, institutions are what he calls "going concerns" that form the broad strokes of social evolution in ways that direct, influence, or challenge this interrelation of modes of production and habits of mind. To analyze institutions is thus to have a medium- to long-term analysis of social evolution. There is, of course, the question of what counts as an institution. For Veblen, the notion is expansive—after all, one can think of many different kinds of going concerns. The state, the church, schools, and the military are all obvious examples of institutions, but Veblen suggests that almost all kinds of social movements (or what we might call "civil society" or "voluntary" organizations) are also institutions: civic groups, sporting clubs, interest groups, corporations, booster organizations of small town development, and small businesses. This extends culturally as well to institutions like fashion, advertising, and etiquette. One might think of how Veblen's institutional analysis would show in an ideal world how these institutions organize human action in a way that harmonizes the habits of thought in concert with the productive demands of the machine process to produce a life that allows for individuals to flourish.

Such an ideal world is not in the offing, however, because in Veblen's theorizing, time is out of whack, producing a number of lags. There are two main kinds of lag in Veblen's framework. The short-term lag is that the technological innovation of the machine process moves faster than the cultural habits of mind, making people ill equipped to confront the current moment (or crisis) because they are operating under habits of thought that are no longer relevant. We only need to consider the lag time between financial "innovation" and the regulatory apparatus of finance to see the consequences of this kind of lag. This insight from more than a century ago spurred Veblen to theorize that economics is not an evolutionary science, because the habits of mind of academic economists were about twenty-five years behind the current state of business enterprise and could offer nothing about the present moment or prognosticate on crises. There is also the lag of a more anthropological time scale, where certain habits of mind that might be undesirable nevertheless persist even as technological innovation continues and cultural habits of mind change as well. The pursuit of honorifics, simulating battle, ostentatious waste, and the subjugation of populations are some of the atavistic impulses that get carried through different social formations, even if subconsciously.

In this sense, Veblen's notion of institutionalism is not a "snapshot" model that might be found in contemporary economics or quantitative social science research. Phenomena are always moving, mediated by other forces, and contextualized historically. For Veblen, institutional analysis must take this longer arc into account; social conditions do not just fall out of the sky or emerge from nowhere. To bring this explicitly to the present project on prepping, Veblen's institutional framework tasks us with diagnosing not only the present conditions of why prepping behavior might make sense but also what kind of institutional developments unfolded for this to be the case. The politics of prepping is as much about explaining the political conditions that produce the prepper as it is about what the preppers do at a given time or in a certain context. For this book to analyze how prepping became incorporated into mainstream life in the United States, it must trace back the institutional roots of what habits of mind persist, how the machine process develops, and what kinds of cultural lag and atavistic instincts persist as America underwent industrialization and the production of a consumer society. We argue that institutions like the Boy Scouts of America, the Arts and Crafts movement, and tinkering culture are the expressions of this cultural lag—the habits of thought that are trying to make sense of and keep up with the fast-changing relations of production of industrialization. We show how some atavistic impulses like invidious emulation, conspicuous consumption, and an imperial frontiersman myth of ultimate self-reliance produce a *bunkering subject*, a subject whose answer to existential problems is to fortify the mythical homestead. It is a subject whose prepping politics is the only vision of a livable future, be that on Earth, in outer space, or on another planet. In this way, the institutionalist story of the politics of prepping locates how the prepper is a legible and mainstream object of economic analysis, one operating as a cultural marker of the rise of neoliberalism even as it holds on to bygone and antiquated myths of political subjectivity. The institutionalist story gives a political valence to the subjects who are told that the state will recede and that citizens are on their own, and it shows the cultural habits of mind that make this a practicable arrangement.

FRANKFURT SCHOOL CRITICAL THEORY

Veblen shows us how culture and institutions combine to form habits of mind and the patterns of production that produce a certain way of being in the world. And while he is dubious of the narrative of progress, the institutional evolution of political society could, ideally, produce a qualitatively better world. By the time the Cold War bunker becomes part of the American imaginary and solidified as the domestic embodiment of neoliberal individual responsibility, the determinant habits of thought and relations of production seem stuck. That is, every social challenge takes on apocalyptic proportions, and the solution to problems is to harden the home's carapace through personal consumption choices.

This is where Frankfurt School critical theory, particularly Herbert Marcuse's notion of one-dimensionality, forms the other main contribution to our theoretical grounding because it is able to diagnose the ideological "stuckness" of neoliberalism and its seeming totality. It also allows us to consider prepping not as an empirical fact or as a matter of utility, something to be analyzed solely by observing the discrete behaviors of preppers or identifying the phalanx of public policy that propels it. Instead, Marcuse lays out the ideological project of a one-dimensional society, a society without opposition and where alternatives are almost unthinkable. As Margaret Thatcher infamously noted, "There is no alternative." In such a register, prepping behavior is not a matter of whether it is effective or desirable or meets the moment in a given crisis but in what ways it reifies the consumer society of prepping as a hegemonic myth. This myth becomes politically dominant to the point that it shapes all possible futures, as if prepping and bunkering are the only reactions to any social or political problem.

Marcuse's one-dimensional society "without opposition" is based on an affluent society that reduces citizenship to mass consumption choices, replaces political decision making with technocratic tinkering, and flattens discursive, ethical, and political objections to the existing order by absorbing or producing ersatz opposition to serve its own ends. For Marcuse, the ability to negate the existing order is not an attitudinal posture, like pessimism, but the precondition for social and political change. Negation is the ability to think and strive for a qualitatively different world, one that refuses the existing order so that a new one might be built. Marcuse's thesis is that a one-dimensional society prevents that negation from even emerging, making social change illegible, even unthinkable in everyday life.[12]

We take from our institutional analysis that prepping becomes inscribed into habits of thought and an everyday practice as a matter of mass production and consumer society. We can then integrate Marcuse's analysis to argue that prepping is a one-dimensional activity that precludes forming non-consumer-society alternatives. This helps us avoid getting bogged down in normatively evaluating certain modes of prepping to find the "good ones." As Marcuse reminds us, such negativity can be found, but that search should also serve as a caution about how one-dimensional the dominant cultural myth is. Movements with genuine negativity and that engage in collective preparation are certainly worthy of identifying, but doing so can hide the fact that one-dimensional society can subtly absorb such movements or even produce ersatz "resistance" movements of its own. It would therefore be dangerous to point to a particular group or social movement and hang the hopes of negative thinking there. Therefore, cataloguing the different kinds of prepping movements, from white nationalist compounds to deep green anarchist collectives to ethnic minority prepping groups and evangelical movements, is interesting but beyond the scope of this project. The one-dimensionality thesis is also useful for our analysis because it avoids placing arbitrary markers for public policy, for example, setting the number of days of provisions one should keep on hand. Regardless of whether it is one day or one hundred days, the bunkerized prepping subject is called to enact a certain kind of everyday life that reifies the existing order. The prepping/bunkering individual becomes a legible subject at this juncture where institutional development meets the ideological project of one-dimensional neoliberalism—not in deciding whether one versus two weeks' worth of potable water is optimal.

Finally, Marcuse is unique among Frankfurt School critical theorists in that he especially focuses on the fact that domination is never complete. One-dimensional society portends to absorb all opposition and sources of negation, but like an over-poured concrete structure, that attempt at totality just makes the inevitable cracks all the larger. With this in mind, Marcuse's theory offers scholars a way to engage social movements that tempers expectations for liberatory potential. Maybe some movements were once sources of opposition but are no longer. Perhaps they have always been in the thrall of the one-dimensional society. Conceivably, they may show a promising way out of the bunker. In any case, the political questions this raises go far beyond what kinds of preppers are "good" and which kinds of prepping "work." Rather, it raises the underlying political question of how prepping reifies existing structures and to think through what it would actually look like to strive for a different world.

READING NEOLIBERALISM

With these two theoretical poles in mind, we also read neoliberalism in two registers: as an ideology and as a set of institutional arrangements. Ideologically, neoliberalism operates like many other dominant ideas of the ruling class; it is a set of ideas that support the ruling class and circulate through society as natural truths. The ideological tenets of neoliberalism function in this way, making it appear to be an expression of human nature in institutional and relational form, which shapes everyday life. We apply this everyday life of neoliberalism to the conditions for disaster and for preparing in limited, individualistic, and market-based ways that reify those ideological assumptions. Operating between these poles provides flexibility to analyze how the ideology works on the ground and as a set of ideas that participates in the foreclosure of collective and democratic responses to collectively experienced catastrophe. That is, while neoliberalism as a global order might be on the way out, it explains why the everyday life of a neoliberalized subject may persist in our habits of mind. This also points to the institutional strictures of possible futures and why habits of mind persist even as structures change. We cannot simply wish away or opt out of institutional arrangements.

Neoliberalism has a long history, first in Europe and then in the United States. Neoliberalism diverges from liberalism in key ways, which track with some assertions made by the neoreactionary movement. Advocates of neoliberalism and liberalism agree that "there is no such thing as a stable free market or pristine capitalism," but "whereas social liberals consider social and economy inequality the devil of capitalism, neoliberals believe in the need to achieve greater stability under conditions of capitalism and inequality." In 1951, Milton Friedman wrote the essay "Neo-Liberalism and Its Prospects" well before neoliberalism took hold as a global phenomenon. Friedman anticipated a slow drift from what he perceived as the collectivism of the midcentury toward a new liberalism that borrows from its nineteenth-century predecessors but updates the role of the state in relation to the economy. Neoliberalism "gives high place to a severe limitation on the power of the state to interfere in the detailed activities of individuals; at the same time, it must explicitly recognize that there are important positive functions that must be performed by the state." Instead of the laissez-faire, "hands-off" state, neoliberalism requires the state to "police the system, establish conditions favorable to competition and prevent monopoly, provide a stable monetary framework, and relieve acute misery and distress." The citizen would be buffered from state overreach by "the existence of a private market; and against one another by the preservation of competition." Friedman sees the individual as an economic unit who can only be efficiently and freely organized through the private, free market. The market must be protected by the state, which can provide a stable operating environment. Unlike libertarianism, Friedman's neoliberalism sees the state as more than the enforcer of bare minimum rules to maintain social order; rather, the state is in service to the market, which is the guarantor of personal liberty. Collective action, unionization, and other means of working together toward common goals are antithetical to the neoliberal "faith," as Friedman calls it. The state's absence is selectively managed to protect corporate capital flows instead of producing for the common good.[13]

Phillip Mirowski and Dieter Plehwe argue that neoliberalism developed as a response to liberalism and socialism and as such is "flexible in its intellectual commitments [and] oriented towards forging some new doctrines that might capture the imaginations of future generations." Mirowski and Plehwe identify key tenets of neoliberalism that tend to persist across a range of neoliberal writings and applications, including a tight link between individual freedom and a competitive market anchored in private property; the right to plan one's life without surrendering will or liberty to a central planning organ; viewing the state as an all-consuming juggernaut that limits individual freedom; holding that politics weakens the practice and use of science to make informed, rational decisions; and believing that a limited government means limited politics in a given society.[14]

Wendy Brown offers a useful view of contemporary neoliberalism not just as a way to organize economic policies and practices but as an ideology that conditions the political subject as the economic subject. Neoliberalism does not call for state absence from economic affairs; it is not a strain of libertarianism. Instead, it calls for the right types of regulation and deregulation to liberate capital and labor from state-imposed restrictions while regulating markets in ways that allow corporations to set their own labor and environmental standards. The neoliberal state is one of managed absence of the state from social life, whereby the state turns over responsibility for social needs like healthcare, employment, childcare, public safety, and the right to be housed to the market while allowing these markets to operate with little state interference. The state exists and is still powerful, but it wields that power in such a way to be cooperative with the needs of capital. What then of the neoliberal subject? The individual is exposed to the conditions of everyday life with few social safety nets and diminishing opportunities for democratic activity as public decisions are increasingly made in boardrooms and over dinners paid for by any given special interest's lobby. Brown argues that the political subject of the state is remade as the economic subject of the market, a person for whom participating as a citizen is routed away from collective decision making on public issues in public spaces and instead toward privatizing public concerns and decisions as individual problems solved through consumption. Individual consumer choices are simply a product of rational choice or just people duped by marketing schemes. As Adam Kotsko puts it: "Neoliberalism confronts us with forced choices that serve to redirect the blame for social problems onto the ostensible poor decision making of individuals."[15] Kotsko critiques Brown's commitment to the binary division of the sphere of economy from the sphere of the political and further holds that "the political" is not necessarily where "the good life" exists but is where people *fight* for the good life. Therefore, it is worth noting that to critique neoliberalism is not to suggest that there exists a sharp distinction between economics and politics and that neoliberalism simply destroys the sphere of politics. It is also worth pointing out that neoliberalism as an ideology of everyday life and institutional behavior gets inscribed at a deep level of political subjectivity. While it is certainly true that the international neoliberal order may be ending (or has been over for some time), that does not mean that the habits of mind or institutional arrangements do not carry over. Instead, we put forward that neoliberalism is a set of ideas, institutions, and practices that restructure the relationship between economics and politics such that political commitments are in service to mobilizing and liberating capital and institutions that benefit from this arrangement at the expense of a political and economic order that prioritizes democracy, alleviates suffering, and produces the conditions for living well in a way conceived of that goes beyond the mere accumulation of wealth and power.

PREPPING TOWARD BUNKERIZATION

In discussing prepping, we spend considerable time on the material manifestation of the bunker in American society and the way the bunker as a discourse circulates across socioeconomic levels and political ideologies and identities. We use the bunker not as a case study or as a central object for inquiry but rather as a discursive site that we extend to build a theory of *bunkerization*: an organizing logic of the everyday practices of what appears to be rational behaviors for preparing for and managing risk and disaster in American life, which are shaped by institutional configurations. Because of this, the purpose of theorizing bunkerization is not to determine the ontology of bunkers once and for all or to create a typology of people who bunker, even less to gawk at bunkering and the ways in which people choose to avert and survive disaster. Rather, the bunker provides conceptual utility as a way to frame and extend the characteristics of a bunker into a more generalizable way of organizing life around threat and risk. This way of organizing life does not even require a physical bunker; thinking with a bunker mentality is how people mobilize, we will argue, for possible unknown futures.

Neoliberalism as ideology and institution becomes a hegemonic idea that is emblematic of the foreclosure of democratic and collective institutional arrangements for addressing climate change and other disasters. It creates an eternal present with a path dependency that makes prepping or bunkering appear rational. The politics of prepping is not what people are doing or what their behaviors are but rather how prepping came to be legible and what possibilities come out of it. Here we find options from green authoritarianism to solar punks and green anarchism; they contain many overlapping behaviors but different aims for the future. We are not making political prescriptions, but we are also not quietly championing these alternatives.

Indeed, we are not advocating for any of the prefabricated green solutions to these defined and described problems. Instead, we work to take stock of where we are, how we got here, and why we struggle to create alternatives that are novel and qualitatively different.

One of the commitments of this book is to describe and understand subjects in a cultural, ideological, and institutional configuration, not to describe what individual Americans do when they fear horrifying conditions. The "we" or subjects of this volume are people who are conditioned by this context. Different groups scout, tinker, and bunker. We hope different Americans will also be called to step outside of the bunker and address crises differently. "We" is, then, a stand-in for subjects who are called into various subjectivities that are shaped by the coproduction of cultural, economic, and political forces that are, in turn, shaped by people who are also embodied subjectivities. Ultimately, the "we" is not an aggregate of individual Americans and their collective motivations; "we" is a way to describe those of us who live in these configurations, in these times.

SIDESTEPPING PSYCHOANALYSIS

We will use a lot of what might look like traditionally psychoanalytic terminology in this book—*fear*, *anxiety*, and so forth. And while there is a rich tradition of using psychoanalytic concepts that emerge from Freud and those he influenced as a way to engage in a critical theory of society, we sidestep it in this analysis.[16] We have made the conscious decision to avoid this terrain because we are committed to an *institutional* analysis. We make no claims about whether psychoanalysis can offer a complementary, contradictory, or parallel analysis, but what we think keeps our project out of the psychoanalytic register is that we have structured the argument in such a way that does not question the intrinsic motivations of people. Nor do we seek to explain through individuated means why members of given groups engage in prepping behavior. In other words, we are not able to diagnose what Americans "really think" or if they actually believe that their prepping behavior is an effective way to confront the manifold crises of the current context.

The justification for this move is twofold. First, one of the upshots of Veblen's theory of institutional evolution is that it centers institutional development as the driving force of historical development. The codeterminant interplay of institutional survival—both the habits of thought that the machine process imparts to people who engage it as well as how those same people then shape further iterations of the machine process—works to explain the historical circumstances in which certain behaviors are valorized and provides an instinctual analysis that is not rooted in the general psyche of humanity as such. In other words, the machine process and institutional arrangements produce iterations of instincts at different times that could, but might not always, carry over as Veblen's cultural lags build up. Thus, institutional analysis from a Veblenian perspective means that humans have instincts for things like idle curiosity, a parental bent, or workmanship and that these are tempered by the machine process and the habits of mind that are imparted through the lived experience of people caught up in the process, rather than being expressions of the individual psyche and unconscious. This also goes for how institutional development also brings with it old habits of mind that get expressed in peculiar ways, such as invidious emulation, honorifics, or conspicuous consumption. When we discuss certain modes of everyday life or behavior in the United States, then, we will make instinctual claims but ones that are mediated by the machine process, without any normative or teleological reasoning behind them, such as that they are repressed, deformed, or productive/destructive. Veblenian analysis resists such teleological thinking.

Second, our survey of "prepping" has yielded a wide array of prepping behavior that resists connecting a specific intrinsic motivation to a specific kind of behavior—that is, what makes a prepper look different in a number of registers. We will make the case that prepping historically looks different at different points in time. We also find that even in the current context, the stated motivations of preppers vary so wildly that although they may often be portrayed as part of a reactionary right, there are many leftist, anarchist, or minority groups that engage in prepping behavior as well.[17] We think it is too easy to lose the specificity of these vectors of prepping behavior and collapse them into psychoanalytic drive theory. It is also too dispersed a concept as a matter of intensity. That is, part of defining "prepping" is purely contingent in the first place. The prudence of keeping, say, ten days' worth of supplies (and which kinds of supplies) might not be "prepping" behavior, but maybe keeping twenty days' worth of supplies is. Where one draws the line from prudence to prepping is purely a matter of context. It is therefore not possible to demarcate the boundaries of prepping as a matter of intrinsic drives, like we might with obsession, melancholia, and so on. We also must remark that part of the reticence to tread on psychoanalytic grounds is a lack of expertise on our part. This might be a disciplinary or dispositional problem, but in any event, while we cannot foreclose the psychoanalytic dimension of our analysis of prepping, a Veblenian institutional evolution analysis explains behaviors in its own methodologically sound way that hopefully can provide the material basis for, support, or complement psychoanalytic inquiry.

THE LAYOUT

The Boy Scouts issued a turn-of-the-century warning to "Be Prepared," and the handicraft movement elevated tinkering to an ethical response to the conditions of industrialization. The nuclear age reiterated the tight linkage between being a good American and being prepared, which, coupled with the rise of neoliberalism and another tide of anticommunist panic in the United States, helped shape what being prepared meant and against which dangers. As the Cold War anxieties slowly opened into generalized anxieties about violent clashes fighting centuries-old racist institutions, fear of the widening wealth gap, and eventually climate change, turning to the market to prepare for anything and to have the provisions of bunkering, even above ground, became just good sense. Outer space, preserved as a permanent exterior to the planet and an object of environmental management, is an ideal place to project escapist fantasies as the final frontier of bugging out. Commercializing outer space for rocket fueling stations, mining, building moon forts, and rationalizing the Boy Scout astronauts to "be prepared" in the extremes of a void is a logical conclusion to prepping as a way of life in the American scheme of institutionalizing consumption as the best way to provision for individual survival and the survival of the American way of life.[18]

THE EARLY TWENTIETH CENTURY: PREPARATION THROUGH SCOUTING, HANDICRAFT, AND TINKERING

While the role of prepping as a function of statecraft or the purview of preurban populations who produced much of their own needs has a long history, the kind of contemporary prepping we discuss is only possible given a production process that is capable of delivering the mass-consumption opportunities that allows for commodities to be hoarded and stored for long periods of time. The book therefore starts with the mass consumption introduced by the unfolding industrial revolution in the late nineteenth century, which we consider as the wellspring of the anxiety about the dissolution of traditional social bonds, new modes of production, and the loss of the self-sufficient subject who is able to fashion the ends of life from start to finish. The path to consumer society is not smooth, however, and looking at how people made sense of, reacted to, or resisted industrialization is illustrative. Urbanization was not only a result of industrial development but also carried with it xenophobic reactions to migrant populations, a fetishized reiteration of the "frontiersman" imaginary of westward expansion, and a renegotiation of the yeoman masculinity prevalent since the nation's founding. These movements spoke to a general unease about the resilience of traditional bonds of social relations and how easily they might be frayed, as well as what might be done about this fraying. This anxiety takes numerous forms, but the book will focus on the following: first, scouting as a way of managing the anxieties of xenophobia and the polluting results of industrialization, specifically by looking at the Boy Scouts of America (BSA). Second, the Handicraft (or Arts and Crafts) movement, which sought to develop the moral and aesthetic sensibilities of start-to-finish production as a way to counter the dirtying and stultifying impacts of the industrial division of labor. Third, the "tinkering" push that found its footing with the rise of automobility in America as a way of mastering the machine process of industrial production and bending it in a way to serve individual ends, even if people were no longer able to procure their own versions of certain commodities from start to finish. Analyzing each of these movements and how they relate is best done through the lens of a contemporary critic of the same period in American history, Thorstein Veblen.

Chapters 1 and 2 lay out the institutional rationale as well as the theoretical landscape of scouting, tinkering, and handicraft. Scouting, handicraft, and tinkering are not mutually exclusive understandings of social reproduction or responses to industrialization. They merge with one another or negate aspects of one another at certain historical junctures. The goal of analyzing these movements is not for historical presentation, but the book establishes these movements as exemplars of an ideological terrain that sets the stage for doomsday prepping in the Cold War and beyond. Even when these movements were in their fullest bloom in the early twentieth century, they were criticized contemporaneously. In particular, the critiques of these movements in this text are drawn from the work of the American political economist and sociologist Thorstein Veblen. Veblen is a good choice for at least three reasons. First, his analysis, as exemplified by his most famous work, *Theory of the Leisure Class*, is a seminal analysis of consumption as an ideological component of class domination. To wit, the leisure class asserts its dominance over the laboring classes by consuming so visibly that they communicate that they do not have to rely on laboring for their lifestyle; this is the crux of Veblen's famous formulation of "conspicuous consumption."[19] As a result, the politics of opting out will be theorized as a form of conspicuous consumption—by those who have the capital, resources, and time to choose not to engage in the dirty, stultifying world of industrial production. This will be useful for a reconsideration of much of the "back to the land"-style environmental movements and the more obvious bunkerizing habits of the ultrarich. Its moral or aesthetic development notwithstanding, conspicuous consumption broadcasts a privileged position of being able to remove oneself from the necessity of work and, indeed, a shared fate. Second, Veblen is a good theorist of American politics because he also offers a methodology of "cumulative causation." Cumulative causation is the anthropological insight that humans in the current context carry a kind of baggage of bygone modes of life. That is, even in the twenty-first century there are still vestiges of the frontiersman (we need look no further than the "going off the grid" genre on cable television), the do-it-yourself-er (which at present might look like the fetishization/Etsyfication of commodity production), and the tinkerer, who may not be able to reproduce all the ends of life but is knowledgeable enough about certain processes to bend it to personal ends (via hacking or by being a savvy consumer, endlessly hunting for the best deals in commodity accumulation). These phases of American history are not discrete but persist into the current context. Finally, Veblen also gives a nonteleological trajectory of analysis. His idea of the "machine process" is a co-constitutive process whereby the interaction of humans and the means of production yields a dynamic where they each determine the other. If the process of industrialization led to ecological degradation and an unfulfilling laboring life, then scouting presented an alternative to preserving the landscape and the reclamation of the kinds of knowledge that would let a person be self-sufficient. As people tried to hold on to that self-sufficiency by making their own things via handicraft, the industrial process that made the standardized ends of life became more complex but less expensive and more broadly available. In the face of complexity, the response of tinkering was not to master the production process itself or produce the same things from start to finish but only to have enough of a sense of its logic so as to make it work for the individual, or at the very least not be stymied by ignorance of the process, such as being stranded on the side of the road with a flat tire. Veblen saw this process in real time and critiqued a good many of these movements contemporaneously; the theoretical tools also allow for carrying this critique through the American experience and into doomsday prepping, bunkering, and the dictates of neoliberal subjectivity. It is important to draw that continuity between the present and the rise of consumer society via mass production, and Veblen's analysis is ideal for just such an endeavor.

Near the turn of the twentieth century, "scouting" in many forms became popular as a youth movement. Imported from England, it was seen as a way to instill national pride and ecological conservation. The BSA, in particular, whose motto was and is "Be Prepared," emerged as the foremost organization of this kind. While the goals of conservation and national pride are on their face uncontroversial, they hide an undercurrent of xenophobic anxiety about immigrants befouling pristine ecologies (that, it goes unsaid, are better off preserved for the exploitation of heavy industry) and lacking the correct kind of character. Scouts could lead by example and show a spirited civic superiority, as well as learn some of the skills of daily life that had become deemphasized in an industrialized society, such as domestic construction, fire building, and orienteering. This is an important move in the American imaginary that builds a throughline from the notion of radically self-sufficient individuals and that is still present when Americans are asked to build makeshift fallout shelters during the Cold War. Scouting serves as a foundation of understanding how a certain kind of national character is articulated and reproduced. Being prepared is thus a matter of having the fortitude to withstand the external shocks of immigration and the ecological degradation of industrialization.

Relatedly, the Handicraft movement of the early twentieth century was a particular response to the environmentally degrading and dehumanizing aspects of new industrial production processes and serves as an entry point to the character of "opt-out" politics in the United States. Arts and Crafts movements were separate and distinct from the struggles of early labor movements and their attempt to unionize and agitate for legislation for workplace safety. Rather, the Handicraft movement focused on the aesthetic development of the artistic faculties by emphasizing start-to-finish production. These reinforced notions of rugged individualism as well as a removal from the monotony of industrial processes. Essentially, this movement sought to valorize artisanal production as a better alternative to the literally dirty aspects of industrial production and its resulting socioeconomic ills, like criminality and the stupidity that such a division of labor entails. Being prepared to make the ends of life by oneself was not only a matter of aesthetic sensibility; it also ostensibly made people self-sufficient, allaying the worry that the division of labor in industry rendered people unable to live out the frontier imaginary of setting up a homestead using only one's own wits. Being prepared, in this instance, would mean knowledge of being able to set up the home, as well as the homeland (essentially a reproduction of the nation-state in a Manifest Domesticity),[20] by eschewing urban industrial production (with its attendant immigrant and presumed criminal populations). In other words, the fantasy of the Handicraft movement is one in which individuals could opt out of the ravages of industrial production, assume responsibility for their own aesthetic and moral development, and carry on the reproduction of the nation-state on their own. In this register, prepping looks like a kind of "carrying on" for people with the proper moral development and skill set.

The final point of emphasis is "tinkering" culture, which emerged alongside the rise of automobility in the United States. Automobile manufacture is a unique conjuncture of the threads described earlier in this introduction. Automobile manufacture is a highly complex mode of industrial organization that easily goes beyond the scale of handicraft; while some people did build their own automobiles start to finish, the Fordist organizational model of production and affordability outpaced the ability of individuals to compete with that kind of production at any meaningful level. However, this did not diminish the myth of the do-it-yourself individualist; it only changed its register. Rather than being able to handicraft the ends of life from beginning to end, the myth was subtly recast to one of *understanding* the logic of mass production and thus being able to repair, customize, or otherwise master the output of industrial production for one's own individual and idiosyncratic ends. Tinkering culture was thus able to propagate the myth of self-sufficiency through, for example, being able to custom fit products onto one's car or by not being waylaid by a mechanical problem. This idea of being a savvy consumer able to understand the logic of production and thus able to make it serve individual goals finds its current manifestation in notions of hacking, hoarding, or couponing. Prepping in this register is no longer about being able to fully reproduce all the ends of life by oneself but, through a savvy knowledge of the process of commodity production, *bending* it to serve individual goals in the face of social collapse, by, for example, creating a cache of mass consumables.

While these movements in the early twentieth century are not exhaustive, they are nevertheless illustrative of the fits and starts of cementing the consumer society made possible by industrial production. They show a trajectory of opt-out politics that will retain its valence in the contemporary moment, from managing the anxieties about new procedures, populations, and pollutions; to the class politics of moral and aesthetic development through handicraft; to the savvy consumer who may not know how products are made but can always get the best deal and knows how to "beat the system." This trajectory is important for understanding prepping now, and, as Veblen reminds us, these reactions are the baggage that are carried into the Cold War bunker imaginary as well as contemporary prepping movements, and we will use them to analyze the behavior of neoliberalized, responsibilized, Americans.

COLD WAR PREPPING: NUCLEAR BUNKERS AND NEOLIBERALISM

After the Trinity bomb test in 1945, shortly followed by the bomb drops in Hiroshima and Nagasaki, the world entered the atomic age. Prepping as a do-it-yourself response to the numbing and dumbing of industrialization took on new urgency as a necessary safeguard against nuclear warfare. Chapter 3 bridges the institutional framework for prepping with the midcentury practices that appear as rational planning in the atomic age. Here, thinking like a scout to "be prepared" was a means to protect American individualism through preparation, and tinkering and stockpiling like a savvy consumer always a step ahead of the hiccups of mass production and consumption coalesce in the mid-twentieth century into a moral and practical prepping subject called upon to defend the United States against communism. As the United States led its population toward mutually assured destruction with the USSR, the federal government struggled to psychologically and materially prepare citizens for survival against a nuclear attack. After debating the merits of constructing public shelters and distributing funds for private family shelters, the state ultimately provided everyday people with only basic information about safeguarding the home and body from nuclear violence. Prepping, then, became a new marketplace in which the good American-as-consumer should shop and tinker their way into a survival strategy should the big one fall. It was a bad decision, but there were no other possibilities.

The bunker became a stand-in for prepping in the nuclear age. While bunkers are not the only means of self-protection, the bunker represents the individualized fortressing approach to disaster prep and survival. Unlike their European counterparts, American bunkers were not conventional wartime fortifications, such as the encasements along the Atlantic Wall from which to shield oneself from attack or to hide from an enemy during on-the-ground invasion or aerial bombardment. American-style bunkers were conceived of and structured to be an extension of the domicile, only fully encased, and meant to be a second family home in order to ride out a worst-case scenario.

The bunker's role as a domicile does not negate its role as an emblem of national mobilization; indeed, imperial ambitions are often wrapped up in narratives of domesticity.[21] The imperative to turn one's home into a bunker is not simply a matter of meeting certain technical specifications for withstanding apocalyptic events: the everyday maintenance of the domestic sphere became wrapped up in apocalyptic preparedness as a matter of hygiene, cleanliness, and personal responsibility.[22] This also means that the bunker increasingly became less about a separate space but rather designated a reorganization of everyday life around the "claustrophobic" and "cadaverous" dimensions of living in a hardened carapace. As Paul Virilio notes, bunkers represent a shrinking space of the livable world, as well as a flattening of time, given the functional instantaneousness of nuclear warfare. The speed at which apocalyptic warfare could be initiated had the effect of permanently mobilizing populations, making their homes become bunkerized fortresses and prompting adherence to regimes of surveillance, discipline, and hardening as a matter of personal responsibility and risk management.[23] Thus, when the U.S. federal government was devising its nuclear fallout plans, the instantaneousness of nuclear war meant that they could not logistically get Americans into municipal blast shelters, which must be entered before detonation. Instead they devised a system in which Americans would take responsibility for building their own fallout shelters, which had the supposed benefits of giving Americans time to get into (assuming a certain spatial distance from ground zero), being able to be made cheaply, and showing the Soviets that Americans were ready and willing to endure a nuclear conflict.[24] This is not because fallout shelters are particularly effective (the "Gaither Report" argues that the casualties would indeed be "unacceptable") but because the speed of warfare meant that this was the least bad option.

By having Americans take responsibility for identifying, assessing, and preparing for risk, bunkerization is emblematic of the convergence between the everyday neoliberalization of American political life as strategic personal risk management and the federal government's messaging around individualized preparation in the event of a nuclear attack. Neoliberalism encouraged the market-based approach to provision for one's family and individual safety and fit hand in glove with the U.S. government's decision to provide guidelines and recommendations for surviving nuclear fallout. Rather than providing shelters and resources or even reshaping public policy to avoid such a conflict, the government's plan was instead to frame the public's acting individually to save themselves as patriotic. In so doing, the antidemocratic tendencies of neoliberalism linked up with the antidemocratic tendencies of doomsday prepping, further institutionalizing prepping as a mode of life that affirms a commitment to being a certain idealized type of American that rejected communism, had faith in capitalism, and appreciated the exceptional suspensions of the state during certain emergencies as business as usual.[25]

PREPARING FOR THE (NON)FUTURE: OUTER SPACE AND THE LIMITS OF NEOLIBERAL AUTHORITARIANISM

Doomsday preoccupations have traveled into the twenty-first century and adapted with the shifting (but not radically changed) ideological grounds. Silicon Valley provides a convergence zone between prepping and ideological formations increasingly hostile to democracy. As individuals were conditioned to account for themselves during the height of the nuclear scare, the marketplace for prepping met a grand but failed experiment in selling residential bunkers. Yet in the wake of this attempt to marketize the personal bunker, federal agencies like the Federal Emergency Management Agency (FEMA) formed out of atomic age nuclear defense agencies and began publishing do-it-yourself guides for assembling at-home emergency preparedness kits and instructions for keeping yourself and family members safe during active shooting events, tornadoes, and power outages. FEMA is now part of the Department of Homeland Security (DHS), an interesting bureaucratic nest for promoting community resilience. The DHS mission is: "With honor and integrity, we will safeguard the American people, our homeland, and our values." The mission is driven by the post-9/11 security landscape, during which "we rallied together for our common defense, and we pledged to stand united against the threats attacking our great Nation, fellow Americans, and way of life." Taking national defense as a mechanism to safeguard Americanism, not just Americans, indicates that homeland security and making a culture of "relentless resilience"[26] is not about saving individual lives regardless of who they are and what values they embody, but it is about saving America and with it the representatives of such values. Those who are fit for survival are those who are not are drawn on intersectional lines of race, class, country of origin, ability, gender, and whatever else is caught on the wrong side of the domestic friend/enemy distinction. What is at stake for prepping, from the BSA to our current time, is a patriotic subject that knows how to engage their core values and has the market savvy to ensure their survival and thus the survival of the nation; this sentiment is alarmingly close to the collapse of state and individual found in fascist systems.

This part of the defense-driven FEMA mission aligns with the approach to personal safety during the atomic age, during which the federal government worried about salvaging American values from the ravages of communist propaganda and liberalism's moral erosion, which invited the wrong kind of consumerism, religious decline, and poor social behavior. Chapter 4 moves into the twenty-first century, where the goals of national security have not radically changed, despite accounting for new vectors of weakness like cybersecurity and climate change. The marketplace again met the do-it-yourself spirit of "relentlessly resilient" communities, selling DIY emergency kits already chosen and packed for your convenience, leaving the do-it-yourself part to making the right choice in the burgeoning marketplace of kits and bug-out bags. Silicon Valley's self-hagiography of upsetting tradition, or "disrupting the market," has provided fertile ground for developing products for the resilience market that fit in line with national security goals not just to "strengthen preparedness and resilience" but to "Preserve and Uphold the Nation's Prosperity and Economic Security."[27] As this particular goal is addressed in Silicon Valley, it meets a set of ideological commitments that pitch resilience against democracy and prepping against collective action. Quietly, a guiding ideology in Silicon Valley is the Dark Enlightenment, a movement and set of writings by multiple authors that makes a case for technoneofeudalism, which would remake state governments as corporations with a CEO instead of a president. This ideological pastiche embraces an exit-ramp approach to preparing for end times or merely disaster. The political subject is collapsed into the economic subject and is granted the ability to shop for a state that suits its interests and to opt out of politics, exposure to harm, and living among others. Of course, many of the torchbearers of this ideology are preppers as well, as has been documented by Douglas Rushkoff through his experiences with superrich prepping culture.

In chapter 5, prepping extends all the way into the new space race, which in some ways has become the ultimate opt-out plan for those seeking survival. The new space race is driven in part by anxieties about the loss of Earth's habitability as climate change radically alters the conditions necessary for life for humans and scores of other species. The efforts to become multiplanetary provide a new way to turn over the central contradiction of bunkerization: an event may produce a fundamentally different future, but the only imaginable future is the status quo, with its class dynamics intact. Going to space to build industry, stake private sector and state claims to space resources, and establishing colonies may sound fantastical, impossible, even exciting. Finally, it offers a last hope to rocket away from doomsday, particularly a climate change doomsday. But space exploration as a response to climate change and related disasters depends on alienating outer space from earthly environmentalism. Exploration requires an enormous market to sustain the efforts, plans to produce markets in extractive industries, a market for tickets on a rocket ship and subsequent colonization, and the requisite class stratification between those who provide labor, those who own the space travel companies, and those who can afford to relocate off-planet without committing to a life of hard labor. Space exploration is now touted as an avenue to avoid total human extinction on Earth as the planet warms and drowns. Becoming multiplanetary has become an imperative and one that can be met through outer space entrepreneurs working in partnership with state space agencies, particularly to address the legal barriers to commercial access to space found in international treaties managed by the United Nations. Rather than waiting for the sky to fall in subterranean bunkers, going to outer space entails going into the sky in a rocket bunker to create bunkered life on uninhabited (and uninhabitable) planets.

Outer space appears as a new frontier of untouched cosmic wilderness. In the outer space imaginary, the colonial and frontier dreams of the United States are redeployed to promote the technological and commercial race against China and Russia. In order for outer space to function as a screen onto which survivalist and imperial fantasies can be projected, it must remain *exterior* to the planet, rather than an *extension* of the environment or understood as, ultimately, the place where humans *already* live. In fact, outer space is already a managed environment, with treaties, domestic public policies, and continuous human presence in low Earth orbit, aboard the International Space Station. Silicon Valley's penchant for disruption not only produces prepping gear for terrestrial needs but participates in producing the infrastructure, public policy, and technologies for space exploration beyond the capacity of state actors. SpaceX has disrupted the traditional pipeline between defense companies and NASA, and in doing so it has become a beacon of hope for those who think its CEO will fulfill his cosmic destiny as the man who makes humans multiplanetary and thus saves humanity from doomed conditions on their home planet. The rocket need not even be the bunker; it can just as effectively serve as a metaphor for the bunkerization of life and the institutionalization of prepping. Via the rocket, everyday people confront their collectively experienced harms through the economic practices and fantasies of economic titans creating a survival plan.

THE STAKES

This may seem an odd place to wonder, why prepping? So far, we have established what prepping is, how we approach the study of prepping, and the major themes contained in this volume. Yet the question remains, why this subject in the first place? Prepping can appear both quotidian and extraordinary. Prepping for a moderate storm that may knock out power and make getting to the grocery store a challenge seems somehow not prepping; that's just good sense and responsible actions. Prepping, as a cultural convention, often appears radical, the irrational activities of people driven to extreme ideologies and spiritual beliefs who typically live in remote communities removed from the flow of everyday life. Between these two poles, prepping may seem either too normal to be of scholarly interest ("of course I have energy bars and water bottles stashed in my closet, this is not a politics") or too kooky to be representative of the public or universalizable ("the end is near"). We argue that prepping is a meaningful activity that speaks to political institutions that govern the United States and produce a subject within this context who is conditioned to approach threat, disaster, and climate doomsday as individualized consumers who, in these acts and orientations, are attending to their responsibility as good Americans. Beyond "just good sense" and the fringe of mainstream society, prepping is an American way of life that encourages people to harden the shell of their personal security not only by physical bunkers but by orienting the way they live into a state of "relentless resilience" that requires constant vigilance, surveillance technology, data management and analysis, smart planning for uncertain futures, and the preservation of a particular set of American values to carry forward whether into a bunkerized home or onto a spaceship.

Prepping, then, can tell us quite a lot about the fault lines in the American liberal democratic project and where those discontinuities and rumbling, thrusting, grinding energies of a kinetic and unstable democracy make themselves felt. Precisely because prepping is an often-overlooked vector of activity in the political body, we interrogate and explore it beyond the behaviors, practices, and conventions of prepping but rather by asking how prepping is woven into the American subjectivity and how it functions as an institution in the political landscape. Better understanding how prepping sits in American politics does not suggest that this book serves as a seer stone to reveal the ultimate and hidden truths of the relationship between uncertainty and American politics. However, pulling back

from prepping as either too normal or too abnormal, or treating it as
a neurosis (or psychosis), and taking it seriously as a century-old phenomenon allows for it to provide another window into U.S. politics
and what guiding institutional practices are currently deployed, with
historical precedent, toward collectively experienced crises like the
ever-present threat of nuclear war and the unfolding global climate
crisis. Prepping here is theorized, rather than gawked at, and brought
into the tangle of critical theory, social theory, critique of neoliberalism, and politics of American subjectivity. We may not all be preppers in the sense that we Americans all stockpile, horde, or bunker,
but we all live in a bunker society that entails thinking of ourselves
as vigilant foot soldiers in the war against instability and ideological
change.

1

PREPPING AS AN AMERICAN INSTITUTION

ANALYZING DOOMSDAY prepping can and has taken a variety of shapes.[1] For instance, one could look at what seems like a curious behavior and flesh out the dimensions of that peculiarity as some kind of aberrant limit case or diagnose something wrong in the body politic. Alternatively, doomsday prepping could be looked at as a phenomenon of popular culture, with basic cable television shows enraptured with the motivation and daily life of preppers; perhaps this is done while bemoaning the dearth of more worthy cultural expressions. International relations scholars might look at doomsday prepping as being part of a security apparatus employing domestic extensions of state strategies of defense. Our point of departure is that whereas most analyses of prepping movements take the valence of the behavior as a given, we will attempt to excavate the social, political, and cultural setting of the behavior. In other words, while prepping may be an empirical given, an institutional approach can help explain how certain habits coalesce into the prepping behavior that has become increasingly mainstream in American political society. This approach works because institutions shape responses to broader social forces; they condition human behavior in ways that mediate/govern ideological frames and provide a situated series of cultural sequences to explain social change. This gives us a better sense of where certain behaviors emerge and why. This chapter explains our approach by laying out the framework of Thorstein Veblen's theory of institutional analysis, showing how institutions and habits of thought are codetermined, locating where this particular version of institutional analysis falls in the broader discipline of political science, and framing the institutions that form the basis of our analysis.

Broadly speaking, in our institutional conception, the politics of prepping as consumer culture in the United States starts with the rapid industrialization underway by the turn of the twentieth century that ushered in mass consumption as a mode of life. Industrialization not only brought new modes of production and consumption but was also a novel renegotiation of national identity caused by urbanization and immigration. These new social relations of production challenged the "yeoman farmer" myth of the American founding and reconfigured the ethical content of the spirit of capitalism: valuing punctuality as opposed to adventurism, for instance. Yet, the industrialization process alone does not necessarily explain how and why social and cultural changes emerge or why certain behaviors like prepping become recognizable. How people respond to broad social changes, individually or collectively, is not a foregone conclusion. The first task, then, to establish what makes prepping a legible directive is to theorize what drives the social and cultural change that yields the prepping directive in the first place. One could look at the "Great Man" version of history, where certain world-historical figures, by dint of individual volition and fortitude, heroically change the course of humanity, a broadly held notion at the turn of the twentieth century.[2] But this Victorian notion had fallen out of intellectual favor by the time industrialization took hold, and the then still new fields of psychology and sociology, influenced by the evolutionary theory of Darwin and how sciences (both natural and social), tried to build theories of how societies change based on evolutionary insights from the natural sciences.[3] On the other hand, the "German Historical" school of thought, coming from Hegelian philosophy, is often characterized as the driving force behind the line of analysis that there is a teleological endpoint to which human endeavors were ultimately geared and that the goal of the social sciences was to chart the progress along that path.[4] The American political economist and social critic

Thorstein Veblen offered a different way of understanding social change: institutional evolution. This theory provides a way of reconciling individual agency within broader social structures without resorting to hero worship, positing the institution as a mediating force that does not insist on a predetermined teleological endpoint for human action. For Veblen, the task of social science is relatively straightforward, even if not always that simple to execute. Institutional analysis addresses the "lag" between the machine process, which Veblen refers to as "facts-on-the-ground" or the "matter of fact" of a given mode of production, and individualized expressions of cultural habits of mind, which Veblen takes as behavioral expressions of bygone social relations that are often at odds with the current facts on the ground. Institutions bridge this gap or manage this lag, but not cleanly; bygone habits of mind remain and are holdovers from a "barbaric" past.[5] Veblen often terms them "invidious." This atavism is the subtext of the otherwise seemingly benign observation that Veblen made in 1923 that most small towns in America had an everyday life mostly unchanged since the end of the Civil War; social frictions would emerge from this lag between urban industrial centers and rural, still mostly agrarian small towns.[6] Institutional analysis is thus primarily an exercise in a multilayered, multidisciplinary tracing of the trajectory of political society. It rejects the assumptions of neoclassical economics, for instance, about perfect information, the utility of a "snapshot" analysis of one particular moment in time, instrumental rationality, and the tendency toward equilibrium.[7] Institutional analysis also takes the approach "that economic activities cannot be isolated from other cultural practices."[8] Essentially, in regards to doomsday prepping, this means that questions of consumption cannot simply be consigned to the rational motivations of atomized economic units, maximizing their own utility. Rather, consumption is a social category and cannot be disentangled from political and social considerations, like the institutions that shape behavior. Jean Baudrillard names consumption as a "social destiny" that is a class project of displaying waste; as it is not about individual gratification, analyzing consumption requires a historicized contextualization.[9] Wasting, hoarding, consuming—all of these behaviors of consumption are laid out in an institutional arrangement of class power. Prepping is no exception, and institutional analysis gets at the fundaments of this arrangement of class, consumption, and power that goes beyond individual human behavior.

The goal of laying out Veblen's institutionalism is not to apply Veblen's social theory whole cloth. Those kinds of analyses have been done well already and do not necessarily help theorize prepping per se.[10] However, we rely on Veblen's institutionalist perspective to illuminate his theory of general social change for three reasons. (1) It is an attempt to explain what drives political development in a holistic way to explain lags, mismatches, and contradictions among habits of mind and the given relations of production as the United States underwent the process of industrialization. This is an important aspect of prepping because it overcomes the possibility of dismissing the behavior as merely aberrant or bizarre along the otherwise smooth continuum of progress. (2) Internally, Veblen's institutional account establishes an alternative grounding of the dominant strains of institutionalism in political science that is prevalent in the United States, which essentially treats institutions as formally developed civil society organizations or organs of the state, within which agents engage in strategic rational choice to meet their ends. While we certainly do not dispute that the state is an institution, such a confrontational approach misses a good deal of the cultural milieu and daily habits that shape people's behavior. (3) Veblen was writing during the early period of America's industrialization, and he was attempting to diagnose the condition in real time. He saw institutions not necessarily as vehicles of progress but rather as often becoming preservationist, "imbecile" vehicles that smuggled archaic, atavistic, and invidious habits of mind from bygone eras that frustrated the democratic promises of technological evolution.[11] In Veblen's framework, the term "institution" may be taken synonymously with "custom" or "convention," which highlights their propensity to carry over habits from the past into the future.

This expansive sense of what institutions are can make everything look like an institution, so while some care has to be taken to not simply refer to any social phenomenon as an institution, it is also important to note that there are more than the "official" institutions (e.g., the state) that have force in this analysis. As we move forward through a broad sweep of American political development, we will construct a constellation of institutions that we believe form the basis of prepping behavior and a subjectivity of the prepper. Though we make no claims that the institutions we offer to analyze are exclusive or exhaustive, they provide a compelling way to understand the evolution of the prepping subject in American politics. Part of that story is U.S. government policy via the institution of the state, but just as—if not more—important is the cultural milieu of civil society groups that navigate the evolving habits of mind. To wit, the government asking citizens to build backyard fallout shelters has a social, cultural, or political context that makes the request seem reasonable.

Veblen is unique in that he does not assume, as Emerson averred, that institutions are simply the "lengthened shadows of individuals."[12] Nor are institutions remote loci of formally concentrated power that fit tidy categories of some public policy analysis. Rather, institutions "fundamentally condition human behavior in groups" and have myriad vectors of expression and emphases of these various behaviors.[13] Veblen offers a different lens for looking at cultural, social, and political change, one that focuses on the ceremonial, rational, superstitious, or class-based registers, which he analyzes as the evolution of institutions.[14] Indeed, the subtitle of his most famous work, *The Theory of the Leisure Class*, is *An Economic Study of Institutions*. In this text, the story of institutions is a class analysis of "conspicuous consumption." Conspicuous consumption is the dynamic of acquiring and disposing of wealth, especially—indeed spectacularly and visibly— wastefully, to confer a class status whose genesis is the result of the atavistic habits of thought of preindustrial, timocratic society, establishing leisure as a class marker of one's not needing to engage in wage labor. Institutions also describe things like organized sports, which ritualize honorifics in battle, and women's fashion, which for Veblen is an atavistic manifestation of property and dominance—adornment as the display of one's prizes.[15] In this way, institutions become an imbecilic force that transmits these archaic habits of mind to make them compatible with the developing modes of production in industry. Institutions thus both manage and perpetuate their cultural lag, especially when they degrade to the point of only being concerned with their own reproduction, which Veblen argues manifests as a steadfast commitment to the status quo.

VEBLEN'S POLITICS OF CLASS, EMULATION, AND SABOTAGE

Of course, institutions and individuals are not simply two sides of the same coin, interacting with each other on occasion. By setting the conditions for human action individually or in concert, Veblen argues that institutions create social classes to coordinate human endeavors. Here Veblen is recognizable from a Marxist perspective but offers his own formulation of class dynamics. In *Theory of the Leisure Class*, he offers a three-part class structure for an industrial society geared around the business enterprise. In his anthropological writings, Veblen argued that after a state of peaceable savagery (which might be regarded as a rhyme of Marx's notion of "primitive communism"), a "barbarian" predatory class emerges that uses honorifics, waste, and violent protection of private property to signal its power and ability to opt out of the labor process. So that it may pursue these honorifics, the predatory class appropriates the useful things produced by the labor undertaken by the rest of the population. It is noteworthy here that Veblen does not call the predatory class "capitalist." That would give too much credit to a class that did not create capital but instead leeched off of its creation by the underlying population, and this is why the display of excusing oneself from the need to labor makes the predatory class and the leisure class synonymous.[16] In any event, this two-class overview appears more or less in line with the Marxian analysis of an ownership class siphoning the surplus of a laboring class.

In the machine process of institutional production, however, Veblen adds a third class that is unique to the business enterprise: the business class. The business class is a conduit that directs capital flow and skims some off the top; it is basically an intermediary, rent-seeking, salaried class. How these three classes relate to one another is encapsulated by Veblen's theory of conspicuous consumption. This concept has been reduced in mainstream economics and psychology to "keeping up with the Joneses," which is a shorthand for trying to explain a propensity to spend beyond one's means. This reduction, however, does not capture all the social relations that drive the emulative impulse of conspicuous consumption. For Veblen, conspicuous consumption is a behavioral manifestation of the class dynamics at work in this tripartite model of the predatory class, business class, and underlying population. Veblen used "underlying population" instead of something like "working class" because they are not a class for itself in the way the predatory/leisure and business classes are. The leisure/predatory class has removed itself from the need to labor, and while it once did this by accruing honorifics through battle and conquest to appropriate the labor of the underlying classes, it has now ceremonialized these displays of honorifics in institutions like organized sports, civilian medals that mimic military achievement, and discursively treating corporate competition as war. The central point in these ceremonialized pursuits of honorifics is to retain the privilege of predation: to ostentatiously display—to conspicuously consume—the goods that demonstrate one's ability to remove oneself from the need to work.[17] This lack of the necessity to labor comes from inherited wealth, landlordship, or other kinds of passive rent claims; in short, *the leisure class does not need a wage to make a living*. Indeed, as Veblen notes, the more ostentatious, the more extreme the leisure, the more social power is derived from that ceremonialism. The more socially important a person is *is because* of that display.[18] Here it is important to note that this is clearly at odds with the "Protestant work ethic" and narratives of industrial efficiency that reward the effort of labor. In fact, for Veblen it is quite the opposite. The business class attempts to emulate the leisure class because leisure is a show of power and standing. The business class thus acts as a kind of aspirational intermediary between the working class and the leisure class. As a result, the business enterprise is less concerned with the production of goods than with the accumulation of money, and the business class skims some of the exploitation of the working/industrial class on its way to the leisure class.[19] For Veblen, these kinds of enterprises look like private insurance, real estate, advertising, banking—basically anything beyond making the necessaries of everyday life.[20] The business class does not own the means of production in the way that the leisure class might, but it is able to secure rent streams by directing and exploiting the fruits of industry via banking, finance, or economic development. The business class seeks to emulate the leisure class by displaying its increasing remoteness from the necessities of wage labor to make the ends of life and to conspicuously consume to try to show their social power. From the C-suites of high-powered executives to the flexible entertainment arrangements of the "creative" and "innovative" workplaces of the self-styled creative class, the emulation in these arrangements is the pantomime of the business class removing themselves from the labor process even while nominally still having to be at work.[21]

This emulation trickles down through other classes. The underlying population, or working class, though unable to emulate the leisure class by removing itself entirely from the labor process (because the working class must, in fact, work), can act like the leisure class through the purchase of consumer goods, at a price point made possible through the sheer quantity of industrial production.[22] This emulation of the leisure class through mass consumption is the impetus to spend beyond one's means, mimic increased standards of living, and fall sway to the advertising industrial complex. This does not speak to the moral character of working people but shows how the business class creates markets of consumption that provide opportunities for the business class to redirect money to their pockets.[23] Though this emulation of the leisure class is induced, it is still less invidious than the relationship between the business class and the working class. Because the business class relies on exploiting flows of money from industry and the economic necessity of wage labor, a problem emerges: the working class would prefer to meet their ends of life in as efficient and non-irksome way as possible. But doing so would eat into the pecuniary flows that the business class can exploit. Veblen recasts the term "sabotage" to mark this friction between exploitation and industry. Sabotage is the "conscious withdrawal of efficiency" and is an activity of the business class, not the working class.[24] This includes throttling production, price fixing, and planned obsolescence, which for Veblen are ways to secure monetary flows at the expense of industry. The business class "(mis)directs the competitive system's pecuniary traffic so that it will flow through gainful channels. By gainful channels, Veblen meant business channels that yield a pecuniary gain."[25] This business usufruct funds the status emulation that the business class employs as it strives to display its leisure. Effectively, the business class funds its emulation of the leisure class by inducing leisure emulation in the working class, and the working class's emulation is made possible by mass consumption.

The tripartite class model for Veblen in industrial society, then, has two classes trying to emulate the leisure class, but the intermediary business class does so by grifting the working class and frustrating it from meeting its aims of labor efficiency and non-noxious work environments. The working class emulates via consumption, and the business class emulates via siphoning the fruits of labor. What this means in terms of prepping keeps much of the same shape: the leisure class is able to remove itself from social life, and their fantastical private islands and extravagant interplanetary escape plans will continue to be featured in tony lifestyle magazines. The industrial/working class, left to fend for themselves and with only mass consumption as a mode of action, will try to purchase preparedness as best they can. And, sensing a market to be made, the business class will sell bunkers, disaster timeshares, and shelf-stable food to arrogate to itself some of the monetary flows of the industrial production of apocalyptic readiness. This logic will be amplified in a neoliberal order, but first, we seek to show how have institutions evolved for this kind of prepping logic to make sense.

INSTITUTIONAL CHANGE: EVOLUTION, CUMULATIVE CAUSATION, AND (NOT SO BLIND) DRIFT

The thrust of the analysis of institutional development, for Veblen, is essentially that the speed of technological development, particularly during (and, we would argue, continuing after) rapid-onset industrialization yields a new "machine process," or relation of production.[26] Veblen's ideal machine process has the potential to be a source of liberatory social change, making people more matter-of-fact, less superstitious, more efficient, and focused on the efficiency of labor, and providing ample ends of life.[27] However, culturally embedded institutions, what Veblen refers to as "settled habits of thought," represent a cultural lag that puts a drag on the possibilities of social change stemming from the onset of the machine process. As Plotkin and Tilman put it, "Prevailing institutions . . . possess an uncanny ability to retard the rationalization and secularization of consciousness, without which there is little chance for progressive political change." The task of institutional analysis tracks this lag, uncovers which habits of mind are smuggled in by this institutional drag, and how these settled habits of thought shape, change, or frustrate qualitative political change. Plotkin and Tilman use the example of digitalized music sharing as a technology that is frustrated by the institution of private property, turning "sharing" into "theft" not out of some ontological moral truth but purely from institutional arrangements shaping habits of thought having to do with relations of private property.[28] Similarly, we argue that the potentials of central planning and rationalized production of collective action are frustrated by the settled habits of thought of neoliberal institutions of hoarding, waste, possessive individualism, and the hollowing out of public purpose. The following traces Veblen's methodological construction for institutional analysis, and then we offer a nonexhaustive list institutions we wish to track for the purposes of our study. Any attempt to offer alternatives or a vision of a different set of social relations must account for these institutional lags/drags and take seriously how to overcome particular settled habits of thought, rather than simply wishing things were otherwise.[29] This lag also would explain how settled habits of thought persist in everyday life even if the institutional configurations are changing, as we will explore in the analysis of neoliberalism.

Such a contradiction between part-myths of competition and the half-realities of cooperation might seem difficult to navigate, but the job of an institution can bridge, as well as intensify, that gap. Consider, for instance, the myth of the "self-made man" in Sinclair Lewis's novel *Babbitt*. A businessman becomes disillusioned with a life of unproductive salesmanship and tries out an ersatz bohemian rebellion, but after a very brief dalliance, he quickly rebounds back to the creature comforts of upper-middle-class life. Lewis's titular character, set in the period of rapid industrialization in the United States in the early twentieth century, prides himself on being self-made even though he very clearly relies on a network of "boosters" and good-ol'-boys to maintain his social position. Aside from simply being a tidy if implausible story, the question emerges of where this myth comes from and what end it serves in the contemporary moment. Veblen's cultural lag helps us see this development in the way he theorizes the preindustrial category of the "masterless man [*sic* throughout]" to periodize bourgeois development. Masterless men were an emergent class of craftspeople not tied to the land and could handicraft a surplus of the ends of life for personal profit as opposed to enriching a lordship.[30] For Veblen, masterless men kept the romance of competitive adventuring to make a life for oneself (a precursor to the contemporary "being your own boss") alive, and this romantic notion from a preindustrial period persisted even as industrialization standardized production and wage labor became the primary form of pecuniary accumulation, which produced a lag between the wage labor of industry and the pecuniary gain of adventure and exploit.[31] The industry of making things and the exploit of business (which, again, is making money, not goods) are two very clearly different things and can indeed put industry and business at cross-purposes. Still, they are often conflated, such that accumulating money is assumed to be a reward for those who produce useful things. This sentiment becomes a fully naturalized fiction that serves as a "spiritual foundation of law and custom."[32] As Lewis shows in his novel, this romantic notion of adventure and singularly masculine creativity carries through into the business world, but the realities of the business world are based not on individual derring-do but on fratriarchy. This group model of support, which sustains masculinity and keeps open opportunities for exploit, maintains class positions via mutual recognition. After all, Babbitt is not the masterless man who creates his own ends of life and can provide the same for his community; his job as a realtor is purely in the business of "selling houses for more than people could afford to pay." Sinclair's Babbitt has a self-perception as an adventurer who is doing battle on the field of business, echoing the ceremonial habits of predation and their honorifics in battle. Nevertheless, he relies on his circle of civic institutions to make sure he maintains his standing and his masculinity; his sense of self is fully contingent on a socially constructed masculinity that must be conferred onto him, rather than being an emerging quality of his *bildung*. While this seems like a direct contradiction, both in its literary deployment as well as for the internal coherence of Babbitt, this is precisely what Veblen argues the institution of masculinity is set to manage. It allows Babbitt the chance to stage a faux rebellion against the hollow hucksterism of the business enterprise and its inability to provide a meaningful life, while at the same time just as easily allowing him to relinquish these strivings and slide back into the trap of the comfortable network of conformity that might otherwise seem at odds with his realization that life is more than making a buck. As we will see with the Boy Scouts, similar dynamics are at play: a mythical masculinity of the adventuring frontiersman confronting the realities of needing obedient wage labor, and an organization bridging the gap between the latter and the lag of the former. Masculinity within the institution of the business enterprise sustains a certain kind of vision where "business *is* manly, and manliness is businesslike."[33] This is at odds with preindustrial visions of masculinity, particularly in the United States, where masculinity is perceived as being a fully autonomous frontiersman, one able to establish a home and provide for his family without needing to be obedient to any external authority.[34] We can hear echoes of Jefferson's yeoman farmer, to be sure, but the job of the institutions of industrialization is to rationalize the yeoman into being an obedient factory wage laborer *while* sustaining the fantasy. Babbitts can go have their fun as long as they come home before the next mortgage payment.

So far, this story of institutional change is rather tidy. Institutions, by dint of their longevity, are able to bridge the gap between a given mode of production and the habits of mind that precede it, thereby mollifying the contradictions that might emerge between the two. The story cannot remain tidy, of course, because institutions often serve as reactionary forces, smuggling old habits of mind and resisting change. In addition, the evolutionary notion of institutional change holds that these two forces—habits of mind and the machine process of industrial production—are codeterminative. The habits of mind that are rationalized into the machine process in turn shape and change the machine process.[35] This evolutionary process holds the promise, at least potentially, of instilling in people a more matter-of-fact, materialist, indeed socialist, approach to life, rather than a façade of vocational fulfillment through drudgery, patriotic manhood to make the country great, or vicious competition to secure that profit flows upward.[36] While Veblen hoped for such a "Soviet of Engineers," he was also deeply pessimistic about such an arrangement coming to pass.[37] This pessimism stems from these atavistic holdovers from ages past; the pursuit of honorifics and emulative waste would more likely be absorbed into the current process. But still, the potential! If only we could just leave these old habits of mind in the past, but as Marx reminds us in *The Eighteenth Brumaire*, "The tradition of all the dead generations weighs like a nightmare on the brain of the living."[38]

This institutional stuckness means that institutions are not haphazard amalgamations of individuals who are hedonistic globules of desire, pursuing their own strategic ends in a utilitarian frame somehow cohering into a broader social force greater than the sum of its parts. In political science, this is our point of departure from the "rational choice" school of institutional analysis. On the other hand, Veblen's institutionalism is not a firewalled dichotomy of officially constituted organizational transactions or relationships like state/citizen or vendor/consumer. This is where our analysis will differ from the "historicist" school of institutional analysis, which is focused on the interaction between individuals and levers of power (Congress, bureaucracy, etc.) and how responsive they are to popular demands. Rather, our conception of institutions is that they are organized habits of thought that come from culturally embedded practices and that mediate the lived experience of people, in ways that can blur the boundaries between institution and behavior. In our analysis, culture comes from the habituated behavior of the surroundings in which one acts, which, to paraphrase Sahlins, means that cultures are the meaningful orders of persons and things. This puts us most closely to the "sociological" school of institutionalism within political science and can admittedly make it difficult to assemble a tidy list of things that are institutions and things that are habits of minds of the individuals within them. For instance, masculinity can be analyzed as an institution, but it can also be an affect that evinces individual behaviors. It can further be a habit of thought that is animated and reanimated at different times for different reasons, such as the westward expansion of American imperial ambitions, protecting one's family from a potential nuclear war, or the bravado of adventurism into the reaches of outer space. As groundwork, then, we will lay out what we take to be our institutional touchstones, fully understanding that they are not final or even fully separable from the behaviors and habits they enshrine. This codeterminative aspect of institutionalism is an important component of Veblen's theorizing, one that has been deemphasized in more contemporary strands of institutionalism.[39] This is unfortunate because such an interplay can be explanatory of how social change emerges. That is, it is not only the facts on the ground but the attitudes about those facts, and that the habits of mind act as a filter for subsequent behavior means that institutional analysis must try to account for the vast cultural, social, and political impulses in which people operate. It can explain the lag between the facts at hand and peoples' attitudes; it can explain contradictions between habits of mind and matters of fact.[40] This positioning opens up ways to analyze phenomena like prepping, where the question is less whether a particular behavior is rational given certain contemporary facts but what are the cultural lags being expressed in a given behavior. It simultaneously avoids questions about what people "really believe," because the cumulative habits of mind and atavistic impulses are not simply a matter of personal preference but are a broader cultural phenomenon that emphasizes the cultural sequences in which people live and act.[41] To lay out our argument: in the United States, prepping is an institution that serves as a regressive force against collective action by animating archaic and atavistic habits of mind such as emulative waste, frontiersmanship, and conspicuous consumption, and it is fully compatible with the neoliberal development in American political society because neoliberalism animates those same atavistic impulses.

Here emerges the uniquely Veblenian vision of what institutionalism looks like. Institutions do not *cause* social change, but they are repositories of archaic behavior that rationalize an individual's relationship with an evolving set of facts on the ground. The contemporary context abounds with examples of institutionalized cultural lag to resist or rationalize social change.[42] In Veblen's ideal world, a different kind of organizational system would supersede institutions and provide better ways of meeting the ends of life, preferably led by the people whose rationality is sharpened by the machine process.[43] While he thought this unlikely because the atavisms of institutions was too great to overcome, he was at least optimistic that America might trend toward something of an industrial republic, producing goods efficiently, and pursuing a common good, not private profit— very much a kind of American socialism. Institutions nevertheless insist on a bygone habit of mind that makes them regressive, and because the only thing keeping institutions alive is perpetuating these habits of mind, which increasingly have little purchase as political society changes, institutions become consumed with perpetuating themselves as their reason for being.[44] This is what Veblen means when he refers to "imbecilic" institutions. Institutionalism is a gradual process of imbecility, producing shortcuts or short-circuits around critical faculties and excusing people from having to confront the challenges they face or coalesce around collective-action solutions.[45] Imbecilic institutions may even be well meaning, but their need to perpetuate the status quo prevents them from actually spurring meaningful social change.[46]

A consequence of institutions and habits of thought being codeterminative and influencing each other is that institutions also change, evolve, and adapt to their circumstances as they interact with habits of mind. To be clear, what this often looks like practically is that while institutions are a regressive force that insists on a status quo built on archaic habits of mind, they nevertheless adapt to changing circumstances to perpetuate their existence. Institutions, however, lacking the full agentic force of human subjects, are subject to what Veblen calls "blind drift." This is not to say that institutional drift cannot be guided; quite the contrary. Institutions are essentially there for the taking, to serve the consciously articulated ends of humans who can wrangle them. Thus, directing institutional drift can be an attempt to provide direction for evolution through concerted efforts. Without such attention from people, institutions can passively resist new forms of social relations in their default mode of reproduction of the status quo through totally blind drift. In either event, for Veblen, this institutional drift is nonteleological; it may be blind, adapting and lagging behind updating relations of productions, or it might be directed toward determined ends, but in neither case is there a final, first, or transcendent endpoint to which institutions are moving.[47] Like a dinghy in a body of water, it will drift blindly, but with a paddle, we might make it go where we desire.

It might seem at first blush that institutional drift contradicts the notion of imbecilic institutions insisting on a status quo of previously held habits of mind. However, true to Veblen's evolutionary stance, institutions did have to navigate changing landscapes and changing habits of mind in order to persevere, so they would inevitably alter as time went on, to better maintain their purposes, even, in the case of blind drift, if their explicit purpose was no longer clear.[48] Veblen suggests, contrary to the "great man" notions of social change, that institutional drift meant that social changes of conduct would be a "drift of habituation rather than a dispassionately reasoned adaptation to the circumstances of the case. It appears always to be a matter of 'forced movements' rather than an outcome of shrewd initiative and logical design—even though much argument may be spent in the course of it all."[49] This, of course, cuts both ways. It means that while people may have personally held affinities for certain courses of action or outcomes (the good life, for instance), the actual conditions of social change are more diffuse and contingent on previous habits of thought. Perhaps even more interesting, however, is that it also means that top-down directives do not simply establish new patterns of behavior or habits of mind. In the case of prepping, we will see that government initiatives explicitly called forth certain cultural habits of mind from early industrial America. If nothing else, it patently makes little sense to think that a certain subset of Americans simply wakes up and decides to prepare for doomsday. With this double movement in mind, the vital part of Veblen's diagnosis for our work is that the basically ineffectual "argument . . . spent in the course of it all" about prepping is unhelpful in producing shrewd designs of effective statecraft to meet existential threats. Government directives, social movements, and charismatic millenarians may try to call new worlds into being, but Veblen's institutionalism insists that analysts keep an eye less on the bombastic arguments "spent in the course of it all" and more on the drift of habits and institutions that might show us where we are headed, perhaps to wrangle institutional drift in a particular direction. Leering at the prepping habits of the ultrarich may be quick tabloid fodder, but it is more important to trace the habits of mind that produce prepping as a mode of life if we are to answer pressing collective action questions.

Because institutions condition human behavior in groups, institutions do not need to act directly; indeed, one could argue that the strength of institutions is that they are not dependent on the conscious decision making of one or a few individuals for their persistence, not to mention their ability to endure beyond the typical human lifespan. Rather, institutions drift blindly, but blind drift can mean one of two things. First, it can be a nonteleological opportunity for newness, where novel junctures emerge as conditions change that require response or adaptation. But more likely for Veblen, second, blind drift can serve as a naturalizing or essentializing force to reify an institutional arrangement as an implacable given that cements a prior status quo. Indeed this drift may not be so blind but is instead some combination of "problem-solving for improvement [that is] *partially* realistic and *partly* mythical beliefs, producing some misdirected intentionality," and "'standards of improvement' [that] are informed by self-congratulatory commitments to the status quo." While this drift might still be considered blind in the sense that it lacks a fixed teleology or final end, there is an intentionality in shaping the institution that tries to direct that drift in a less than benign way.[50] It is easy to imagine what this kind of institutional blind drift looks like—old habits of thought that adapt to contemporary problems with half-truths and outright fantasies, steadfastly insisting that the way to fix a new problem is with business as usual, which has the added benefit of coming with the self-congratulatory plaudits of those who benefit from the perpetuation of the same. Our position is that this through line of institutional development has strong explanatory power for how habits of mind are institutionalized in the United States. Indeed, this text operates on the premise that the "main institutional drift of the twentieth century foretold continued predation, irresponsible power, and chronic warfare."[51]

As institutions change or drift, they often exhibit the status quo–preserving aspects of habitual change, sometimes blindly, sometimes with an attempt at conscious drift, but, in any case, with cultural lag. The institution of the business enterprise on ecological problems is a case in point. The atavistic habits of mind of pecuniary accumulation and private profit have occluded the wholesale changes that need to be made to stave off the worst effects of global climate change. This gap is not attributable to some nefarious plot by a ruling cabal but instead to a blind drift of accepting the profit motive as the correct driver for all social change, including for ecological considerations, where pollution simply becomes an "externality," as well as a conscious drift of soft-pedaling denialism and fantasies of "clean"-burning fossil fuels. That these do not comport with the facts at hand or the urgent need to reorganize production to forestall ecological collapse is clear, but there are vested interests in keeping these habits of mind, and this is engrained at an institutional level, essentially turning "solutions" into reifications of the status quo thanks to a bit of wishful thinking.[52] The attempt to achieve a certain vision of social change can be stymied by imbecilic institutions that get in the way.[53] Indeed, Veblen argued that "the government was little more than a collective representation of the business community whose actions reflected that community's interest over the common good."[54] We will detail, for instance, when discussing the new space race, the partially realistic notions of resource extraction off-world with the partly mythical belief that humanity can become a truly multiplanetary (and beyond) species. We will also show how in the middle of the Cold War, asking citizens to manufacture private fallout bunkers was a commitment to the status quo that preserved American life and, indeed, that could achieve the impossible task of preserving the nation in the face of nuclear conflagration. We will specifically lay out how prepping relies on the institutional development of neoliberalism to (re)animate habits of mind such as emulation, conspicuous consumption, and competitive honorifics and shape the discourse of the future of off-worlding, the new space race, and off-planet extraction.

In this way, the institutional approach allows us to build a political diagnosis of prepping: where it comes from and which habits of mind persist, adapt, change, or find unique expressions to make prepping a legible course of action. Politics is about directing drift, overcoming lag, or otherwise coordinating for a particular outcome given the facts at hand to shape futures of collective action and create new organizations, ones that do not rely on the neoliberalism entrepreneurial self with only mass consumption as a vector of action. The question is how to get there from here, and that requires a sense of the political. To wit: "Veblen's sense of the political can be as easily put in a nutshell: that actual situations require responses. What politics is: response to situations. What politics is not: anything more first, final or transcendent."[55] There is no teleology of politics, at least not one that can be produced in a reliable way. Social science is about understanding and explaining reality, or, as Veblen called it, a "matter of fact" approach. Tracing institutional drift and the habits of mind that determine the other sets the stage for political analysis. It is impossible simply to wish things were otherwise, but it is equally impossible to imagine that bygone habits of thought might somehow be appropriate orientations to the changing social relations of the machine process.

Veblen's institutional development is one built on a notion of cumulative causation for institutions that is dynamic, interrelated, and open-ended. He effectively argued that "the ongoing process of institutional adjustment to altered circumstances could be understood through cause-and-effect reasoning [that] reflected the evolutionary character of human culture."[56] This is how he can root the machine process as both evolutionary and nonteleological. It is evolutionary because institutions are part of a "cultural sequence," and human behavior within them is "where cultures evolve as behavior changes and as cause of that change."[57] It is nonteleological because it has no predetermined ends or aims, only those that are pursued by conscious agents.[58] For Veblen, a committed socialist, his critique of capitalism was neither that it was failing to live up to its own standards nor that there was an inevitable transition to a higher/better political economy. Rather, it was that it was asleep at the wheel, and its vested interests were happy to indulge their atavistic habits of mind to enrich themselves at the expense of everyone else.

The upshot here is that there is no simple business-versus-technology dichotomy, or even a dichotomy between a blind drift versus a consciously directed drift. Some combination of blind drift and conscious drift, plus some technological innovation, likely changed habits of mind or retrenched other atavistic ones or had some other kind of change over time.[59] But Veblen also complicated the analysis by suggesting that individuals were shaped by "the force of habituation to different technological exigencies and possibilities and to different institutionalized regimes."[60] There is thus the possibility for things to be different, but only to the extent that these technological exigencies are graspable in some kind of totality that is socially useful. This will cast doubt on the ability to land humans on Mars. In other words, overcomplexity and inaccessibility can hinder the possibilities of the working class in controlling the helm of institutional drift. Institutions may sneak in old habits of thought, but to blindly let them develop is almost certainly a recipe for disaster as cultural lags widen.

This institutional approach also reminds us that gawking at the peculiarities of certain sects of doomsday prepping movements, of all kinds and orientations, is not a politically useful analysis. Doing so could sneak in a teleological approach or a diagnosis based on a reductive vision of rationality. Perhaps some kind of prepping is justified or normal, but these thresholds are socially determined. Perhaps prepping is a rational response to an irrational system, but diagnosing the response does not change the system. For the same reason, we also avoid normatively cataloging preppers, determining which ones are good, which ones are deluded, or whose prepping quanta is enough versus just a little too much. Rather, our institutional analysis asks which habits of mind are being deployed and how are they institutionalized to make this behavior rational, mainstream, or otherwise unobjectionable. Indeed, preppers come in many forms, from different ideological persuasions and within different circumstances.[61] Rather than saying that urban farming cooperatives are good and white nationalist militia compounds are bad (though, to be clear, that is where we would stake our own normative claims concerning the two), the political question is: How this has become a rational response to existential risk, and what other organizational possibilities can be pursued to push collective action, rather than individuated, responses? These questions prompt thinking through institutional arrangements like neoliberalism, nationalism, imperialism, and the like to uncover how prepping becomes an accepted habit of thought and how it discursively shapes the assumptions about organized human behavior going forward. No small task, to be sure, but that seems to us to be the job of political analysis—to find the immanent possibilities within the given facts at hand.

BUILDING AN INSTITUTIONAL DEVELOPMENT OF PREPPING

Institutions are "settled habits of thought" in a social ontology.[62] We would add that these habits of thought give shape and form to modes of everyday life. Because institutions are dynamic and are always already in the process of (un)settling, it makes little sense to definitively differentiate between institutions and other kinds of noninstitutional social behavior. This is undoubtedly frustrating for the empirically minded, but it is an attempt to capture the habitual drift of social change to explain contemporary phenomena. To answer the charge that in this Veblenian model *everything* can be an institution, our response is that we are not taxonomizing but attempting to display a process—so whether a given "thing" is an institution is less important than analyzing the process of (un)settling habits of thought. Trying to take snapshots of individual psychological attitudes or beliefs does not allow us to get a sense of this dynamism, and we run the risk of losing the forest for the trees anyway, given that institutions are what settle those habits in the first place.

We operate from the vantage that institutions allow us to make claims about the patterns of variability that are present in human behavior. Here we argue that Veblen's institutionalism comports with Max Weber, who notes that the

> attempts which have been made hitherto to interpret economic phenomena psychologically, show in any case that the procedure does not begin with the analysis of psychological qualities, moving then to the analysis of social institutions, but that, on the contrary, insight into the psychological preconditions and consequences of institutions presupposes a precise knowledge of the latter and the scientific analysis of their structure. In concrete cases, psychological

analysis can contribute then an extremely valuable deepening of the knowledge of the historical cultural *conditioning* and cultural *significance* of institutions.[63]

Human action remains variable, as do the instincts, rationale, and impetuses for doing things outside the realm of institutions, but the method of institutionalization provides an explanation for

> both personal forms of activity and institutional behavior . . . by tying them to the actions of individuals as they evaluate their meaning. Because social action necessarily involves individual behavior that can be and is acted out only in the context of the past, present, or future behavioral expectations of others, [institutionalism] seeks to grasp the subjective intelligibility of action to those persons acting in the social context. Any given number of individuals may take comparable actions on the basis of different motives, or, at the same time, seemingly comparable motives may lead to many dissimilar modes of activity. By connecting these diverse motives and meanings of action to a socially determinable range of outcomes, one can begin to construct interpretations with considerable explanatory power.[64]

Our institutional analysis, then, does not try to give a totalizing account of the entirety of human existence but rather is a culturally constructed attempt to think through the "theoretical schemes for going on in life."[65] Sometimes habits cross domains or influence others; sometimes behavior is erratic or inconsistent. The job of the social scientist is to account for these variabilities. This is a task distinct from a psychological analysis. To put this in terms of prepping, there are numerous groups that engage in the behavior, and for different reasons. We argue that to build a politics of surpassing this behavior we must provide a level of analysis that goes beyond the individual belief, both in terms of ostensible ideological motivation and in terms of determining the "genuineness" of those beliefs. We instead use institutional analysis to theorize how prepping became an organizing habit of thought of American life and what it might take to overcome that. This is not an easy task: institutions often are imbecilic and wear a groove of path dependency, pointing in the direction of a future that looks the same as the present. Habits are not simply individuated behavior but are social, and when an institution such as prepping is "continued, duplicated, and replicated it carries with it a causative impact to a degree, bearing on the likely shape of institutions with similar roles in the future."[66] With this in mind, we offer three institutions that help explain the emergence of prepping in American political society. We will lay out their institutional rationale here with some of the habits of mind and culturally embedded expressions during a period of rapid industrialization and the onset of a society of mass consumption and go into the detail of their development in the next chapter, and we operate from the position that even in the face of apocalyptic catastrophe, the business enterprise and its atavistic habits of thought persist and that they remain archaic, unable to meet the moment of present threats. Instead, they reify class divisions and animate other archaic atavisms, to the extent that even when looking at how we envision the future, these same atavistic habits of thought persist as an assumed driver of human behavior. Ignoring institutional change is also fraught: "Institutions that become steadily more encrusted with ceremonialism, that is, more emulatory and predatory, will not enhance 'fullness of life.' On the other hand, institutions that facilitate scientific curiosity, proficient workmanship, and altruistic behavior are more likely to meet the generic ends of human existence."[67] This institutional trajectory is cumulative, and we run the risk of amplifying the damage done by animating old habits of thought and building regressive forces that amplify cultural lags. The goal is to root them out in their embedded context. This gives us a chance at doing something differently.

INSTITUTIONS THAT SHAPE PREPPING: SCOUTING, HANDICRAFT, TINKERING

Conscious of the fact that we are speaking in the context of the United States, our selection of institutional arrangements seeks to reflect this very specific condition. There is a ripe possibility for comparative studies of prepping across countries, but those are beyond the scope of the present work. To excavate the idea of prepping as an institution, we look at the early twentieth century as the United States was rapidly industrializing, expanding westward, waging war, and experiencing mass immigration. Specifically, we look at the Boy Scouts of America, the Arts and Crafts movement, and tinkering culture and how they coalesce at the point where, in the middle of the twentieth century, the federal government asked Americans to construct their own homemade fallout shelters in preparation for nuclear war.

Scouting might seem like an obvious institution to take up, especially given that the motto of the Boy Scouts of America (BSA) is "Be Prepared." Indeed, it is almost an invitation to ask: Be prepared for what? We will posit that institutionally, the BSA prepared Americans to manage the transition to an industrial society based on wage labor, rationalizing the virtues of the myth of the self-sufficient "frontiersman" with the realities of the need for obedient, disciplined workers, managing the cultural lag of conceptions of masculinity. The BSA also preserved the imperial ambitions of westward expansion by inculcating stewards of the land in a certain kind of environmental preservation that kept the natural environment pure in order to be rationally managed and exploited by industry. Scouting is thus the stirrings of a "wise use" ecology in ways that valorized imperial expansion and the removal of indigenous peoples. The BSA, finally, was institutionally fundamental in cementing purity in terms of mass migration patterns during industrial urbanization. Discourses of cleanliness and stewardship of the land managed anxiety about the xenophobic "dirtiness" of rapid urbanization and mass immigration, both environmentally and in terms of the national character. This institutional story is not to suggest that the BSA was an explicitly xenophobic, racist, and imperialist organization but that it participated in the renegotiation of what it means to be an American, and in so doing it represents the cultural lag of early American myths about what kinds of people citizens were meant to be and rationalized it into the tumult of industrialization and international conflict (most specifically the two World Wars). Being resourceful, obedient, and self-sufficient still infuses what it means to be an American; many astronauts, for instance, were advanced scouts in their youth.

The Handicraft or Arts and Crafts movement was an institutional intervention that was also in reaction to the rapidly advancing industrialization process of the United States. Much like the BSA, these movements rationalized mass production and consumption in ways that preserved an ethic of start-to-finish bespoke production. This was presented as a matter of social and moral hygiene, by resisting the dinginess and stultifying effects of industrial divisions of labor and cultivating an appropriate aesthetic sensibility through alternative production methods. Handicraft was thus another way to smuggle in atavistic habits of thought around mass immigration, cleanliness, and the maintenance of a class structure. Veblen's theory of conspicuous consumption will come especially to the fore here because handicraft is a way to distinguish between the kind of consumption engaged in by the leisure class, who can afford the more expensive handicraft goods—as well as display the ethical, economic, and aesthetic superiority that such ostentatious consumption provides. The institutions of handicraft preserve the idea that certain kinds of consumption are better than others, and thereby they reify class hierarchies, which in turn solidifies the political project of neoliberalism, where purchasing power sustains political power and social hierarchy. Savvy consumption and the right quality and quantity of purchasing are the hallmarks of a consumer society that come through an emphasis on handicraft. Although ostensibly an alternative to industrial production, it comfortably sits alongside it as an aspirational mode of consumption, for the ostentatious consumption of those who are able. In the case of prepping, handicraft is the institutional basis for savvy consumers who can build their own backyard shelter as well as judiciously accumulate, manage, and discharge a stockpile of mass-produced, shelf-stable goods.

Finally, the institution of tinkering manages the lag between the complex machine process of production and its finely tuned and specialized division of labor and the habits of mind of "masterless men" who can fashion the necessities of life from start to finish. Tinkering replaces the complete knowledge of production (in modern times, impossibly complex) with a mastery of commodities. In this way, rather than being able to produce a commodity (say, a radio), tinkering, for example, being able to "take it apart and put it back together," is a way to demonstrate mastery of the logic of the commodity production. Tinkering provides the basis for "hacking," that is, making commodities perform in ways that may not have been intended. Tinkering is most evident in U.S. automotive culture. Given the highly coordinated and intricate division of labor of car production, tinkering becomes a response to Fordism and Taylorism, both in the way that it maintains the habit of mind of self-sufficiency, in that a person might still exert a kind of control over the mass-produced, impossibly complex products of industry, as well as solidifying the habit of mind of industrial discipline, in that the same person must still understand the logic of industrial production in order to tinker or hack the result.

These institutional negotiations lead, undoubtedly, to social contradictions. The self-sufficient frontiersman and the happy worker in the thrall of the business enterprise may not make logical sense, but managing this contradiction is precisely the role of these institutions. The aesthetics of start-to-finish production does not square with the hoarding tendencies of mass production. The mastery of commodities to make them do things they might not have otherwise been designed to do is incompatible with a mythos of bootstrapping do-it-yourself-ers. To the extent that these institutions make legible the directive to take "personal responsibility" and construct a homemade fallout shelter, it also helps make legible the responsibilization of citizenship in a neoliberal epoch and beyond. That is, we use this institutional framework to show that by the time the U.S. government confirms, in the "Gaither Report" of 1955, that the federal government will not provide shelter as a matter of government policy, it is harking back to the habits of mind of frontiersmanship, fortification, and self-reliant Americans who take responsibility for their own fates. We have pulled out these three institutions because we argue they do the best job of cultivating those habits of mind, even as the facts on the ground tell a different story, both in terms of the extent to which Americans are still those things (to the extent that they ever really were), as well as how they pull the habits of thought and adapt them to a machine process of mass production and mass consumption.

2

CRAFTING A PREPPING AMERICAN

As **WE** argued in the last chapter, the conditioned social behavior of individuals in groups and the political possibilities of action and social change can at least in part be explained by institutional development, particularly the version of the institutional analysis presented by one of its founders, Thorstein Veblen. The goal of this chapter is to try to use these insights to develop an institutional analysis of the prepping American. Doing so establishes an Americanness such that, by the time the U.S. government asked citizens to construct do-it-yourself (DIY) fallout shelters in the mid-1950s, this request made sense and connected to old (atavistic) habits of mind. This, along with the machine process of mass production and consumption, sets the stage for prepping as a way of life and as part of the institutional development of an American identity.

To be clear, we are not adjudicating whether the policy of Americans building their own shelters against nuclear attack was wise or effective.[1] Instead, this institutional development carries the promise of illuminating how Americans were primed to build bunkers as a matter of national identity, how such a self-conception shows what a postbunker America might look like, how bunkerizing one's home is incorporated into everyday life as an ordering logic, and how that displays the same kind of atavistic habits that are on display here. For now, the politics of prepping emerges with an activation of habits of thought that carry through what it means to be an American—namely self-sufficiency, frontiersmanship, imperial expansion and its xenophobia, and taking responsibility for one's own survival by being able to produce all of life's necessities. This chapter takes up the question of the kinds of institutional arrangements that activate these habits of mind and these predatory or archaic expressions.

To map these institutional trajectories, we discuss the Boy Scout, the handicrafter, and the tinkerer as cultural archetypes that form the basis of a politics of prepping in the United States. We reiterate that we are not attempting to crack into the psyches of Americans to find out what they "really think" or to find some biological drive, impulse, or instinct that produces this behavior. We also do not seek to give a comprehensive history of discrete social movements. Our task is to show how these institutions smuggle in atavistic habits of mind that shaped what it meant to be an American, then how they persist in the prepping behaviors of contemporary Americans, and how that shapes the political situations and possibilities of the present moment. These three institutions help us contextualize broader social phenomena such as imperialism, expansionism, xenophobia, industrialization, fears about ecological degradation, and the division of labor as intellectual and moral development. These institutions explain the uniquely American politics of prepping and bunkerization through mass consumption, such that by the time the U.S. government is in the thick of the Cold War, it is a legible request when it asks citizens to build their own fallout shelters for nuclear war. These institutional thrusts provide fundamental, if not fully exhaustive, insights that help us analyze the current trajectories of neoliberalism, the new space race, and the mainstreaming of prepper culture.

THE INSTITUTIONAL EVOLUTION OF AMERICANNESS IN THE BSA

The Boy Scouts of America (BSA) is a ubiquitously embedded American institution. The organization is so wrapped up in the mythos of American youth that it has a cultural valence regardless of the recent fiscal or demographic challenges of the organization. Still, the BSA was not monolithic at its inauguration, as it was competing with other scouting organizations. This was true both abroad, particularly in England and Germany, which had scouting organizations that pre-dated the BSA, but also in the United States, where different scouting organizations, often regional, vied for the time and attention of (mostly) boys. The well-documented story of the BSA's founding reflects this. The British scoutmaster Robert Baden-Powell, as well as the founder of the "Woodcraft Indians" scouting outfit, the Canadian Ernest Thompson Seton, along with the American Daniel Carter Beard, the founder of the "Sons of Daniel Boone," a scouting organi-zation that valorized frontiersman exploits, all gathered at the Waldorf-Astoria Hotel in New York City in 1910 to found the Boy Scouts of America.[2] Uniting (or eclipsing) rival scouting organizations is a smart way to make an institution a going concern, but a Veblenian analysis prompts the questions: Why then? What habits of mind were being changed or preserved? And what was it responding to? Our analysis of the BSA focuses on how it managed the cultural lag of the difference between the dictates of the new machine process of industrial production and the habits of mind of the masculine American imaginary of self-sufficient citizens living off the land. The BSA thrived where other scouting organizations might have failed precisely because it was a successful adaptation to new modes of production that did not violate the mythos of what it meant to be an American. Notably, the BSA become the standard of scouting, separate and distinct from the overtly militarized "American Boy Scouts" organization founded by William Randolph Hearst, which in our institutionalist framework failed to take root because it did not rationalize boys into the changing social relations but offered an alternative mode of life modeled on the soldier.[3] The BSA was able to avoid the twin poles of overly sentimentalized romantic yearning for a bygone mode of life and a regimented militarization that would remain separate from the world into which boys would enter. It provided the basis for the conception of masculinity to adapt to the new industrial mode of production, which prized con-formity and efficiency rather than adventurism and brashness. The BSA helped bridge this gap.

Scouting has particular relevance here, especially as the BSA became eponymous with scouting itself and in comparison to other fraternal organizations that were also prevalent in the early-twentieth-century United States. Unlike the Freemasons or Odd Fellows, the BSA did not claim to offer an escape from the stultifying conformity of corporate life but instead "instilled values for navigating corporate-industrial life and thriving in it."[4] This encapsulates the institutional development of rationalizing old habits of mind into new social relations. In the same way, Baden-Powell's vision of scouts won out over the Sons of Daniel Boone or other fraternal organizations because it was not offering an alternative to emerging social relations but bridging the gap between the habits of mind and sense of self that was being challenged by these new modes of production. The BSA was able to take the Victorian concept of "self-made manhood," which was emblematized and guaranteed by producing one's own provisions from start to finish, and rationalize it into the "monotonous, specialized goods production" of the industrial machine process.[5] The Fordist and Taylorist production process may have offended moral and aesthetic sensibilities, such as in Max Weber's depiction of industrial processes in Chicago stockyards, but the tangible result was that workers were "dispossessed of an overview," where they are "stripped of 'a single thought or emotion.' "[6] The BSA's task in the face of Taylor's scientific management was to get boys past the apprenticeship system of labor training and to adapt to a stratified workforce where knowing the whole of the process was not important.[7] The BSA turned these anxieties about industrialization into a mark of confidence about how well boys could turn into men that integrated themselves into the system of industrial production:

> Modern corporations needed employees to work together seamlessly on segmented routine tasks in order to compete against rivals. . . . While maintaining the character of heritage [habit of mind] of self-reliance through outdoorsmanship and individual rank and merit badge standards, half of the BSA's Twelve Laws and portions of the Americanized Scout Oath helped teach members a fitting new work ethic for the twentieth-century's large-scale industries and management by expertise.[8]

The derring-do of swashbuckling businessmen and the aloof yeoman farmer were being displaced by being trustworthy, clean, and reverent. The BSA provided a vision of masculinity that hung on to the outdoorsmanship of the frontier ethos while making obedience to authority and rigidly hierarchical social control prime moral motivators. This obeisance is important because, otherwise, it might encourage boys and young men to challenge the hierarchies of work that disrupt the smooth flow of profits.[9]

To distill this dynamic into the topic of prepping, we appeal to the Boy Scout motto: *Be Prepared*. The BSA was able to provide a vision for Americans (and to be clear, this is a mostly masculine vision of what it means to be an American, even as scouting organizations for girls were emerging at the same time) that rationalized the cultural lag between industrialization and self-sufficient yeoman farmers (someone like Thomas Jefferson), brash businessmen (like John Rockefeller), and adventurous field generals (such as President Theodore Roosevelt).[10] The BSA adapted to the machine process of mass production with its industrial divisions of labor and need for concentrated, cooperative wage laborers, as well as the preindustrial habits of mind of self-sufficient American yeoman farmers, living off the land. At the historical juncture of the early twentieth century, such an institution was vital to manage what might have otherwise been a very clear contradiction between the dictates of industrialization and the cultural image Americans had of themselves. The BSA was able to articulate this new political economy; its attendant imperial ambitions and militaristic social organization, as well as the reification of the idea that self-sufficient American individuals were to be prepared to withstand the travails of such imperial adventurism (be that westward expansion, managing/disciplining immigrant populations, or the Cold War of bunkerization). The BSA is an emblematic institution of the idea that the mythos of individual responsibility can be made compatible with the homogeneity and interdependency of a society of mass production and consumption. The following will demonstrate this institutional specificity by looking at the broader social context in which the institution was founded and how it sought to overcome this lag and redefine "preparation" as a habit of mass consumption by analyzing what it means to "Be Prepared." This notion of preparation was shaped during the imperialism of westward expansion and account for how scouting incorporated militarism, the anxieties of mass immigration and how those relate to conservation efforts, and the onset of a society of mass consumption. "Be Prepared" meant to establish "civic superiority" by taking responsibility for the "less prepared."[11] This idea of civic superiority through preparation as a display of masculinized responsibility will carry forward in the development of a prepping American.

MANAGING/DENYING IMPERIALISM

Part of the process of industrialization in the early twentieth century involved increasing international and, as a byproduct, imperial entanglements for the United States alongside other world powers. This growing imperialism, which served as a way both to source raw materials and create export markets, is one of the economic "facts at hand" that Veblen argues must be confronted directly, even if it is unsavory or otherwise undesirable.[12] The imperial aspect of industrialization in the United States is also emblematic of Veblen's idea of a cultural lag, in the sense that empire conflicted with the self-sufficient, land-working, isolationist notion of what it meant to be an American. Part of his institutional analysis was to theorize what kinds of institutions or organizations could manage this contradiction or lag. As an institution, scouting was able to provide "a beguiling solution to America's imperial dilemma, furnishing a template for doing empire in a nation notoriously invested in negating its own imperiality," which provided the space for Americans to indulge in a "luxury of innocence."[13] In other words, institutions like scouting were tasked with overcoming the lag between the realities of empire and the habits of mind of an isolationist citizenry; scouting helped sustain a myth of an empire without imperialists. This also explains why Hearst's American Boy Scouts floundered; its mimicry of militarism with drills and weapons handling was too close to the imperialism that Americans understood themselves to be opposed to.

This is why, in general, the BSA was able to survive when other scouting and fraternal organizations failed to take root. In a Veblenian sense, the BSA could manage this lag. It could update habits of mind to accommodate the current facts at hand while not completely negating the mythos of self-sufficiency—a tricky balancing act. Other scouting outfits that also were not as overtly militaristic as the American Boy Scouts, such as the Woodcraft Indians, focused almost exclusively on performing, whether accurately or inaccurately, a preindustrial alternative that operated in opposition to ramping up industrialization efforts and the nascent empire's many foreign engagements.[14] Such organizations would be unable to overcome that gap between those more isolationist habits of mind, however appealing, with the changing face of American production, because they could not habituate their members to the reality of industrial production. Such movements immediately seemed anachronistic, and they soon withered away. The BSA, on the other hand, was able to split the difference between being overtly imperialistic and too anachronistic. It did "the imperial work of for a society without causing an affront to its nonimperial identity," making the ideological job of the BSA's efforts to update habits of mind "the white boy's burden . . . Boy Scouts were to learn empire, not question it." Although the BSA was founded a few years before the outbreak of World War I, the institution was attentive to the growing imperial powers and struck a decidedly nonmilitaristic organizational model to facilitate a civilian imaginary for international engagement.[15] Such a move allowed youth organizations like the BSA to engage in projects of nation building, belonging, and citizenship, as well as imperial acceptance, even if they did not conceive of themselves as imperial actors.[16] Far from being a peacenik organization, the BSA claimed to mobilize the peace. The BSA purported to be a vector of cross-national ties, harnessing the dynamism and goodwill of a youth movement in the United States in a way that allowed the imaginary of isolationist Americans to remain undisturbed—a nationalism that could ignore imperial expansion.[17]

This is not to say that the BSA was an overt mouthpiece for empire or that it explicitly behaved in such a way to facilitate international expansion. In fact, the BSA was careful during and in the aftermath of World War I to not be an explicitly promilitary institution. It was generally supportive of the war, in the sense of a patriotic approval well within the mainstream of other civil society organizations but resisted being conflated with the institution of the military.[18]

Thinking about the BSA as a civil society institution that operated as a conduit to launder American innocence about imperial expansion by holding on to archaic notions of self-sufficiency clearly demonstrates at least a part of BSA's ideological task. It manages the cultural lag and seeks to shape the habits of mind of Americans into something that is more friendly to the changing reality of imperial expansion. The BSA helped manufacture an international innocence in the midst of a changing political economy of international industrialization. It is also important to note that in terms of its ideological function, the point of the BSA is not to *overcome* the cultural lag but to *manage* the contradictions that it might otherwise engender. In the early twentieth century, after a massive campaign of westward expansion through a doctrine of Manifest Destiny, it certainly seems risible that Americans did not see themselves as citizens in a project of empire, but as Kaplan notes, masking the project of empire in the trappings of domesticity can make imperialism look like a simple enlargement and maintenance of the domestic sphere.[19] This dovetails with the Veblenian institutional analysis to show how lag, or contradiction (we may use these terms interchangeably),[20] is managed through myriad institutions and allows the myth of the landed yeoman farmer or striving solo entrepreneur to persist even as the facts of everyday life indicate otherwise.

Scouting served this role of empire well, but as Veblen reminds us, the habits of mind also change the institutions that change them. The Boy Scouts were themselves changed by the habits of mind that animated the myth of the frontiersman; it had turned, by midcentury, into a nationalistic institution ready to defend the empire with the knowhow of the frontiersman and the disciplined ethic of a soldier.[21] Nationalist support for the war effort began to conflate scouting with military service.[22] This would still count as an ideological success, updating the habits of mind that united adventurism and discipline for military ambition, wrapped up in a harmless nationalism of civic superiority as a kind of peaceful mobilization effort. The BSA may not have had imperial collusion at the front of its mind, but its institutional evolution alongside the facts at hand of American empire in the twentieth century would make it so.[23] In this way, being prepared as a scout nominally resisted but substantially extended the militaristic notion of preparedness to defend the nation in a way that recasts prep-aration as a peacetime project that forms masculinity as a civic supe-riority.[24] It is precisely this ambivalence that gives the BSA a unique valence as an organization that can rectify old habits of thought with the new machine processes of industrial production and attendant phenomena such as imperialism. It allows Americans to walk the fine line of being nationalistic but antiwar, even as the world descended into war in the early and middle twentieth century.

ORGANIZED ADVENTURISM AND
INTERNAL BUREAUCRATIZATION

An essential way that the BSA was able to become synonymous with scouting and become perceived as "American as apple pie" was the extent to which it was able to integrate itself into the trajectory of Amer-ican society by harmonizing old habits of mind with new realities—in this case, an isolationist people confronting the imperial ambitions of an increasingly global United States. This tactic also updated mas-culinity from its Victorian context of Veblen's "masterless man"—the adventuring entrepreneur living off the land and according to their own cunning—toward what William Whyte referred to as the "Orga-nization Man," representing a masculinity geared toward identify-ing with and meeting the needs of workplace organizations, rather than presenting an alternative to them.[25] One job of the BSA was to make equivalent the masculine qualities of plowing the soil and punching a time card.

Much like the case of the BSA's ambivalence of its (initially) nation-alist nonmilitarism, the institutional task of the scouts was to reorient what it meant to be an American in the increasingly urban, industrial mode of production. And, again much like how the BSA smuggled in an archaic sense of what it meant to be an indepen-dent, isolationist American even in the face of imperial ambitions, the BSA also ported the archaic habits of adventurism and daring entrepreneurialism into a machine process that expected almost the exact opposite: conformity and unflinching obedience. Thus, as the BSA Scout Law says, scouts are not only to be "loyal, helpful, friendly, courteous, kind, obedient, cheerful, thrifty . . ." but also "brave."[26] Such a shift was especially important in the aftermath of World War II, where militaristic ambivalence but fervent nationalist support preserved youth and boy-men to navigate post–World War II difficulties by emphasizing obedience and denying imperialism in favor of a more innocent, managed adventurism in scouting.[27] Scouting expeditions to the Arctic or Antarctic poles or to Africa as a way of turning boys into men are stark examples of this kind of organized excursion.[28] Playacting an old habit of mind to both valorize and update it fits with Veblen's framework. Specifically, Veblen discusses collegiate athletics as arenas where achieving honorifics in battle can be dramatically—but safely—reenacted.[29] This further sets the stage for the predatory leisure class and the aspiring business class to reflect this seeking of honorifics through the business enterprise itself.[30] Masculinity through battle is replaced by business cunning.

These institutional changes in the way American masculinity are understood, updated, and preserved are also reflected in the institutional development of the BSA. The BSA was not only an attractive organization because of its content but for how it fit itself into the changing American landscape. Every U.S. president since Theodore Roosevelt was the BSA's honorary chair during their time in office and remained an honorary vice chair for the rest of their lives.[31] Rather than the other scouting organizations, which affirmed masculinity by denying the industrial organization and hierarchy of American life, or the civic organizations that relied on a byzantine, quasi-secret structure to carve out a space for men like Babbitt to affirm their masculinity in a safe fratriarchy, the BSA modeled itself after the kind of organization taking hold in a Fordist and Taylorist industrial America. By mimicking the organizational structure of the changing industrial landscape, the BSA provided a model for updating habits of mind to new contexts in a way that preserved bygone ideas of what it meant to be an American, particularly a masculine one. From a Veblenian institutionalist perspective, this makes perfect sense. The codetermination of habits of mind and machine process updated the idea of masculinity from one of rugged individualism and complete self-sufficiency into one that is meticulous, organized, and efficient within hierarchies.

Being prepared is, at least in part, a manifestation of adaptation to industrial production and rationalizing oneself with the new machine process. Being a good American meant synchronizing with the Taylorist production schedule, the rhythms of the machine, and being respectful of the time and property of the ownership class. Going to the frontier, working the land, and providing for one's family was reduced to a dramatized and managed series of experiences that could be done through an organization such as scouting, while at the same time instilling new habits into masculine identities like cleanliness, punctuality, cooperation, and diligence even as it provided those "rugged" experiences.[32] Now repackaged as "fun," for example, going camping, scouting is able to present itself as a socialization effort to turn boys into responsibilized citizens.[33] Being prepared, then, in part meant savvy consumption in order to effectively accumulate the ends of life in such a way as to purchase a good life; scouting taught how to attempt being a responsible citizen in an era of mass production and consumption and providing for one's family in a different kind of modality.

In a bygone, yeoman version of American masculinity, being prepared may well have involved going into the frontier, establishing a safe perimeter, working the land, and running a household to allow for a family to thrive. Whether this is historically accurate, this archetype was a driver of American masculinity. In an industrial mode of production, however, this conception of masculinity is not only no longer needed but detrimental to the concentrated, cooperative labor process of mass production. As institutions develop to rationalize people into these new processes, the BSA presented a way to hold on to these old ideas of masculinity while changing this conception of masculinity to meet the needs of the new machine process. Being prepared is part of this rationalization process but also a reorientation of how one prepares: moving from working the land to savvy consumption. Preparation, in this way, is reflected in the broader organizational trends of the machine process. Scouting serves as a way to socialize boys within a disciplinary apparatus to construct them as men who can take responsibility for preparedness in the way that mass consumption allows and rationalizes the older version of American masculinity into obedient industrial subjects that still valorize the moribund visions of masculinity.[34] The BSA produced obedient wage laborers who nevertheless have the skills and knack for adventure to survive in the wilderness if they must.

CONSERVATIONISM, XENOPHOBIA, AND HYGIENE

The American president who encapsulated the hortatory effects of scouting as an activity that was synonymous with what it meant to be an American man was Theodore Roosevelt.[35] Roosevelt is also often associated with the start of the American conservationist movement in the early twentieth century, with special attention paid to a supposed romantic impulse to keep pure the natural beauty of the American wilderness.[36] This largely tracks with the Leopoldian, Muirian vision of conservationism writ large; the impetus behind conserving nature was premised on the idea that it was there to behold and was vital for proper moral and aesthetic development.[37] This version of conservation runs headlong into the same problem of organizational orientation noted earlier. Much like the competing fraternal orders and scouting organizations that sought to provide an alternative space separate and distinct from the encroachment of industrial society, making integration into the new dominant mode of production difficult, this romanticized version of conservationism as carving out pristine outlets to be kept as a reprieve from industrial society put it at odds with the new machine process. In the same way that habits of mind of organization, empire, and masculinity needed to be rationalized into the emerging machine process of industrial production, so too did conservationism. Rather than try to reify the romanticism of nature as a pristine alternative to an increasingly urbanized life, conservationism shed the transcendentalism of Emerson and Thoreau and became a matter of managing resources lying in wait, a stock for men to display their mastery over nature.[38]

The BSA was explicit that rather than marvel at the unknowable mysteries of nature, scouts would master it, "unlock" its secrets, and "recognize the forces and the laws of operation," and in so doing engage in a "struggle with nature." The natural environment is not a redoubt that offers solace from the rigmarole of modern life but rather is the feedstock from which scouts can identify new valuable resources, as well as preserve existing ones. The BSA's version of nature scouting—through increased scientific knowledge and resource identification/management—trained boys to become men who could eventually be expert managers of a nation's economy and resources.[39] Boys could go into nature and marvel but were expected to come out as men who knew how to leverage the wilderness to meet the needs of a modern industrialized society. It is unsurprising that the mastery of natural resource management would also extend into human resource management. The BSA was crafting a masculinity befitting the emerging American empire, and as military needs increased, human resources were more easily mobilized into war.[40] Natural resources for national development, imperialism, and war supersede the nature that awe-struck scouts might encounter; a scout's job was to assume responsibility for achieving national ends through the rationalization and domination of their lived environment.

Mass immigration during the early twentieth century also fueled anxiety about what it meant to be an American and whether recent immigrants might be rationalized into Americanness through things like scouting. On the one hand, the BSA, like many other institutions at the turn of the twentieth century, operated from an assumption of biological engineering and entertained, as part of the civic superiority of scouting, an attempt at outreach to communities of immigrant boys to mold them into proper Americans. Though often done in an explicitly racialized way, the assumption here is that while perhaps immigrants are not eligible to have full Americanness bestowed on them, perhaps their male children could, if reached early enough. This attitude toward immigrant populations encapsulates why the BSA as an institution did not insist on providing alternatives to the dominant social order but rationalized itself into it. The BSA understood the bodies of its boys to be the future components of the men who compose the body of the national Leviathan, and so those bodies would also have to be clean for the national body to function efficiently. [41] Natural conservation mimics practices of hygiene, expanding the notion of what it means to be "clean" in the scout oath. Being prepared here means being on guard against pollutants in the body politic, as well as offering opportunities to discipline entrants into the rationalized, mechanical social body.[42]

Besides setting a standard for Americanization and rationalization into the new industrial society, disciplining immigrants also tied into the conservationist efforts of the BSA as a matter of human resource management. On the one hand, the BSA saw itself as part of a technocratic vanguard, with organizational advantages for dominating, extracting, and managing natural resources. On the other hand, it assumed responsibility for producing disciplined subjects capable of performing Americanness in its new iteration at the turn of the century. For the BSA, these two aspects went hand in hand when dealing with mass immigration to the United States in the early twentieth century. Here it is important to note that the assumptions behind whether immigrant populations could attain Americanness through scouting were based entirely on the immigrants' being from Europe. While nations all over the world produced scouting organizations more or less modeled on the BSA, it seems the American imaginary only extended to immigrants of European descent. Managing natural resources and managing human resources were not separate things: "Some scout conservation sources also implied that working-class European immigrants lacked the intelligence and foresight needed to protect the nation's resources, but that they might develop such skills through joining Scouting."[43] The BSA managed this anxiety of a populace that saw itself as isolationist (even if not necessarily homogenous) dealing with an influx of immigration by presenting scouting as a way to assimilate and discipline immigrant groups. This gave the BSA "a unique opportunity to win public approval. If ethnic pluralism was a reality, preventing the disuniting of America would become a major task."[44] The BSA provides the institutional bridge to confer Americanness upon the right kind of people for acquiring the right kind of skills and for participating in the right kind of nation building. The logic of natural resource conservation comes through here—a large group of immigrant boys can be managed and rationalized into productive units, much like natural resources lying fallow in the wilderness.

The unity between managing natural resources and human resources, as well as the unity between the hygiene of the scout and the social hygiene of the body politic, reaches a high point regarding early-twentieth-century juvenile delinquency. The xenophobic anxiety of mass immigration certainly fueled much of the concern of juvenile delinquency, but this also ties directly into another institutional job of the BSA: to rationalize the increasingly dense urban life that emerged during industrialization. The assumption was that "working-class youths and youths of color" were "more likely to exhibit delinquent behavior."[45] Whether such criminality was inborn was openly debated, but certainly, "a corrupt environment or unsavory companions would strand an adolescent boy in childlike selfishness and cruelty, leading him into juvenile delinquency and lifelong criminality."[46]

As a result of managing the new urban environment to try to prevent juvenile delinquency, these youths would have to be managed and disciplined like natural resources. However, lurking behind this assumption—at least in part—is an anxiety about urban density and the changing character of Americanness that is based on rural yeoman landowners and the assumed moral development such a life imparts.[47] The BSA took it upon itself to be the institution that develops boys in such a way that "is an effective antidote for the poisons of undisciplined lawlessness," while noting that "there are no bad boys, but some misdirected boys," notably the youth population of the "warring nations of Europe," whose children would be in the thrall of the rescue project that scouting could promise.[48] The magistrate and scoutmaster Joseph Finch offers as much in 1915:

> This morning a young Italian of 18 or 19 was arraigned before me on a charge of insubordination and vagrancy preferred by his own father. The old man is a street paver, a rammer, the father of seven children, a wizened day laborer, about half the size of his delinquent son. . . . His education in the public schools had so thoroughly instilled in him the idea of keeping clean that he carried to the point of keeping away from any manual labor which might possibly soil his hands. . . . The whole trouble was that his education had been such to make him look down on manual labor. . . . The discipline of the Boy Scouts would have met this particular case in two ways. He would have been trained to be clean, to omit cigarettes or anything else that was impairing his health. . . . Secondly, he would have been

taught the dignity and decency of common labor. As a scout, while he would have been stimulated to prepare himself for a more skilled position, he would have felt that even a pick and shovel were not only permissible, but desirable.[49]

Here hygiene, managing immigrant populations and priming their offspring for earning Americanness, and the idea that the BSA is the vehicle to prevent what might otherwise seem a foregone conclusion of juvenile delinquency show how the BSA understood itself as an institution tasked with being a vehicle for self- and social discipline. A key feature of that discipline was to present a path for immigrant populations to be integrated into American society. Increased urbanization would not disrupt Americans' self-conception as frontiersmen who live by their own cunning off the land, but now the goal of conservationism would convert from being an appreciation of the great mysteries of nature celebrated by transcendentalist thinkers like Emerson and Thoreau into, instead, wise resource management for national goals. They would "Be Prepared" to manage themselves and their resources to reproduce Americanness, in the face of any challenge.

HANDICRAFTING CONSPICUOUS CONSUMPTION

The BSA was an institution that helped rationalize masculinity into a new mode of production as the United States rapidly industrialized. Anxieties about American masculine identities, mass immigration, and urbanization were updated by boys who could "Be Prepared" to become the kind of men needed to administer the managerial apparatus of natural resource and human management. Yet it is clear that more work was needed to manage these anxieties. As far back as Adam Smith and his famous pin factory, the industrial machine process and its attendant division of labor was a source of worry about the holistic development of people under its sway. Even though Smith points out that industrial production's use of machinery and the division of labor yields drastic improvement over craft production, he also notes that

the man whose whole life is spent in performing a few simple operations . . . naturally . . . becomes as stupid and ignorant as it is
possible for a human creature to become. The torpor of his mind
renders him not only incapable of relishing or bearing a part in
any rational conversation, but of conceiving any generous, noble, or
tender sentiment, and consequently for forming any just judgment
concerning many even of the ordinary duties of private life. . . . The
uniformity of his stationary life naturally corrupts the courage of his
mind. . . . It corrupts even the activity of his body . . . in every
improved and civilized society, this is the state into which the labour-
ing poor . . . must necessarily fall, unless government takes some
pains to prevent it.[50]

As a result of Smith's formulation, the myth of the self-sufficient
American yeoman farmer at the frontier comes into sharper focus as a
perceived bulwark against such stultification. The Handicraft or Arts
and Crafts movements (we will use the terms interchangeably) offered
an institutional framework for such a reprieve. While many of these
movements popped up in the United States at the turn of the twentieth
century, we will broadly take the term to mean a constellation of movements that extolled producing the ends of life from start to finish as a
salutary mode of life. Of course, where one starts and where one fin-
ishes are somewhat arbitrary (very few of those who make their own
bread also mill their own flour, for instance), but these movements
promised to overcome the deleterious effects of industrialization by
asking people to hew to a prior mode of production that envisions production in its entirety so that they might develop creatively and aesthetically. Even though prepping may be less concerned with aesthetic
development, the idea, as with scouting, that good Americans should
apprehend production to provide for their everyday needs is still amplified as a sign of good moral character and civic superiority.

HANDICRAFT MOVEMENTS:
NEW EMULATIONS IN OLD CRAFTS

Turning back to Veblen is instructive even if only for the fact that he
wrote about these movements while they were happening. Veblen's

perspective on the machine process was one of perpetual motion, so he heavily criticized movements that sought to turn back time or reclaim a bygone mode of production. He criticized the Arts and Crafts League of Chicago and other such handicraft movements in two particular ways. First, he critiqued the supposed aesthetic sensibilities that would awaken the moral drive of people to become better citizens, turning away from the filth of the city toward a beautiful bucolic life, as a tertiary outcome. Primarily, handicraft served as a marker of class distinction, for people to hold up their handmade goods as superior to others' mass-produced ones.[51] Second, he critiqued the material impossibilities of handicraft production to meet the actual needs of life in an efficient way that was as non-irksome as possible. These critiques gain even more salience in the face of the complexity of the machine process and will come into even sharper focus when discussing the shift from tinkering to hacking. The machine process, in earlier stages of production, may have been visible in its entirety to a given individual, such as Adam Smith's pin factory. But as labor is divided, skills increasingly specialized, and technologies are applied to the machine process, the ability of a given individual to command the apparatus of production to make things start to finish becomes difficult to fathom, especially given that the machine process is increasingly composed of products of past machine processes.[52]

At the turn of the twentieth century, the Arts and Crafts/Handicraft movement had taken hold in some urban areas of the United States. These movements held that industrial production prevented the moral and aesthetic development of citizens and could impart such development through producing more of their own commodities from start to finish, imparting a more virtuous moral and aesthetic development onto Americans.[53] Doing so would ostensibly ward off the various social pathologies of industry, such as the criminality and filth of rapid urbanization. For Veblen, however, these movements were an anachronistic attempt that amounted to little more than a wistful yearning for a bygone era to remedy the evils of the current context.[54]

In this regard, Veblen is not a critic of handicraft as such, but he is against its deployment as archaic romanticism as a bulwark against new forms of production, which turns it into a vector of conspicuous consumption. Handcrafted goods display the kinds of defects that prove the item was handmade, with all the time and skill that such an endeavor requires, and these defects signify rarity and, as such, high price points.[55] In this respect, Veblen's critique of the Handicraft movement fits with his overall prescription of cultural lag described in the previous chapter, where the social status conferred by acquiring rare artifacts easily overwhelms the possibilities of aesthetic development. Even if handicrafters believed there was an egalitarian or liberatory potential in crafting, the urge of the predatory/leisure class to conspicuously consume such fineries to show social distinction overrode that.[56]

Looking at the facts of production and the stubborn cultural lag, Veblen historicizes the era of handicraft as emerging from the feudal relations that laid the groundwork for modern statecraft.[57] No longer tied to specific plots of land ruled over by warlords, crafters not only fashioned their own goods from start to finish but also spurred a development in the instinct of workmanship that instilled a sense of ownership of production.[58] As Veblen puts it: "In the medieval speculations . . . these religious verities run back to the question, 'What has God ordained?' In the course of the era of handicraft this ultimate question of knowledge came to take the form, 'What hath God wrought?'" Instead of resigning themselves and their production processes to the unknowable will of the divine, craftsmen began considering the divine as a kind of master crafter of nature from whose stock and bounty they were to fashion their own ends of life. For Veblen, this means the beginning of exact standards of measurement, replicable empirical science, open lines of trade, and experimentation with an eye toward material production and enlargement as a care of the divine's bounty. As craftsmen honed their techniques, they became far less dependent on the specific land they might have otherwise been tied to and from which came the "masterless men." The relationship to the rise of empiricism and mercantilism comes into focus as well, since masterless men relied on being able to reproduce the goods of life reliably, quantifiably, and commercially.[59] This broadly correlates to Horkheimer and Adorno's notion of instrumental reason but also harks back to the notion of a scout being able to assess and care for the natural bounty of the national frontier.[60]

The old vestiges of feudal life were still present, however, and in this reorganization of labor in urbanized centers modern heads of state corralled handicraft production to make implements of war.[61] Veblen explains this cultural lag by suggesting that craftsmen, having reorganized themselves to facilitate trade in urban settings, lost more traditional bonds of solidarity because of a (perhaps overstated) self-sufficiency and were happy to lend their energies to building and sustaining a war machine for perceived industrial ends. In reality, it was the atavistic pursuit of honorifics that so easily swayed the masterless men; whereas a new mode of production might produce a better society, Veblen is quick to warn that the lag is still there, and so social development is plodding, uneven, and hindered by these archaic habits of thought. While Veblen's actual anthropological evidence for this sweeping claim is scant, it echoes the analysis of theorists like Paul Virilio, who argues that the process of urbanization itself is a war technology that arranges and monitors peoples and goods.[62]

This archaic glory seeking that drove urbanization elevated war and destruction, as well as the justification for the leisure class's claim on the social surplus.[63] From this insight, far from being simply a matter of moral development, craft—much like the BSA—smuggles in notions of colonialism, imperialism, and adventurism. While it is conceivable that masterless men, having thrown off the yoke of feudal lords, could have aimed to build a qualitatively different set of social relations, the cultural lag instead kept barbarian tendencies alive, and the advances in scientific reasoning through handicraft production is then directed at pursuing honorifics through battle.[64] In short, handicraft instilled a habituation for self-sufficiency as well as smuggled in an archaic preference for hierarchies, explaining how masterless men became wage laborers.[65] Within industrial production, it is easy to see how these attitudes of self-sufficiency and reverence for hierarchy are preserved—again to potentially deleterious ends. Urbanization, specialization of knowledge, and quantification continue in even more extreme ways in the current context, and the mobilization of the population (in warfare either symbolic or actual) is still part of the landscape of production, urban planning, and architecture.[66]

In Veblen's analysis, handicraft was much more than a hobby, something that might be easily reduced today to mean the goods that people show and sell on Pinterest and Etsy. It was a mode of production that explained the cultural habits of the immediately postfeudal and transitional stages of industrial production. As such, handicraft is suited to explain those historical relations. As Veblen sees it, going backward or insisting on the moral superiority of a previous mode of production is not a realistic option, because the current mode of production has already subsumed the prior mode and the cultural milieu in which individual habits of mind have already changed. In addition, the anodyne version that is on offer fails to come to grips with the enormity of the mode of production it is aping.[67] In this light, his critique of the Handicraft movement is that it cannot possibly rise to the occasion that the stakes of industrial production actually present, with its own specific cultural lags and atavistic tendencies of the predatory/leisure class and the business class to appropriate the surplus from the underlying populations. Veblen does not critique the idea of handicraft itself, but he critiques appealing to it as an ahistorical salve because it too becomes a marker of predation and conspicuous consumption, just as it was when handicraft was indeed the dominant mode of production. Handicraft movements amplify, rather than overcome, the cultural lags that emerge during the industrialization process.

The Handicraft movement did not necessarily see itself in this way, however. It tried to split the difference by setting itself apart from old modes of production while at the same time building a utopian vision of industrial production. One particular iteration of the Handicraft movement that Veblen criticized directly, the Industrial Art League in the United States, gave a mission statement of sorts:

> This movement is not to be understood as a fanatical protest against machinery, and not as a return to the abandoned domestic system of mediaeval days, but rather as a modern conscious effort to advance a step beyond the factory stage of industry, and to inaugurate a new industrialism wherein the interests of both the producing and consuming classes are guarded—the one class demanding the opportunity of individual expression, and the other the satisfaction of its higher wants.[68]

The text is an exposition of the Handicraft movement's founders' desire to reunite art and labor to supersede mechanical drudgery, yet even the discourse of class harmonization fails to overcome the antagonism between art and industry.[69] Veblen would also point out that the way the machine process is refined is by those who are in it and looking to make it less degrading. As such, in a critical review of the Triggs text, Veblen is blunt: "The movement . . . runs on sentimental grounds rather than on grounds of reasoned practicability." Veblen further indicts this sentiment of the Handicraft movement's seeking to opt out of industrial production by excusing itself from the everyday effects of that mode of production: "Modern industry, in so far as it is characteristically modern, means the machine process; but according to the arts-and-crafts apprehension, only outside of the machine process is there salvation."[70] He insists that the only way to overcome a mode of production is immanent in that mode of production, through the coevolutionary relationship of machines disciplining workers and workers imparting new habits of mind into production.[71] This does not mean that Veblen necessarily disagrees about the downsides of industry; in fact, in many ways, Veblen's concern about a rapidly alienating technological apparatus is a far graver matter. Rather, he seeks to find a way out through overcoming the barbaric hangover of domination, glory seeking, and pecuniary gain that has carried over into an industrial mode of production. This is impossible by simply insisting that people opt out of the system, even if they could return to a handicraft era that was itself marked by the same habits. As chapter 1 argues, only the predatory leisure class can opt out, so building a politics around emulating that behavior is doomed. As Veblen puts it: " If these habits of thought are to be shaped by any propaganda of ideals, they must be sought out and laid hold on in the field where they grow. The machine process has come, not so much to stay merely, but to go forward and root out of the workmen's scheme of thought whatever elements are alien to its own technological requirements and discipline."[72] Changing those habits that are already being changed by the process must similarly be endogenous. Industry can be artful, but only if artfulness is brought into industry by those in the machine process. There is no going back in time, and craftsmanship that eschews the advantages of machine production runs the risk of displaying conspicuous waste, not artisanship.[73]

HANDICRAFTING PREPAREDNESS

If the only aim of the Handicraft movement was to impart an aesthetic impulse for workers to bring artfulness into the realm of industrial production, that might be an easy program to endorse, even if all it amounted to was "a romanticism with a smear of lackadaisical aestheticism across its face." This disdain from Veblen is not only from handicraft's inability to seriously engage the material foundations of its mode of production and countenance why it was supplanted by industry. He is also skeptical of handicraft as a class marker, by analyzing who is able to opt out of industrial production in favor of handicraft and why they might choose to do so. Veblen notes that exceedingly few people actually have the means to decline the products of industry in favor of handicraft. The vast majority then look on at those who are able to opt out and attempt to emulate them. The practical effect is that the Handicraft movement offers yet another kind of conspicuous consumption on the part of the business and leisure classes, who have the pecuniary means to show that they have accumulated enough surplus to consume expensive goods. In fact, handicraft products must necessarily be more expensive: "if they are to pass inspection by the adepts, they must be sufficiently expensive to preclude their use by the vulgar."[74] Conversely, the very imperfections that result from handicraft are themselves taken to be a prerequisite of good taste.[75] Regardless of its stated intentions, Veblen helps us think through the Arts and Crafts movement of the early twentieth century as heralding conspicuous consumption to cement the class status of the predatory class and not as being a failsafe skill set for people to produce the things they need if a catastrophic event interrupts power grids or supply chains. This is another example of how handicraft movements reify class hierarchies.

Making artfully crafted goods is not a realistic option for many people, but conspicuous handicraft implies its inverse for those who cannot fashion their own ends of life. Workers who are conditioned by the machine process and lack the skill to produce things start to finish or who lack the purchasing power to consume handicrafted goods must make do with the mass consumption of standardized goods offered by industrial production processes. The mismatch between the supposed moral and civic benefits of handicraft preparation and the realities of mass consumption as the only viable way of keeping alive highlights how being prepared is a class project. Those in the predatory leisure class who have the funds can consume the start-to-finish skill of craft production in an attempt to meet their needs if mass production supply lines falter or agricultural production is interrupted. The myth of the free American who can do this on their own is precisely what animates the fascination with the prepping habits of the ultrarich. Lavish private islands with fully staffed medical facilities are, of course, conspicuous consumption at the surface level of making expensive purchases, but they are also conspicuous handicraft in that what they display is that the leisure class can opt out of industrial society and reproduce their daily needs by dint of their purchasing power. These differences in purchasing power, not skill, are what determine the ability to buy one's way into different tiers of preparedness. Still, against the myth of the yeoman farmer who can thrive on the land by their own labor, handicraft was a way to make mass consumption the proper prepping portal as well as conceal the class dimensions behind it.

TINKERING, HACKING, AND THE SELF-SUFFICIENT AMERICAN

As the machine process develops and the habits of mind around industrial production continue to shape each other, the archaic assumptions about Americanness find their expressions. If the BSA recast American masculinity as, at least in part, a matter of scientific inquiry and cataloging of natural and human resources for nation building, and if the various handicraft movements tasked Americans with being able to reproduce the production process on their own, then tinkering represents a way of relating to a mode of the machine process where the complexity of production is inaccessible or not reproducible. With tinkering, Americans are asked to demonstrate savvy by making mass consumer choices in ways that bend production to their will or even subvert the original intent of mass consumer goods. Tinkering is less concerned with being able to mimic production on one's own or taking good care of the natural and human stock of production than it is with subverting, hacking, or gaining informational arbitrage on mass production. This both cements mass consumption as a prevailing mode of life and sets the stage for a neoliberal politics of individual responsibility.

Tinkering is colloquially defined as an activity that a lay, nonexpert person engages in by way of a hobby. It is something one does on the side, or imperfectly, or as a low-stakes affair. Etymologically, tinkering seems to emerge onomatopoetically from the sound a repairer of pots and kettles would make as they worked. Tinkering often carries with it a connotation of something that is inexpert, imprecise, and unscalable. Tinkering will be defined here as "where small changes are made to something, especially in an attempt to repair or improve it . . . to reveal the inner workings of physical artefacts and afford transparency in underlying systems, structures and functions for subsequent alteration and improvement."[76] In a philosophical register, tinkering is "a mode of work that can be both passionate and playful, and which takes its cues from curiosity as much as necessity. As such, tinkering carves out a middle ground between an absorbing Heideggerian lifeworld and the 'mere presence' of an environment of objects or a mere stockpile of resources."[77] Tinkering is its own kind of *techne*, of knowing by doing, at an intimate proximity with the object. Few things represent this intimacy, playful passion, and curious necessity in the United States more than car culture.

AUTOMOBILE CULTURES

The rise of the automotive industry represents an important shift in the machine process, now centered around Fordist/Taylorist modes of industrial production and concerned with enshrining the habits of mind of the consumer society. Against the backdrop of the putative benefits of the "open road," where one can escape the hubbub of urban life and find the "democratic" space of booming across the American landscape, the automobile in early-twentieth-century America presented a carefully curated sensuous experience of "nature"—and situated nature as a place best accessed via automobile. Nature is thus less of a resource reserve for enterprising scouts to conquer but still presents a frontier artifice of escape and appreciation. Americans adapted to this new means of transportation not only through merely purchasing automobiles but by designing, tweaking, or even building their own. Tinkering on cars amounted to "user modification of the automobile body, allow[ing] motor travelers to not only redesign the car but, at the same time, to re-negotiate their cultural identities and their relationships to public space in terms of gender and technical expertise."[78] Of course, this description can be applied to other artifacts of the machine process as well, but the automobile is a paradigmatic example. Inhering in the idea of the automobile is the production of motorists as consumers, as well as the playful passion of understanding its underlying systems enough to modify them, even if they were not fully reproducible at home. Car culture also foreshadows the idea of hacking more generally—bending commodities to the user's will or making the commodity do something it was not designed to do.

Tinkering on cars was born from the limited possibilities of early industrial production. Unlike the current context, where cars can be ordered to bespoke specifications, early automobiles had few frills or were downright inadequate to meet the climates in which their owners lived. For people to tinker on cars was thus mostly to weatherize cars to make them suitable to local conditions or to add some creature comforts that are now taken for granted, such as gas gauges, trunks, mirrors, or padded seats. People also adapted cars to suit different climates or make them camping worthy.[79] The raw materials of industrial production were crudely fashioned into consumer goods that required personalization, and tinkering emerged as a way for automobile consumers to customize their vehicles to suit their preferences or lifestyles. Tinkering on automobiles was often a matter of aftermarket modifications to personalize or localize a commodity in ways that industrial production was unable to meet off the line.

But tinkering was much more than adding side-view mirrors to Model Ts. Tinkering culture also shaped a discourse of invention. It allowed people to "participate in a larger discourse of technological enthusiasm and ingenuity," even if they did not fully grasp the entire production process.[80] Veblen's theorization of the constitutive elements of the machine process remains instructive as a way of seeing the discourse behind automotive enthusiasm and ingenuity. The discourse of ingenuity sits comfortably in early-twentieth-century America, with its rags-to-riches myths of industrious Horatio Algers. Indeed, the relatively blank slate of the standard-but-no-frills Model T was very quickly seized upon as a get-rich-quick opportunity, where Americans, by dint of their intellect, could make a fortune in the automotive aftermarket.[81] This provides the basis for automotive enthusiasm and again shows the co-constitutive forces of Veblen's machine process. If ingenuity was an opportunity for the machine process to shape American attitudes, then automotive enthusiasm was the way that American attitudes were reshaped to the machine process. Americans, perhaps in an attempt to strike it rich in the OEM (original equipment manufacturer) market or simply out of idle curiosity about this new technology, sought to understand the engineering underpinning automobiles. The promise of the machine process, Veblen holds, is that individuals do not have to know how to handicraft every component part of the industrial production process or even have an exhaustive knowledge of the complexity of industrial production. Therefore, selling niche aftermarket parts does not require knowing how every part of the automobile worked. Rather, the machine process provided people an opportunity to use their knowhow about it to tinker with it to their ends.[82] As Veblen saw it, even in the face of unfathomable precision and complexity, production did not need to be grasped in its totality by everybody involved in the process—and this represented an opportunity.

Automotive tinkering is a matter of being able to repair the vehicle so it continues to work properly and add personalized comforts. Such repairs and modifications can be for one's own vehicle or can be done for others, in an effort to get rich in the aftermarket. Indeed, the boom in patent applications involving auto modification seems to indicate this habit of mind, even if most of the patents did not come from plucky individuals but from the automakers themselves.[83] These vectors of tinkering are based on two things being true. First, there must be a reliable machine process that gets a reliably similar vehicle in front of consumers in a short enough time frame in predictable quantities. Second, the level of complexity of the finished product must be comprehendible by end users. As car production became further refined and complexified over the course of the century, cars become increasingly reliable, comfortable, and feature rich and, along with that, increasingly difficult to modify. As the complexity of cars themselves as well as the regulatory apparatus surrounding them increased, even Moulton Taylor, who built a flying "Aerocar" from scratch in the 1970s, "often had little or no real knowledge of how mechanized factories were organized or the work of engineers who designed them. Tinkerers like Taylor were ill-equipped to deal with new federal safety regulations for motor vehicles that were introduced in the early 1960s."[84] A reliable machine process with reliable consumers who fancied themselves automotive experts—even as opportunities to use that expertise were obviated—produces cultural habits of mind about a kind of amateur expertise in the relations of production. As regulation and complexity make tinkering on the chassis of an automobile more difficult (and increasingly impossible), the habit of mind of tinkering expresses itself in "hacking" the production process itself, that is, to make mass production and consumption serve the savvy consumer's personal ends.

FROM TINKERING TO HACKING: RESPONDING TO NEOLIBERALIZATION

The industrial machine process and its habits of mind produce a rich soil for neoliberalism to flourish in, because it both solidifies mass consumption as the best way for people to meet their needs and provides a way for savvy consumers to display their individuality through smart consumption by intervening in the production process itself. Even as production capacity evolved into a post-Fordist iteration of "just-in-time" production (JIT; also referred to as "Kanban" production), the end result is still ostensibly to produce commodities to meet the needs of a consumerist society.[85] The machine process and habits of mind in this JIT labor process will help us analyze the rise of neoliberalism. The phenomenon of "hacking," like automobiles in the prior section, will be the main example for making sense of this shift.

Whereas tinkering emerges in the early twentieth century as a habit of mind that relies on standardized, reliable production, which end users decode, reconfigure, or otherwise engage to their own ends, the contemporary notion of hacking means intervening at the production process itself to demonstrate consumer savvy and make the process serve one's desired ends.

JIT production is a rerationalization of production generally. JIT reconfigured the spatial and historical processes through which cars (and countless other complex consumer items) are made. The beginnings of JIT production schedules came from Toyota's innovations in the assembly of cars, which defied and demolished the set-in-place production of warehousing, stockpiling, or sustaining a set workforce in a certain place.[86] The production of automobiles under "Toyotaism," while fluid, transnational, and chaotic, is nevertheless still grounded in a material base that flows more or less smoothly, even if the engine is designed in a different place than where the tires are manufactured or where the assembly line rolls the completed vehicle off into the world. However, "running smoothly" takes on a whole new meaning. It means no stockpiles and no labor hiccups, so the tire factory only stocks enough rubber to make only as many tires as needed and only as much union labor as is necessary to get a certain number of automobiles off the line. This is, of course, not to the consumer's benefit but to the automakers'. After all, new cars are not getting less expensive to purchase. Profit margins are healthier when constant capital is not being stockpiled and when variable capital is only used to meet a quota.[87] Of course, if there are any hiccups to material procurement chains or labor hiccups, JIT production unravels rather quickly and spectacularly.[88]

Moreover, tinkering is difficult if a person can neither find a commodity on which to tinker nor afford it. Consider the relative unavailability during the coronavirus pandemic of used cars because chip shortages interrupted new car production, which in turn led to many used cars being bought up or not put on the market in the first place.[89] Because of the way cars are manufactured now, with a reliance on chip manufacture, it is impossible for tinkerers to bypass this industrial arrangement.[90] Even OEM and aftermarket parts are contingent on the downstream effects of new car production. In such a "relentless pursuit of performativity," where the rationalized production process edges out the Heideggerian pursuit of playful sensuousness with the ends of life, what is a tinkerer to do?[91] In other words, there are hard machine-process limits to a tinkerer working around this problem, because nobody can make their own chips.

In 1998, Robert Young of Red Hat Software asked a simple question: "Would you buy a car with the hood welded shut?"[92] As anybody who has purchased a smartphone knows, this question has since been asked and answered—with a resounding yes. Smartphones and computers routinely come glued shut, making end-user upgrades difficult if not impossible. Anybody with a newer automobile knows that only certified technicians have the equipment to interface with the onboard computer. However, the playfulness of tinkering with complex consumer items, which have now become *too* complex, has been replaced with a new habit of mind, *hacking*, which can be defined as taking for given an already existing commodity and making it do things beyond its intended design. "Making it do things beyond its intended design," of course, also applies to tinkering, but the difference is that hacking is less about understanding and uncovering the inner workings of the commodity. With hacking, the knowledge to be gained is not about the artifact itself but about how to deploy that artifact to gather as much information as possible. The habit of mind of hacking as a matter of informationalization is a key component to diagnosing neoliberalism as a catalyst for this change.[93] This illustrates why hacking is so often seen as a matter of getting data past a firewall on the internet.

In many ways, neoliberalism is a Kanban statecraft, and prepping is an understanding by tinkerers and hackers of the frailty of this arrangement. Hackers use that understanding to tweak the brittle system to secure their own ends. JIT statecraft provides the barest of services from a lean, mean government apparatus keen on the "productive restructuring of capital."[94] There again is where the "managed" absence of the state comes to bear. It is quite active in restructuring production for the sake of capital accumulation, but protecting civil rights, public health, maintaining infrastructure, and emergency preparedness are all areas that can be filled in when needed, with maximum flexibility. Prepping becomes not only a matter of preparing for the catastrophe but also preparing for the inevitable breakdown of such nimble statecraft. This represents an opportunity to fill in the gap with even more logistically minded private businesses. For instance, OneGlobe explicitly says that it is "Kanban agile" in helping modernize the Federal Emergency Management Agency to "propagate agile delivery within the agency and improve speed to market." As a public sector partner of Amazon Web Services, it provides "steady state cost savings with urgent disaster scalability."[95] Much like Kanban production, Kanban statecraft is brittle, leaky, and disintegrating, but it can be fixed with the right informatics/logistics/agility. The ability to manage flows of information is crucial to performativity, as presumably less agile actors are left in the dust. Hacking expands the realm of "normal use" by normalizing the "deviant use" of devices.[96]

Given devices that are glued shut or computerized to the point of inaccessibility, the ability to make devices maximize their access to the flow of information is of paramount importance. Hacking JIT production is an attempt to "out-informationalize" some other suckers by using devices beyond their intended design, presumably for their own use. Industrial production produced consumers who tinkered; JIT production produces hackers who strategically accumulate and navigate flows of information so they can better manage risk given a neoliberal order that provides little by way of a safety net. Hacking culture is also consumer culture, but these are consumers of information. Therein lies the neoliberal impetus for prepping.

THE RIGHT TO REPAIR: ARE WE RIGHT TO PREPARE?

The Motor Vehicle Owners' Right to Repair Act of 2005, on its face, seems like a shot across the bow from tinkerers. However, its chief concern was with independent auto repair facilities being frozen out by proprietary software from manufacturers, in terms of diagnostic technology or through strict warranty agreements.[97] More recently, there is an argument for a federal right to repair in part on the grounds that OEM and aftermarket retailers are working together to prevent end users from tinkering with their products. However, the U.S. Copyright Office sees things differently, arguing that people who "brick" their phones through tinkering are best to appeal to existing contract and copyright law.[98] In some ways, this is an admirable argument; there is no reason for smartphone manufacturers to glue their products shut or insist on proprietary screws to secure their smartphone chassis. Yet it is not clear what end a federal right to repair would serve. There is little opportunity to tinker in the sense of building one's own Bluetooth peripherals, for instance. Perhaps the material benefit to this kind of right-to-repair law is not that it will reinvigorate the aesthetic development of tinkering but simply that it will allow users to extend the lives of their products, as well as perhaps introduce "a degree of unpredictability and excitement into the consumer landscape."[99] Discursively, the right to repair is not simply a matter of taking something that is no longer working and making it work again but bending a piece of technology to a person's will, to get the most out of it, to make it yield the most data, or to "propagate agile delivery" and "improve speed to market." It is worrisome if peoples' devices are brickable even as end users, but the right to repair seems more like a right to hack and a right to prepare.

Doomsday prepping purports to be a matter of managing risk by stockpiling enough goods to be able to independently survive disaster.[100] Prepping culture is thus still consumer culture, and its mainstream viability lies in the Kanban structures of neoliberalism. In a JIT state with a JIT production apparatus that is agile, nimble, and logistics driven (read: brittle, leaky, and under-resourced), preppers are hacking this system to accumulate the goods needed to minimize their risk. As production processes become ever more disintegrated, preppers look for ways to stock up on readiness to ride out the worst of it, using information gleaned or hoarded to make "wise use" decisions. Prepping is an attempt at gaining total informational awareness, to borrow a phrase from George W. Bush's National Security Agency, about the potential for natural disasters, civil unrest, or public health catastrophe. Against the backdrop of a neoliberal Kanban state that buckles under the slightest strain, prepping rationality makes sense to hack that JIT production to manage the risk of securing the ends of life. Where people look for this informational arbitrage to get a risk-mitigation advantage varies, but whether it's an Evangelical pastor selling buckets of potato soup or a back-to-the-land commune jarring their own vegetables, prepping culture is predicated on individually savvy consumers filling the gaps of an increasingly dilapidated system of production.

An immediate irony of prepping behavior that emerges from tinkering is that while it is often presented as a means to survive apart from consumer culture, it is itself a consumer culture that creates its own market and manufactures its own new needs, which themselves take on class and gender dimensions.[101] In terms of class, the ultrarich are able to conspicuously consume handicrafted private islands in a practice called "seasteading."[102] The poor, meanwhile, are often unable to gain informational arbitrage, and if neoliberalism rewards information accumulation, then it punishes those without it. This dovetails nicely with the neoliberalism's narrative of personal responsibility, meaning that people who are stuck in first-floor apartments during a hurricane in Brooklyn, a wildfire in California, or a blizzard in Texas might not make it out alive.[103] Meanwhile, prepping is mainstreamed as an almost exclusively masculine activity, about rugged men overcoming impossible odds, pushing to the background the care work that makes communities function, looping back to the "civic superiority" of the masculinized scout ministering to those who are underprepared.[104]

MAKING OUR WAY THROUGH DISASTER

What does this new machine process of tinkering and hacking mean for apocalyptic preparedness? Pitting the two against each other, tinkering's intrusion on the machine process and hacking's bending a completed commodity to channel its information flow could conceivably yield a new set of relations between people and commodities: *makerism*.[105] Makerspaces are emergent but seem to combine elements of both tinkering and hacking as a way to continue the myth of self-sufficiency and mastery of the process of production. That is, some discourse of making is about adapting consumer goods to meet individual specifications (beyond what is offered by Kanban production, at any rate), as well as encouraging hacking devices to channel the flow of information or make a piece of given technology perform otherwise.[106] 3-D printing, shared spaces, and collaborative teams ostensibly produce improved and new products. In some ways, this harks back to the handicraft ethos that tinkering emerged from: an enshrinement of the moral and aesthetic benefits of people designing and making the ends of life for themselves.

The actual content of maker spaces and whether/if it can achieve these ends goes beyond the scope of this analysis. It does seem that many of the atavistic emulative impulses that Veblen warns us of emerge here, too. The meteoric rise and cratering collapse of WeWork collaborative office spaces, the bespoke lab result fraud of Theranos, and the rise of 3-D printing firearms seem to suggest that maybe the moral development of making things start to finish leaves much to be desired. It is instructive, however, to cast doomsday preppers in this tradition of DIY to tinkering to hacking to making; in drawing out these same lineages of atavistic emulation, we can diagnose this phenomenon.

Prepping purports to be a matter of managing risk by being able to independently survive disaster.[107] In the trajectory presented, it seems prepping is both a matter of tinkering, that is, adapting consumer goods to become survival ready, as well as hacking, that is, using consumer goods to other ends, even something as simple as using home improvement buckets to store nonperishable goods in a secure location. As such, prepping is a kind of maker space of the apocalypse, where consumers are invited to share ways to independently survive whatever social, political, ecological, or eschatological disaster befalls. To say that preppers exhibit a neoliberal rationality is accurate in the sense that its vector of performativity relies on market transactions to secure security. What this analysis attempts to do, however, is draw that lineage back from hacking to tinkering to DIY production as a way of highlighting the atavistic impulses of prepping. Prepping is becoming mainstream not because the world is any more or less dangerous at any given moment but because a consumer market has been carved out for it. In the same way that DIY production was supposed to create thoughtful consumers in the early twentieth century, and in the same way that tinkering was supposed to create inventive consumers in the mid-twentieth century, and in the same way that hacking was supposed to create informed consumers at the end of the twentieth century, prepping is supposed to create secure consumers today. But the atavistic impulses that run through them all are present now too—grifters trying to get rich quick on prepping schemes, discourses of ingenuity and knowhow, and the need to manage, challenge, or change the flow of information—all are in the prepping arena.

BUILDING THE BUNKER

The three institutions highlighted here—scouting, handicraft, and tinkering—are attempts to inscribe a certain kind of mastery into Americanness. Scouting seeks to conserve natural resources and marshal human resources to rationalize masculinity from the frontier adventurers into the social needs of an obedient and hierarchical workforce. Scouting did not make soldiers but aimed for the efficient mobilization of the workforce, emphasizing "precision of movement, proper posture, and discipline."[108] Handicraft movements anachronistically asked people to eschew the degradation of industrial production, the social pathologies of urbanization, and the pitfalls of the division of labor, even as it upheld class distinctions via the predatory leisure class conspicuously consuming expensive handmade goods. Tinkering culture realized that while the machine process may be too complex to grasp or reproduce in its entirety, creative Americans can make modifications or even subvert the production process itself to make production serve their ends. These attempts at mastery are based on changing modes of production as they try to smuggle in archaic myths of what it means to be an American.

Whether these myths are true is beside the point; we need scouts who can catalog, conserve, and control nature; crafters who can forge the things they need without the larger industrial process; and tinkerers who can use their savvy to bend systems to their will. Self-sufficiency, imperial expansion, environmental domination, individuality, and savvy remain core components of American identity, even as the industrial machine process produced reliably standard goods. These institutions, that is, both reinforce the idea of the American "masterless man" and the reality of mass-produced commodities. This is an important tension to overcome because placing prepping in the realm of individual responsibility as well as on the mass production of consumer society otherwise falls apart. Similarly, the neoliberal bromides about displaying individual initiative and savvy are incompatible with the interlocked and standardized production process.

Americans may not see themselves as scouts, handicrafters, or tinkerers, but scouting, handicrafting, and tinkering are key components of what makes up the identity of a prepping American. The prepping American takes responsibility for their lot in life and is able to produce the things they need, even if that is reduced to wise choices among myriad mass consumer choices. The mass production apparatus is brittle and leaky, but because they are in a constant state of being prepared, they do not need a government to help them.

This chapter has been a prelude to the question: what kind of American self-bunkerizes? We argue that by the time the Cold War is in full swing and Americans are asked to build their own private fallout shelters, the scouting, crafting, and tinkering American is ready to respond appropriately. Thus, when the Federal Civil Defense Administration states bluntly in their 1958 annual report that "there will be no massive federally-financed shelter construction program," this was not a scandal but a challenge for Americans to dig deep—both in the American construction of identity and into the ground itself.[109] The report continues: "Common prudence requires that the Federal Government take steps to assist each American to prepare himself—as he would through insurance—against any disaster to meet a possible—although unwanted—eventuality. . . . When a free America was being built by our forebears, every log cabin and every dwelling had a dual purpose—namely, a home and a fortress. Today the citizen should be called upon to make the same contribution as our forebears—not for building a free America, but for sustaining a free America."[110] The scouting, handicrafting, and tinkering American was ready to answer this call, build the bunker, and become a prepping American.

3

FROM THE BUNKER FAMILY
TO BUNKERIZATION

CLIMATE CHANGE AND THE ATOMIC AGE

The atomic age is closely associated with both the biophysical markers of climate change, like carbon parts per million in the atmosphere, and the genesis of a bunker society. Climate change is more than the cycles of biophysical changes occurring in our planet's ecosystem; it is a semipermanent catastrophe of epic proportions that exists as a long-term crisis that shapes our social and political lives, and it lingers overhead as an existential disaster waiting to happen. Likewise, the atomic bomb has changed the biosphere, as seen in Hiroshima, Nagasaki, Bikini Atoll, the USSR, and by the hundreds of detonated test bombs across the American Southwest. The remaining stockpiles of warheads exist as a potential disaster. The atomic bomb sits within the Anthropocene as one of the many scientific marvels that threaten to end human existence and to radically alter the planet. The term "Anthropocene" was used in 1922 by a Soviet geologist, again in the 1980s by Eugene Stoermer, and finally in 2000 by Paul Crutzen. It marks the time when the impact of human activities overtook the natural geological activity of Earth. For those with a stake in the use of the term "Anthropocene," scientists and social scientists debate when the Earth-altering impact from organized human life "officially" started. Ian Angus presents evidence that the Great Acceleration, after World War II, marked by the intense use of petroleum-based energy, is the start of the new geological epoch of human dominance over Earth systems.[1] Recent studies argue that the Trinity bomb test and the subsequent release of atomic isotopes into the geological record marks the beginning of the Anthropocene.[2] Petroleum-based energy is only one such source of energy that should worry humans; atomic energy unleashed as a weapon is likewise a powerful force of the Anthropocene. This chapter looks at the federal effort to address possible nuclear disaster during the Cold War, particularly civil defense efforts like recommendations for bunkering, and then draws parallels to the current modes of doomsday prepping and bunkering in anticipation of climate change–caused disasters.

While doomsday prepping predates climate change, some preppers are anticipating powerful storms, out-of-control wildfires, tidal flooding, and other disasters associated with rapid ecosystem change. There are a wide range of responses, from climate change migration to buying disaster preparation kits at Costco, from scouting bug-out locations to buying expensive shelters and compounds in which to ride out the worst of a social and environmental crisis. Access to the tools of survival in the Anthropocene are not distributed evenly to all globally, nationally, or locally, nor is there agreement on what those tools should be, or agreement about the causes of—or even existence of—climate change. In the United States, a neoliberal nation of climate change activists and deniers and the home country of the two richest people on Earth, both of whom are investing heavily in taking the species multiplanetary as a way to prevent climate change from claiming civilization, climate change preparation is largely left to the private sector, where conscientious citizens and residents can conspicuously consume luxury and budget provisions, transportation, insurance, and multiple homes. The Green New Deal continues to be controversial, but the disaster and doomsday preparation markets are less so.

Climate change is not the first time the United States has wrestled with how to survive the bitter fruits of its technological and political choices. In 2023, the *Bulletin of the Atomic Scientists* issued their most recent doomsday clock statement to explain why they've chosen to advance the clock to ninety seconds to midnight, "the closest to global catastrophe it has ever been."[3] The statement explains that this decision is largely influenced by the war in Ukraine with Russia, the Russian leadership's threats to deploy nuclear weapons, and the Russian takeover of Chernobyl and Zaporizhzia, locations of nuclear reactors. The report describes climate change and nuclear weapons as two great existential threats to humanity. We consider them together and how the first of these, nuclear disaster, relied on institutions of frontiersmanship, nationalism, self-reliance, and masculinity to prepare U.S. citizens to consider private redoubts and market-based survival consumption rather than democratically mobilized collective action to address nuclear risk.

BECOMING A NUCLEAR WORLD

In July 1945, the Trinity atomic bomb test in New Mexico successfully detonated, inaugurating the nuclear era. Shortly afterward, in August, the United States dropped atomic bombs on Hiroshima and Nagasaki, justifying that act as the only way to end the brutal Second World War. Since 1945, nuclear nations have detonated 2,056 nuclear test explosions, and the United States alone has detonated 1,032 nuclear tests between 1945 and 1990.[4] The bombs by themselves did not constitute a nuclear world, but they were connected to a new era of nuclear security: "Indeed, a surprise nuclear attack has served as the formal authorizing nightmare of the U.S. security state since the U.S. atomic bombings of Hiroshima and Nagasaki in 1945, an anticipated existential danger . . . that energized the building out of the intelligence agencies . . . a permanent military commitment . . . and the ongoing mobilization of a counterterror state."[5]

Ongoing preparations for and anticipation of a nuclear event, accidental or purposeful, meant the United States and its citizens needed to be on alert and prepared in ways that echoed, if not amplified, the same existential fears that arose during industrialization. As Joseph

Masco reminds: "All residents of planet Earth reside somewhere within a fifteen-minute window of nuclear warning," which he reads as part of the condition of the Anthropocene, in which "the accumulating force of historical greenhouse gas emissions is shifting all ecosystems and climate potentials, creating planetary conditions that are increasingly both hypervolatile and violently in motion." The state of perpetual near-disaster of the nuclear era has seamlessly flowed into the state of perpetual near-disaster of the climate change era. The nuclear world, dependent on narrow expertise, national security secrets, and intelligence agencies, has permitted an erosion of democracy under the auspices of a secure nation: "In this way, the atomic bomb has always presented a foundational challenge to democratic order, as it was made in secret, relies on the production of existential enemies, provokes genocidal imaginary, and locates sole authority to launch a nuclear war in a single individual, the president."[6] In the 1940s, the period during which nuclear capacity was developed and deployed, the neoliberal model of economic and social organizing began growing from a relatively small intellectual project in Europe into a political project both in the West and in the Southern Hemisphere.[7] This, too, supported the erosion of democracy and the growth of private defense contractors and myriad industries associated with nuclear weapon and infrastructure buildout. The antidemocratic tendencies traceable in this history align with Carl Schmitt's prescient observation that the sovereign is "he who decides on the exception."[8] The role of the president as the nuclear decider makes clear that the features of a liberal democracy are easily bypassed under existential threat. Indeed, the only justifiable use of war, for Schmitt, is when one is under existential threat from an external enemy. On the other side of the private meetings and game-theorist predictions of managing nuclear fallout are the institutionalized mobilization of civil defense, the national posture and associated propaganda, and the distribution of responsibility to survive those decisions sealed off from a democratically sovereign people. These habits of mind that get activated will, much like Veblen despaired of half a century earlier, likely impede the ability to form the collective action needed to respond to the scale of nuclear armament.

DEFENSE BEGINS AT HOME

During the Atomic Age at the height of the cold war, the United States had to confront the possibility of total nuclear annihilation, or at least partial annihilation with drastic consequences, like radioactive water and soil that would linger for an unfathomably long time. "A Report to the National Security Council—NSC 68," distributed by President Truman to the National Security Council, stated: "With the development of increasingly terrifying weapons of mass destruction, every individual faces the ever-present possibility of annihilation should the conflict enter the phase of total war."[9] Guy Oakes similarly argues that the end of World War II was not a period of peace but the beginning of the Cold War. "For the current generation of Americans, anxieties of the Cold War would become permanent features of life." Preparing for nuclear attack was not just a job for the doomsday preppers living on the social fringes. Presidents Truman and Eisenhower saw preparation as a fundamentally familial affair. "The main training site where civil defense discipline would be cultivated was the home."[10] Prepping was a federally endorsed set of activities and recommendations, complete with public alert systems and public-school training for children in the classic "duck and cover" model of surviving thermonuclear annihilation. Preparation was the stuff of presidential speeches and handwringing about the best approach to preparing the public to meet the violent end of Cold War hostilities. In 1951, President Truman produced a statement on the newly signed Federal Civil Defense Act (FCDA), which was "designed to protect life and property" and "affords the basic framework for preparations to minimize the effects of an attack on our civilian population, and to deal with the immediate emergency conditions which such an attack would create." The act permitted "the Federal Government to provide matching grants of funds to the States for constructing air raid shelters. The act also allows certain measures to be taken by the Federal Government directly, such as the procurement and stockpiling of necessary medical and other materials and supplies and the provision of suitable warning systems" in order to "get ready, and to stay ready, to defend our homes."[11] The executive branch could not agree if the government should fund a shelter program or if this was a matter of individual responsibility, and Congress would not fund a public shelter program despite the passage of the FCDA. The Federal Civil Defense Administration was created in 1951, but it did not last long: "In 1958 the FCDA and the Office of Defense Mobilization were combined into the Office of Civil and Defense Mobilization (OCDM). Leo Hoegh, director of this new entity, announced that there would be 'no massive federally financed shelter construction program' and instead proposed a 'national shelter plan,' the essential features of which was an emphasis on private shelter construction and government 'stimulation' and 'guidance.' "[12]

The FCDA made provisions for the federal government to give supplies to states and their associated agencies for emergency shelters, but this remained unfunded, and that responsibility was transferred to homeowners. In the 1950s, public libraries participated in atomic bomb attack preparation nationally and locally. Major city public library systems, including New York's and Chicago's, disseminated government pamphlets about family preparedness, like "Survival Under Atomic Attack" and "Civil Defense Household First-Aid Kit." The New York Public Library showed films like "You Can Beat the A-Bomb," and "the Brooklyn libraries . . . allowed civil defense groups to use library facilities for planning, training, and registration purposes." Libraries even were to serve as bomb shelters, thanks to their "common ownership, thick walls, and reading rooms that could serve as emergency hospitals . . . officials also pointed out that library book stacks offered excellent radiation shielding."[13] The Fifth Avenue library stockpiled food and drink rations and prepared staff to escort patrons to safety. Public schools were often designated as public bunkers, with some experimental schools built underground to assess their efficacy as both a place of learning and as a bomb shelter.[14] Some cities began identifying public buildings that could serve as shelters, but most of these buildings were inadequately stocked with supplies in the event of attack.

Despite national mobilization to prepare the public for a long-term disaster, the federal government could not bring itself to fund extensive public shelters or to fund individual families to build their own shelters on their property. The state would provide some guidance, but "in the end, civil defense was essentially self-help, which meant that its success depended on the traditional American virtues of self-determination, personal responsibility, and voluntary cooperation."[15] This meant it was every person for themselves when the bomb went off, and those ill-prepared suffered as they deserved to for being insufficiently prepared or able to afford such preparation. As attention shifted to the personal family bunker, this raised critical questions about the nature of the average American. Would they open their fallout-proof doors to the neighbors or shoot the neighbors before sealing themselves in? The emphasis on individual preparation for decisions made at the national level encouraged a strange emulation, compelling neighbors to spy on one another (who is building a backyard bunker nearby?), to lie to one another (what backyard bunker?), and to think of survival in a zero-sum way rather than as a collective process. Even the federal government prepared bunkers so an emergency government could continue to operate in the event of nuclear attack. Some businesses prepared to keep the wheels of industry turning underground, although presumably the consumer base shift considerably after an atomic blast. Kenneth Rose pulled a telling quote from an American business magazine in 1950 that stated, "More and more businessmen are wondering what would happen to their investments tomorrow if an atomic bomb landed on their city today."[16] Standard Oil, Chase Manhattan Bank, and the New York Stock Exchange bought shelter space for some employees to use and began to store duplicate records in other locations to decentralize their operations in case their nerve center suffered bomb damage.[17] Yet shelters for everyday people did not warrant national mobilization because the institutions of self-sufficiency and frontiersmanship precluded such a collective effort. Laura McEnaney described the rationale: "A federally funded national shelter program, critics argued, would turn the United States into a Soviet-style state dedicated to military preparedness at the cost of individual economic and political freedom. Privately funded family shelters, on the other hand, expressed a distinctly American-style of militarization, based on voluntary effort, family autonomy, home ownership, and public-private collaboration."[18]

McEnaney found that states asked for funding for civil works projects, like underground parking lots, that could double as public bomb shelters. This attempt to fund infrastructure projects concerned

Congress and raised suspicions of a New Deal–like revival of public works projects, which, during this vehemently anticommunist era, was deeply unpopular. Likewise today, the Green New Deal, a sprawling plan for climate change adaptation and mitigation, employment opportunities, and just transitions supported by progressive Democrats and Democratic Socialists of America alike, cannot find congressional or popular traction for similar reasons. The American right wing lumps the Green New Deal together with the specter of cultural Marxism, the popular term for a vaguely defined movement informed by thinkers like Herbert Marcuse, and the conventional anticommunism deeply embedded in American liberal and conservative ideologies: "Part of a larger Cold War recalibration of American society through nuclear fear, the FCDA campaign attempted to shift responsibility for injury from the security infrastructures themselves to the individual citizen, now positioned as properly informed about everyday risk via civil defense programs and expected to be both alert and resilient in a minute-to-minute confrontation with nuclear war."[19] This alertness and ability to prepare connects sheltering to the habits of mind of the scouting, crafting, and tinkering American, concerned with self-sufficiency and protecting a mythical truth about the American character. As Veblen might say, these half-mythical half-truths produce a political subject ready to accept this responsibility, even if it is a less effective reification of the status quo.

In 1951, a convoy organized by the federal campaign Alert America! set off on an educational and volunteer-raising tour across the country. "The exhibit featured the peaceful uses of atomic energy as well as the changes wrought by new biological, chemical, psychological, and incendiary weapons of modern warfare." The informational exhibits were not strictly for public education: "Displays on local, state, and national responsibility for civil defense in the pre-attack and post-attack periods were linked to catechism on American freedom and the Communist menace. The chance to sign the 'Alert America Pledge' to acquire and implement civil defense training was featured in the last part, 'the pay-off room,' geared to local needs and volunteering opportunities."[20]

The patriotic Boy Scouts of America and Girl Scouts of America were mobilized once again as paramilitary civil servants to keep the national way of life and to await orders as volunteer message runners, medical assistants, and casualties: "In 1956, Boy Scouts had delivered a million civil defense posters within critical target areas, and in 1958 nearly three million Boy Scouts were recruited to distribute The OCD's [Office of Civil Defense] new 'Handbook for Emergencies' to thirty-seven million homes. They had President Eisenhower's direct sponsorship and blanketed the nation's cities as well as rural areas." Responsibilities cleaved along gender lines: "Among women, the recruitment message featured private responsibilities of home and family allied to global politics and the public-mindedness of citizenship."[21] Women's roles in civil defense lay in her already private experience as the mother and wife of a nuclear family, and aside from a few pointers, like doomsday pantry stocking and underground housekeeping, she was expected to fulfill these private duties as part of her civil obligations. In this way, American women could display their civic superiority while fulfilling their roles as vanguards of the manifest domesticity of a nuclear empire.

Nuclear preparation took on multiple dimensions, from internal dynamics to urban and rural planning. Even as the federal government struggled to fund public and private shelters, they funded tests of shelter effectiveness against radiation and the psychological impacts of bunkering, both within families and among strangers. Davis reviewed these experiments, which included environmental manipulations by experimenters to induce and then quell panic. Some researchers concluded that shelter life could even improve family dynamics through quality time. Bunkering and nuclear war preparation became a spectacle: some of the U.S. military's own weapons, designed for communist targets, were detonated instead in the Nevada desert, to test the effectiveness of preparation measures against the world's great superpower. Rural families were not encouraged to build bunkers but instead were given vague and unfunded instructions to accommodate fleeing urban refugees. "Most information [to rural communities] focused on the continuity of rural life following a disaster, maintaining steady farming operations, dealing with contamination, and upholding the moral fabric of this country." Rural home shelters were considered useful handicraft projects for the self-sufficient and prepared family man, with wives responsible for stocking, shelter housekeeping, and preparing children for life in the bunker.[22] They did not need to be funded because the habit of mind of the rural frontiersman who can meet all his needs and produce a surplus held strong. This lack of public funding for a mobilization, however, spurred the business class into making a market advertising and selling preparation.

DOOM TOWNS AND SELLING PREPARATION

Part of civil defense included testing the conditions of everyday living against an atomic bomb. Federal civil defense preparations included practice bomb strikes on model homes with mannequin families. In 1950, the Atomic Energy Commission (AEC) chose the Las Vegas Bombing and Gunnery Range to serve as the proving ground for atomic testing:

> On January 27, 1951, the first atmospheric nuclear test was detonated at the NTS [Nevada Test Site], code-named "Able." A total of 100 atmospheric tests were conducted at the NTS until July 1962. All atmospheric testing was banned on August 5, 1963, when the Limited Test Ban Treaty was signed in Moscow, giving birth to the age of underground testing. The United States conducted 828 underground tests at the NTS. The last underground test, "Divider," was conducted on September 23, 1992.[23]

The extensive and frequent testing has given the United States the distinction of being the "most heavily bombed country in the world."[24] Operation Doorstep in 1953 allowed the FCDA to participate in the tests.[25] Operation Cue was a series of forty tests designed to simulate bomb detonation on typical American communities. The FCDA created suburban neighborhoods on the Nevada Proving Ground "complete with houses, utility stations, automobiles, furniture, appliances, food, and even mannequins simulating the people who might live in the town."[26] The tests were meant to help determine the effects of exposure to a nuclear blast on a typical American home and to test the protective effects of residential underground bunkers. Tests Annie and Apple demolished the houses closest to the blast. The tests altered the surface of the Mojave Desert and created a new class of the environmentally vulnerable and politically insignificant, known as "downwinders," from their location with respect to the nuclear fallout. Released images of the test sites focused on communicating to the public the seriousness of atomic bombs and to arouse "a keener interest in civilian defense." In Andrew Kirk's critique of the official photographs of the doom town test site, he notes that absent from most documentation is desert life and evidence of human habitation. AEC and Office of Civil Defense pamphlets "nearly erased the 5,000-square-mile continental atomic testing bioregion of the Mojave and Great Basin deserts and its inhabitants from public view, referring to the area as, 'landscapes almost as barren as the moon,' 'wastelands,' and 'submarginal places' sparsely populated by politically 'insignificant' people."[27] Included in the category of "politically insignificant people" were the Western Shoshone, who actively opposed nuclear testing as a violation of the 1863 Treaty of Ruby Valley and as an act of destruction of sacred sites.[28] Indigenous political and spiritual leaders like Corbin Harney joined with other downwinders in antinuclear activism as the "virtual uninhabitants" of the irradiated desert.[29] Terry Tempest Williams wrote poignantly about her own experience as a downwinder and antinuclear activist in Mormon Utah in "Clan of the One-Breasted Women." Nuclear testing lingers in the environment and in the bodies of plants, animals, and humans exposed to the bomb detonations and radioactive dispersal through air and water. The Nevada Proving Grounds, the Mojave Desert, and the bodies of those exposed to atomic bomb tests are testimonies to the never-ending disasters that require perpetual preparation. "Where other twentieth century conflict landscapes have later become reclaimed and renegotiated by civilians following the end of hostilities . . . the landscapes of the Cold War are the landscapes of a conflict that never was, and due to the nature of nuclear weapons systems, has never truly 'ended.'"[30] Test towns allowed the state to expose itself—that is, its own natural environment, soldiers, civilian employees, and downwinders—to the long-term, multigenerational, and psychological effects of radiation. Such proximity to detonating bombs was part of a conscious effort to unleash a new state of insecurity and uncertainty across the globe.

The test towns, colloquially called "survival towns" or "doom towns," tightened relationships with industry and business-class retailers as the private sector partnered with the public to bring survival towns to life and turn a profit. "Doom Town served as a powerful symbol of U.S. capitalism and venerated a new suburban way of life. In order to 'sell' civil defense to the U.S. public, the FCDA situated the atom firmly within a contemporary consumer landscape. Backed by corporate sponsors, the FCDA assembled these so-called survival towns." The survival towns encouraged civilians to think as consumers and to take responsibility for their own survival through defensive consumption. "Operating within a constrained budget, the FCDA hoped to pass most of the responsibility for civil defense onto the individual and to encourage a philosophy of self-help and civic duty compatible with time-honored American values."[31] This self-congratulatory approach to reiterating the status quo through animating mythical American values is exactly the kind of imbecilic institutional approach that Veblen critiqued. The FCDA affirmed that Americans did not have to change anything about themselves or their way of life. In fact, they just had to be all the more American.

The budget constraints led the FCDA toward corporate partnerships to enrich the business class. "The FCDA increasingly turned to corporate alliances and company sponsorship in order to function. Exhibitions, brochures, and documentaries featured company branding. In 1955, the agency stated: 'Industrial cooperation is essential to the success of a national Civil Defense program.' "[32] The Behlen brothers of Behlen Manufacturing built two buildings, one 6,800 feet and the other 15,000 feet away from the blast, as did some of their competitors. The Behlen buildings sustained the least amount of damage and remained structurally sound, which proved a clever marketing opportunity: "This dramatic endorsement led Behlen Manufacturing of Columbus to begin marketing a new product—family and community blast and fallout shelters. Later they hired former FCDA administrator Val Peterson as their 'Shelter Products Advisor.' One of the ways they advertised was to rebuild the actual Operation Cue building at state fairs and other venues so people could see the building that survived the atomic bomb."[33]

Industries benefited from this relationship both through access to outcomes from atomic bomb tests on their products and in promoting their products as signature objects. Americans could buy safety from the Cold War not just through bunkers but by adopting the suburban lifestyle, which permitted them the space to bury a bunker, store surplus supplies, and live a safe enough distance from the hordes of city dwellers who, it was presumed, would descend on the prepared middle classes to forcibly avail themselves of the preppers' hard work. Even the test home was built to demonstrate the correct domestic sensibilities of a good American family, as Masco points out in his work on nuclear fallout. He references the 1954 FCDA film "The House in the Middle," showing two dilapidated homes with one between them in an ideal suburban state of high-quality maintenance.[34] The middle house fared the best against bomb testing, proving that good hygiene and American domestic values are literally lifesaving. The hygienic concerns of the Boy Scouts had fully come home. Wills argues that the FCDA tests were a failed attempt to promote consumption-based survival, since the destructive power of the bomb proved that nothing, not even the latest car fresh from the factory, could withstand its force.[35] But the relationship between consumption and preparation is a deeper link than just shopping for safety; this was a public campaign that prepared the American public to think of themselves differently in relation to their government than they had been conditioned to do during the New Deal era. More than having products like bunkers and shelf-stable pantry goods, Americans were taught that the burden to survive disaster, particularly disaster caused by international conflict, was an individual and family-unit responsibility that reached back to the founding institutional myths of the country. Nuclear families were encouraged to run preparedness drills, buy bunkers or retrofit their home basements and cellars to serve as bunkers, and to acquire basic skills in firefighting and first aid to reduce dependence on public support and trained experts who may be unable to help in the event of an attack.[36] Even the do-it-yourself bunker became a buy-it-yourself project no longer anchored in the rejection of industrial production but firmly part of a society of mass consumption, with some assembly required.

MARKET FOR BUNKERS

The home bunker was not universally adopted as the "correct" defense against atomic attack. Debates raged among civil defense planners about whether it was safer and more efficient to train Americans to evacuate quickly or to bunker in their suburban shelters and urban designated safe buildings. Doomsday shelters were praised as a good deterrent (who would dare bomb a people so dedicated to survival?) and a smart resource for savvy people. They were also panned as futile against the strength of an atomic bomb, a sign of cowardice, and a distraction from the more crucial task of avoiding a nuclear war.[37] While the federal government eventually endorsed personal shelters, the bunker belonged to the marketplace, along with every other survival supply for sale. Entrepreneurs, scammers, and construction companies began marketing their new products to the public. The latest in bunker design became displays at public malls and demonstrations. " 'My best salesmen are named Khrushchev and Kennedy,' Chicago's Frank F. Norton, president of the National Shelter Association, cried last fall."[38] Shelter companies popped up around the country, including the Atlas Shelter Company in Sacramento, which continues to operate today, with great pride in its history: "The original Atlas Bomb Shelters which was started in Sacramento, California in the 1950's was a dominate [sic] supplier during the Cold War Era and Atlas Survival Shelters as we are known today is the dominate [sic] supplier to the world as well as the American market."[39] Atlas boasts of coverage from the BBC, Fox Business, and *Keeping Up with the Kardashians.* Not all shelter companies during the Cold War were in it for the long haul: "Meanwhile, fly-by-night shelter companies fought for their own survival. On Long Island, several homeowners paid $1,000 each to a contractor who dug backyard holes, then disappeared. After a shelter roof caved in near Dallas, the owner called to complain. The company had skipped town. Federal inspectors in Tennessee found only 3 of 30 shelters meeting civil defense specifications."[40] The Office of Civil Defense issued bomb shelter regulations and cooperated with some shelter companies to help them meet those standards and advertise that they were

OCD compliant but did not regulate or intervene in the bunker market, allowing hucksters and frauds to thrive.

The Atomic Shelter Corporation took out newspaper advertisements promoting affordable shelters that could be used, during non-emergency periods, as what is now commonly referred to as "man caves," or private spaces for the expression of domestic masculinity within the bounds of the family home but existing apart from the conventions and culture of the family. Thomas Bishop puts the heyday of the bunker market between 1961 and 1963, with the last year marked by six hundred bunker companies filing for bankruptcy. "In plying their trade, shelter businesses attempted to marry two eminently successful ideological constructs of the Cold War era: national security and the self-made, individualistic, suburban consumer family." The promise of shelters as DIY projects for the enterprising family man trying to access his yeoman Americanness ran aground as poorly engineered shelter kits yielded endless variations of poor-quality bunkers or bunkers that required construction feats and resources that exceeded the backyard tinkerer.[41] Bunker companies and their salesmen tried different pitches to consumers to cajole them into buying nuclear survival, some in "frightening and questionable taste."[42] Some emphasized the gravity of international relations, but many others suggested that the bunker could be used as a family recreation room that would double as a comfortable place to ride out nuclear apocalypse. "Survival All and Shelter Inc. sales brochures displayed a range of options from 'basic models "that claimed to offer all the 'necessities of survival,'" to luxury models that were spacious, equipped with rugs, or boasted 'expensive indoor paneling.' "[43] The current luxury bunker market may tap into new ways to conspicuously consume in the twenty-first century, but doomsday bunkering has always been a class-stratified way to mass produce, advertise, and consume safety as well as emulate luxury.

Yet the suburban public was not thoroughly convinced that the private family bunker was a good investment, and the urban public lacked the space and often the means to acquire one. "By early 1962, the fallout shelter business was faltering badly as the possibility of nuclear war seemed to recede and the troubling moral and class questions associated with shelters began to accumulate."[44] Shelter companies reluctantly acknowledged that their gamble had not paid off. "Last week Norton [owner of Atomic Shelter Corp], who has lost $100,000 and estimates that over 600 firms have failed, had changed his tune. Grieved he said: 'The market is dead—the manufacturers have had it.'" Even capitalizing public officials who entered the bunker market, including Val Peterson, head of the Civil Defense Administration, and Leo Hoegh, former director of the Office of Civil and Defense Mobilization, were not immune to the market failure: "Last fall Chicago's Wonder Building Corp., headed by Leo Hoegh, former director of the Office of Civil and Defense Mobilization, was selling 200 fallout shelters a week. Last week Hoegh sold fewer than ten. Says Hoegh, who has 3,000 shelters crated in storage: 'I am bleeding rather profusely.'"[45] Others blamed the market crash on a shift in federal messaging from private shelters to public preparation:

> What killed home shelters was the lull in the cold war plus the Kennedy Administration's decision to stress large-scale, community shelters over backyard bunkers. Says Ray Toland Sr., a Los Angeles shelter maker who failed: "It's been a real loused-up deal. All this blah-blah-blah about a $30 shelter or a $300 shelter, and about private and community shelters. People got so confused they didn't know what was right—and they still don't." In Oklahoma City, the number of inquiries about shelters received monthly by one company has dropped from 40 to 1.[46]

Fellow private shelter entrepreneurs echoed the concern that Americans had been poorly prepared by the federal government for the private shelter market. "Americans are not sufficiently war-conscious to make the air-raid shelter business profitable. Howard Sherwood, who hoped to be a top man in the bomb-shelter business, went out of production today and offered to sell his first and only model at a loss."[47] The private shelter business faltered for many reasons, including lack of consumer interest and a shelter market full of poorly designed products. The public was reluctant to believe that bunkers would indeed protect them from atomic attack and resisted a strictly DIY approach to surviving hot international relations. "Non-shelter owners were generally more optimistic about the prospects for world peace, while shelter owners expressed a corresponding pessimism. Paradoxically, shelter owners believed that shelters reduced the chance of war but were more convinced than non-shelter owners that war would occur."[48] The public, under the influence of anticommunist propaganda, federal civil defense campaigns, and advertisements for doomsday bunkers, struggled to identify who was responsible for their protection, how that should be administered, and how dire the threat of atomic attack really was. What was clear, however, was that the federal government was not going to provide the means of sheltering; this would have to be undertaken as a private matter for the public good.

PUBLIC ATTITUDES ABOUT BOMB SHELTERS

In the Michigan State University study "The Fallout Protection Booklet: A Report of Public Attitudes Toward and Information About Civil Defense," researchers collected 3,541 interviews from eight major cities in the United States. Sixty-four percent of respondents thought it was unlikely that war would break out between the United States and the USSR (or some other country), although only 42 percent thought the United States was generally moving toward peace. "Only about one in four believed that he could do something to protect against blast but better than one in three believed that he could take action to protect against fallout." When asked about perceived risks from a bomb drop that did not directly hit their community, "three out of four believed that they would die or become ill from fall-out radiation." When asked about the utility of shelters for providing protection against fallout, "about one respondent in four saw shelters as providing two kinds of protection: slim and none."[49] The majority of respondents did not think shelter building was cowardly and also thought that people had a duty to try to live as long as they could. Seventy-nine percent of respondents thought law and order could be restored after a nuclear attack, although 27 percent of respondents thought the world was unsafe to live in anymore so we just have to choose our risks, and 27 percent thought a postattack world would be a man-to-man struggle not worth living for. Thirty-five percent believed that the "ending or saving of the world is up to the will of God. Man cannot protect himself," although only 7 percent of the same respondents found that building shelters is not in violation of God's will. Finally, the survey indicated that while 67 percent thought shelters were unaffordable to most families, 64 percent thought that "most people have the space to put in a shelter if they really want one." The public understood that the fallout shelter program rested largely on their shoulders: 66 percent thought the government would like them to build a fallout shelter, although 18 percent of respondents did not know if the government wanted that or not. Despite that most respondents saw some benefit from shelters and that they perceived the government wanted them to build a family shelter, only 1.4 percent of respondents had a shelter at all. Only 5 percent had plans and had investigated their options, while 27 percent had thought about it but had not investigated further and had no plans to build a shelter, and 52 percent had no plans and had not thought about building one at all.[50]

The survey explored the inducements that might encourage people to build shelters. Respondents overwhelmingly favored the government's offering to build a free shelter, with 75 percent in favor of such an option. Interest declined from 52 percent interested in a free shelter from the government but the individual does the construction labor, down to 28 percent favoring someone coming to their home and explaining how to build a shelter themselves. Surprisingly, the communication source most influential to their decision were physicists and scientists, with the church ranking the second lowest, behind neighbors building shelters. The president's influence was unable to garner even 50 percent of the respondents. Although nuclear fallout and sheltering was a national conversation in major newspapers and magazines, only 18 percent of respondents had received their government-issued copy of the "Your Family Fallout Shelter" pamphlet, and only 25 percent had read other government sources of information about fallout shelters. A mere 4 percent had been contacted by a fallout shelter salesman. Of those who felt war between the USSR and the United States or between the USSR and some other group was likely, they tended more to hold "attitudes favorable to civil defense" on several of the survey questions than those who thought war was less likely, although the study authors cautioned that this difference between groups was small. Those who believed a nuclear attack would not hit their community but would hit their area had the most favorable view of civil defense, but of those who believed a bomb would fall in their area, "forty-five per cent said they had not thought about building a shelter" and "fifty-four per cent of the 'my community' group [the group that believed it likely a bomb would drop on their specific community] admitted that they had not thought about building a shelter at all."[51] The result was very little shelter construction against a high perceived likelihood of nuclear conflict: "By 1965, as many as 200,000 may have been in place. If we accept the 200,000 number with the proviso that figures on shelter building are highly speculative, what does this number mean? . . . But in an era in which most Americans (53 percent in 1961) believed that a nuclear war with the Soviet Union was likely to occur, an even more forceful argument can be made that 200,000 is a small number."[52]

Although Americans were reluctant to buy and bury their own shelters, debates raged about shelter ethics and the limits of Christian neighborliness. "When I get my shelter finished, I'm going to mount a machine gun at the hatch to keep the neighbors out if the bomb falls. I'm deadly serious about this. If the stupid American public will not do what they have to save themselves, I'm not going to run the risk of not being able to use the shelter I've taken the trouble to provide to save my own family." The same *Time* magazine article found a similar attitude in Texas. "In Austin, Texas, Hardware Dealer Charles Davis stashed four rifles and a .357 Magnum pistol in his shelter and pointed out its four-inch-thick wooden door: 'This isn't to keep radiation out, it's to keep people out.' " Davis is also prepared in the event that some of his shelterless neighbors get into his shelter before he does. "I've got a .38 tear-gas gun, and if I fire six or seven tear-gas bullets into the shelter, they'll either come out or the gas will get them."[53] Anxiety about the unprepared mounting an attack on the prepared was not limited to individuals but became a point of tension between cities, too:

> Relations between Los Angeles and Las Vegas are still recovering from a flap over a speech by Las Vegas Civil Defense Leader J. Carlton Adair, who proposed a 5,000-man militia against the possibility of wartime refugees from California pouring into Nevada "like a

swarm of locusts." And Civil Defense Coordinator Keith Dwyer of California's Riverside County (pop. 306,191) last week told a group of officials and reserve policemen in the town of Beaumont that as many as 150,000 refugees from Los Angeles might stream into Beaumont if there were an enemy attack, and that all survival kits should include a pistol.[54]

The fear of urban masses invading the home defenses of suburban and rural families echo habits of mind from the worries of the "wrong" populations ruining the nation and that a lack of ability to prepare for oneself was a matter of moral quality. This attitude persists in contemporary prepper movements, as well. On National Geographic's television series *Doomsday Preppers*, many of the interviewed preppers express grave concern about the "marauding hordes" of urban scavengers and refugees who, because of their own refusal to identify and prepare for catastrophic events, will seek their unearned survival off the labor of preppers. Indeed, most of the bunker and bunkerized homes featured on the program include defense systems specifically designed to ward off, maim, and kill intruders. Rather than think of self-defense against a national enemy, defense is leveled against one's own neighbors and fellow citizens, whose mere unprepared existence is considered a threat. The great fear of a horde with underdeveloped survival instincts forged by waning American values, as we have established, goes back to mass immigration during American industrialization. Specifically viewing city dwellers as potential threats implies that these are the effeminate, consumerism-softened Americans that Cold Warriors worried would make America vulnerable to communist propaganda.

FEAR AND DISASTER MOBILIZATION

During the Berlin crisis in 1961, the federal government implicitly threatened to use atomic weapons against the Soviet Union as a deterrent to further communist encroachment in Europe. Domestically, the federal efforts were aimed at producing a population prepared for living under the threat of total nuclear annihilation: "The federal civil defense programs of the 1950s thus represented an institutional means of solving the problem of national morale and securing the moral underpinnings of nuclear deterrence."[55] Civil defense was not only outlined as infrastructural strategy; it also required reigniting a perceived loss of classic American values that made the United States distinctive and superior to communist nations and peoples. Preparation is thus less about preparing for a radically different world than it is about taking the status quo into an uncertain future. Oakes outlines the conservative worries about modern American cultural and moral decline issued by George Kennan, an American diplomat; John Foster Dulles, a former secretary of state under President Eisenhower, and Henry Stimson, secretary of war under President Truman. The three struck various conservative warnings about the decline of American culture and moral integrity. All three argued that Americans were spoiled by consumer goods, which produced a lazier and greedier person and eroded the self-reliant habits of mind of the yeoman farmer and his steady self-control. Dulles blamed a decline in Christian values and the insidious effects of economic success, while "Kennan's pessimism expressed a lament for the passing of the old middle class of independent farmers, merchants, and craftsmen and a nostalgic veneration for its typical locus, the small town and the village of the early twentieth century."[56] Modernization and industrialization, untethered from traditional American values, replaced the self-reliant man with the excessive, one more dedicated to his comforts than to his Christian values and, by extension, his nation. The preoccupation with American moral character influenced the federal government's approach to civil defense training and, in invoking the spirit of the self-possessed man, made bunkering and preparation a largely private affair that would animate old habits of mind as opposed to actually facing the existential threat of nuclear war. Initial planning for civil defense against atomic weapons used by the Soviets against the United States emphasized training the American public to avoid panic and to master their fear.[57] Sheldon Wolin understands this cultivation of values as part of the mission of the state to bind its citizens to its constitutional powers. "The state cultivates the political education of its citizens to instill the virtues of loyalty, obedience, law-abidingness, patriotism, and sacrifice in wartime. Through the practice of those virtues, the State encourages identification of the self with the power of the State, the surrogate of participation and the sublimate self-interest."[58] The role of the state for the conservative leaders of the nuclear efforts was to provide cultural and moral leadership to guard against communism while supporting a robust free market to do the same. Impending nuclear war was the backdrop for these institutional directives of preserving a certain kind of Americanness.

Civil defense manuals and films encouraged Americans to prepare so that they could achieve self-mastery, and, in addition to surviving nuclear attack, they would keep the spirit of the American people alive in their response. These campaigns assumed that without preparation and training to face the threat of nuclear attack with resolve and moral fortitude, Americans would lapse into a Hobbesian state of nature. One of the antidotes to the threat of social unraveling was found in a 1953 *Collier's* article, "Panic: The Ultimate Weapon?," authored by Val Peterson, a former Nebraska governor and director of the Federal Civil Defense Administration from 1957–1961. He argued that panic rather than the atomic bomb was the most effective way to win a war, and since warfare was now beyond the battlefield, "every city is a potential battleground, every citizen a target."[59] One of the suggested "panic stoppers" in Peterson's article was to build a home shelter or at least identify the safest part of the home to shelter in.[60] Peterson leveled that panic is more dangerous to national security than the bombs themselves, and citizens maintaining preparedness at all times is the thin line between a Soviet win or loss, regardless of the impact of the actual bomb and fallout. Fear made a population weak against ideological propaganda, so federal civilian preparedness chose to focus on psychological responsiveness and recommendations for shoring up one's home fortress rather than fund national programs to protect the population from nuclear attack and fallout.

Corey Robin's treatment of fear and politics is instructive and moves beyond psychological explanations for civil defense planning and the private shelter. Kennan, Dulles, and Stimson shared with Burke and Locke a preoccupation with an all-too-comfortable population, and all three saw value in political fear as a mobilizing agent for "collective renewal in the fear of these evils."[61] Fear in politics is often understood as the necessary feeling that stirs complacent people into the civil and Christian spirit that makes the United States a great nation. Just as the federal government anchored civil defense as defense of American democracy and capitalism against the evils and tyranny of Soviet communism, Robin posits that after 9/11, commentary focused on the Middle East as a bastion of anti-Western values and anti-Christian sentiment—oppositional values that threaten the existence of the United States—rather than examine the historical and contemporary power imbalances between nations. These ideas are echoed in popular response to the 9/11 attacks, with pundits and political scientists alike describing an America shaken out of its dreamy materialism and easy consumerism and thrown into a state of high alert and fear about its very foundations. Just as Cold Warriors argued that fear of the atomic bomb would make Americans feel alive again and reprioritize their values, 9/11 was assumed to likewise refresh and reboot the American citizens to take themselves more seriously. Robin works through Hobbes to challenge the conventional belief that fear is either apolitical or that it motivates people to act in accordance with shared cultural values. For Hobbes, fear tames individual impulses for glory and daring, which enables people to act in the interest of their self-preservation. This means staying out of the way of the sovereign and accepting that what is dangerous about breaking the rules of the state is better than what is dangerous about the state of nature. "Where a fear of death is supposed to enable the individual to secure his own good, fear in the state of nature leads the individual to act in ways that subvert his good."[62] In a state of nature the individual must defend themself, but under the power of a state, they forfeit that right in exchange for the protection of the sovereign and the rule of law:

> Under no circumstances is he to come to the aid of someone targeted by the sovereign for punishment, or to refuse to aid the sovereign, should he be asked, in subduing someone targeted for punishment—unless that someone is a family member of a person upon whom he is dependent . . . if an individual retains the right to defend himself but no one outside his immediate circle is permitted to assist him, that individual will find himself confronting a form of power he cannot hope to resist with any efficacy.[63]

The sovereign must act within the bounds of the rule of law and apply punishment fairly, or else fear generated by the sovereign will be no more effective than fear of the state of nature. "The very exclusivity of familial bonds draws the family close and repels outsiders." During the nuclear age, federal civil defense championed the nuclear family unit as the primary unit of defense, the group that must come together to take precautions to protect themselves from nuclear attack, and, while their skills may be useful to neighbors, they should not undermine their self-preservation with self-sacrifice to others. In disregarding the recommendations of civil defense campaigns, families and individuals risked personal annihilation, but they also risked emerging from their bunker into a Hobbesian state of nature—or into a communist regime that replaced their law-bound sovereign with something far more terrifying to the American imagination. In Robin's read of Tocqueville, the democratic individual loses themself in the mass and as such exists in a state of anxiety. "At the height of the Cold War, American intellectuals would revive their line of thought, arguing that the greatest danger to Americans was their own anxious self, ever ready to hand over its freedom to a tyrant."[64] For Peterson and other Cold Warriors, more potent than the bomb was crippling fear, a weapon so powerful it could destabilize democracy and capitalism without even requiring bomb detonation. Peterson, Dulles, Kennan, and Stimson encouraged this sentiment by calling for Americans to manage their fear or risk letting their terror or anxiety drive them into unpatriotic actions, like refusing preparation and, in their denial or terrorized paralysis, allow communism to take hold in the United States after the fallout cleared.

Robin traces Hobbes, Montesquieu, and Tocqueville to Arendt, both in *Origins of Totalitarianism* and later *Eichmann in Jerusalem*. Although not entirely in alignment with the conservative voices of the Cold War defense planners, Arendt similarly worried that the modern person had experienced a loss of the civic and social associations that would enable them to resist terror and terrorizing political forces. Her concern with industrialization was not that it emasculated, softened, and replaced American values with superficial consumption but that industrialization was still a social condition that displaced civic values. In the call for Americans to bunker as individual families, civic and social association was mediated through the individualized and marketized version of wartime preparation at home. As Robin points out, Arendt was less preoccupied with the sheer volume of deaths caused by the Holocaust than with the impacts on individual psychology, that terror of totalitarianism reduced people to their barest state of existence, more a set of animal reactions than complex human beings.[65] These concerns are echoed by Peterson and FCDA administrators who cautioned that fear of the Soviet bomb would be more detrimental to the American person than the bomb itself. The number of people vaporized and irradiated by the bomb would be secondary to the impact of the threat of the bomb on the resolve of the public if they were unable to summon essential American characteristics of self-preservation, self-control, and maintenance of cultural institutions. These institutions, like the nuclear family and prepping through bunkering, would fortify the American way of life before, during, and after an apocalyptic event. The concern was that Americans would be less resistant to communism if they were weakened by terror and could not mobilize their fear to act rationally, productively, and protectively.

DEMOCRACY AND OUR WAY OF LIFE

The American way of life that personal bunkers were meant to protect was described as antithetical to the political, cultural, and economic formation of the Soviet Union. In the official U.S. position, expressed in National Security Report 68 (NSC-68), the "fundamental purpose" of the United States is

> to assure the integrity and vitality of our free society, which is founded upon the dignity and worth of the individual. . . . Three realities emerge as a consequence of this purpose: Our determination to maintain the essential elements of individual freedom, as set forth in the Constitution and Bill of Rights; our determination to create conditions under which our free and democratic system can proper; and our determination to fight if necessary to defend our way of life.[66]

By contrast, the report described "The Kremlin" as a menace that undermines or destroys non-Soviet governments, replaces them with its own absolute authority, and absorbs them into the Soviet communist body. The United States took care to position itself as the USSR's polar opposite. "The United States, as the principal center of power in the non-Soviet world and the bulwark of opposition to Soviet expansion, is the principal enemy whose integrity and vitality must be subverted and destroyed by one means or another if the Kremlin is to achieve its fundamental design."[67] Not only was the Soviet Union discursively constructed as a competing political system to the United States, but it was also considered incompatible with the very existence of the United States. The report described the U.S. political system in the terms of classical liberalism, with an emphasis on individualism, rule of law, civil rights, and freedom. By definition, the USSR represented none of those values. An atomic bomb became the final barrier between a free world and a Soviet one. If freedom was to survive, that meant Americans must as well, even if that required taking freedom underground.

The free democratic society the United States wished to protect via nuclear threat does not map onto the United States as it actually exists. Wendy Brown, in reference to Sheldon Wolin, points out that capitalist democracies, rife with inequalities, are incomplete. She argues, "In sum, an orientation toward democracy in the context of nation-states and capitalism requires state support for public goods ranging from health care to quality education, economic redistributions, and strong prophylaxes against corruption by wealth."[68] Truman and Congress refused to fund public shelters, even while nearly baiting the Soviet Union into nuclear contest and endangering the lives of its own citizens to do so. The state's refusal to redistribute wealth, and by extension its refusal to stabilize and make accessible a functioning democracy, also made surviving nuclear attack a class-stratified experience, with renters, apartment dwellers, and people living in the economic margins unable to secure for themselves a bunkered retreat while the warring global powers competed for global hegemony. Encouraging individualized and market-based protection loosens the ties that maintain community and social networks. There are those who bunker, those who are shot stealing another's private property and preparations, and those who are simply left exposed to danger with no alternative. Brown writes: "Democracy also requires a robust cultivation of society as the place where we experience a linked fate across our differences and separateness. . . . It is where we are politically enfranchised and gathered (not merely cared for) through provisions of public goods and where historically produced inequalities are made manifest as differentiated political access, voice, and treatment."[69]

If democracy requires the state to remediate wealth, service inequalities, and cultivate a sense of belonging, creating something together out of our vastly different social positions and experiences, then the United States has not cultivated democracy, and certainly not in its approach to preparing the public for nuclear standoff. Instead of experiencing the linked fate of potential atomic warfare as a communal and universal experience, the state left and even encouraged citizens to retreat from public life, figuratively and literally, to address their linked fate as atomized individuals. The "historically produced inequalities are made manifest" in who could afford to bunker and prepare and who could not. "The neoliberal attack on the social . . . is key to generating an antidemocratic culture from below while building and legitimizing antidemocratic forms of state power from above."[70] While the NSC-68 report presents classical liberalism as the great American form of free society, the state failed to live up to its democratic commitments on the one hand, and it undermined democracy on the other. Prepping for disaster discouraged democratic decision making, gathering, and provisioning public goods and resources and encouraged antidemocratic state activity as the Cold War federal government rapidly expanded the security and surveillance branches of the state. The good citizen, then, is always ready for the warning siren, has a fully stocked bunker or other reasonable plan, and has taken precautions to not share, forcibly or voluntarily, with those neighbors who will not take personal responsibility. This variant of institutionalizing preparation shows from a Veblenian perspective that preparation could have been an institutional evolution centered on democratic deliberation. It also explains why it was instead given over to the thrall of bygone habits of mind from a pre-industrial mythical America, with the dead end that results.

The good citizen was produced within a framework of legal coercion, as well. The House Un-American Activities Committee, convened in 1938, led a domestic war against communism under Senator Joseph McCarthy between 1950 and 1954.[71] Truman's Executive Order 9835 permitted the federal government to root out communists and sympathizers in its employment with "a loyalty investigation of every person entering the civilian employment of any department or agency of the executive branch of the Federal Government."[72] Neighbors were encouraged to monitor one another for signs of "subversive" behavior while at the same time discouraged from collectively organizing to address the threat of the atomic bomb. Robin warns that fear in politics is not simply a function of the increasingly atomized individual severed from civil society; civil society itself is often a site of repression. The disunity of everyday people, encouragement to seek safety through the market, and tightening associations between the free market and the free world helped make ideological space for the rise of neoliberalism just on the other side of the height of the nuclear standoff between the Soviet Union and the United States. After the Cuban missile crisis, "civil defense was replaced with 'civil preparedness,' a move towards 'all-emergency planning' solidified in 1978 with the creation of the Federal Emergency Management Agency (FEMA)."[73] While nuclear attack response still falls under FEMA, what started as a risk-specific government mobilization developed into an institutional "emergency" response, acknowledging that not only is nuclear threat a permanent feature of the risk landscape but also that the U.S. government must always be ready for emergency, even as federal legislation to fund preparation failed to pass. Financial responsibility for preparation trickled from the state to the individual, while risks from climate disaster to nuclear war fell under the state as broad national security interests. The state scans for myriad threats, and the citizen, on high alert, is to prepare individually for all of them.

Prepping, even for nuclear attack, persisted into the 1980s, and bunkers became a representation of the American values promoted by Cold Warriors in the U.S. government. With enough gumption, planning, a can-do attitude, and the self-motivation to learn how to tinker your way to safety, anyone could survive a nuclear attack. T. K. Jones, the deputy undersecretary of defense for strategic and theater nuclear forces and a technical adviser to the Strategic Arms Limitation Talks under the Reagan administration, infamously stated in a *Los Angeles Times* interview in 1981 that in the event of nuclear attack in the United States, "If there are enough shovels to go around, everybody's going to make it." The journalist Robert Scheer recorded these conversations in his book *With Enough Shovels*, titled after his conversation with Jones. Scheer continued: "The shovels were for digging holes in the ground, which would be covered somehow or other with a couple of doors and with three feet of dirt thrown on top, thereby providing adequate fallout shelters for the millions who had been evacuated from America's cities to the countryside. 'It's the dirt that does it,' he [T. K. Jones] said."[74]

Jones did more than imagine a primitive shelter that bypassed the need for a homelike bunker. Inspired by the Soviet strategy for accounting for public safety beyond whoever owned enough property and had enough capital to bunker, he imagined that everyone was capable of simply making a hole in the ground and, in working with the materials available, could thereby tinker and craft their way to safety. The "a hole for everyone" Soviet model of civil defense quickly shifted back to American ideological terrain. Scheer explained how to build a shelter with simple household materials:

> You can make very good sheltering by taking the doors off your house, digging a trench, stacking the doors about two deep over that, covering it with plastic so that rain water or something doesn't screw up the glue in the door, then pile dirt over it. If your house is built on a slab, one very good blast and radiation protection is to dig a tunnel underneath the slab. . . . Learn how to make a ventilation pump . . . how to deal with sanitation, supplies, this kind of thing. In the business of nuclear war, what you don't know can kill you.[75]

Here is evident the American imperative to become competent at DIY projects, to be able to tinker with the supplies you have, to hack your home so it can be converted from a single-family dwelling into a bunker, and to embody the BSA motto "Be Prepared" because "in the business of nuclear war, what you don't know can kill you." Jones summarizes the bunkering mentality in his practical advice: "Throughout the evening, Jones was scrupulously, indeed tediously, reasonable as he built his case that nuclear war was something far less terrible than I had been led to believe: that it was survivable, and not just by lonely bands of savages roaming a devastated landscape. What Jones foresaw was the preservation and quick reassembly of our advanced institutions, modes of production and normal ways of life."[76] Jones's preoccupation with getting Americans to shed their fear of the bomb is in alignment with Peterson's *Collier's* article warning that fear is more powerful than the bomb and can win a war for the Soviets if the American public gives in to it, weakening their resolve against socialism and communism. More than digging shelters, preparedness and bunkering were ways to preserve the fantasy of America while doggedly maintaining that this preservation is only achievable through personal responsibility.

The national government balked at providing funding for public shelters but spent enormously on security, surveillance, and military might. Shelters were increasingly thought of as a private matter, and the government provided basic bomb awareness and tips for bunkering down while promising to nuke the communists if needed, or at least strike their missiles out of the sky. This left families and individuals to decide how much bunkering was worth to them as a consumer matter and how much they would or could spend on it. The bunker market has developed considerably in the past few decades, particularly as the American public takes its cues from the federal government's Sinophobia and persistent fear of communism and the federal and state government's refusal to fund infrastructure improvement and protection from the impacts of climate change. Focusing on individual responsibility and market-based solutions to protect oneself from the bomb and fallout prepared the way for the twenty-first-century of doomsday preppers and the booming prepper market. Rather than throw our collective weight behind the Green New Deal or similar sweeping legislation for massive public funding to protect against climate change and prepare cities and systems for a just and humane change, that energy is diverted to the market. Jodi Dean argues that the left has failed to provide a good counterposition: "We have failed to counter the neoliberalization of the economy. Even worse—we have failed to provide good reasons to support collective approaches to political, social, and economic problems. It's easier to let the market decide." With collective action and collective responsibility unreachable ideals, the expectations of a functioning state are

> reduced to consumer choice, [and] government similarly contracts, now concerning itself with traumatized victims. Its role is less to ensure public goods and solve collective problems than to address the personal issues of subjects. . . . Finally, insofar as the economy alone cannot fulfill the functions of government, one element of the state rises to the fore—security. Thus, accompanying diminished political influence on economic and social policy is the intensification and extension of the state as an agency of surveillance and control.[77]

One of the antidotes to neoliberalism and any number of crises of political legitimacy is democracy. Since neoliberalism is hostile to democracy, and democracy centers political power in the citizenry of a given state, it holds an intuitive appeal. Yet Dean is critical of democracy and its possibilities, particularly in the emphasis on deliberative democracy, which seems "limited to the discussions surrounding a decision, the discursive context of a decision, but forever unable to reach the decision itself."[78] Deliberative democracy, then, is about procedure but not outcome. This form of democracy resembles the liberal democracy that Schmitt heartily critiques as the endless chatter of the middling classes that does not impart them any real power. For Dean:

> Because the appeal to democracy presupposes democracy is the solution to the problems of democracy, because it incorporates in advance any hope things might be otherwise as already the fundamental democratic promise and provision, it is a dead end for left politics. . . . The appeal to democracy remains unable to elaborate a convincing political alternative because it accepts the premise that we already know what is to be done—critique, discuss, include, and revise. Left reliance on democracy thus eschews responsibility not only for current failures . . . but also for envisioning another politics in the future.[79]

Simply appealing for democracy does not necessarily dismantle the institutions that design, govern, and execute neoliberal policies that replace state welfare with market-based replacements, nor does it entail that more democratic processes will lead to a qualitatively different politics. Cold War presidents were fairly elected, as was Senator McCarthy. In fact, his efforts were widely available for public consumption, so democracy's enemies could be well-known, watched, and punished. The robust defense of democracy in documents like NSC-68, implied in the decisions to drop bombs on the Mojave Desert, and evident in the justification to privatize bunkering responsibilities (to ensure Americans maintain key values and avoid making sweeping mandates, as the communists might) is aligned with calls for more robust democracy from the center and left.

Not only is democracy remarkably nonradical in Dean's estimation of its deliberative form, but it is also hardly democracy at all in its constitutional form. What, then, is democracy? For Wolin, "democracy is a project concerned with the political potentialities of ordinary citizens, that is with their possibilities for becoming political beings through the self-discovery of common concerns and of modes of action for realizing them." Democracy need not be defined through the institutional and constitutional constraints placed upon democracy as boundaries to the political efforts of everyday people. Wolin's concern with a bounded politics is akin to Dean's critique of constitutional democracy when he writes, "The reality cloaked in the metaphor of boundaries is the containment of democracy and that the critical boundary is the constitution." For Wolin, the constitution establishes the power of the state, particularly "an organization of power that guarantees domestic peace and security, including the security of the State; that promotes, guards, oversees, and interlocks with the corporate powers upon which the citizenry is dependent for their material well-being."[80]

Bunkering is a shared project between the state and the private sector, and citizens' very material survival was purposefully cast back to corporations to produce and sell those means of survival, from bunkers to canned water, thus releasing the state from providing these things at their expense. This approach suggested that welfare liberalism was a step toward communism. Democracy, then, is less about the empowerment of citizens to shape the world in which they live; rather, democracy is fitted to the constitutional confinement and boundaries necessary for the exertion and protection of state power. "Constitutional democracy . . . is not democratic or democratized constitutionalism because it is democracy without the demos as actor. Its politics is based, not as its defenders allege, upon 'representative democracy' but on various representations of democracy . . . a constitution regulates the amount of democratic politics that it lets in."[81] Constitutional democracy depends on a market to extend the reach of the state across national borders and to redirect civic energy into the marketplace rather than challenge or disturb the administration of the state. Those citizens who internalize the habits of mind about self-reliance and a free market as institutions of a democratic and advanced state understand that they are to carry out their civic duties through the consumption of nuclear protection in the free market. A free market, a free society, and the practices of democracy are thus conflated.

Dean's claim that what the government ceded to the market it regained in security is evident in Truman's expansion of the security state. "Congress deliberately strengthened the authority of the presidency with the Atomic Energy Act of 1946 and the National Security Act of 1947, which created the National Security Agency, National Security Council and the Central Intelligence Agency."[82] In the NSC-68 report, the authors concluded that the U.S. economy primarily supported improved quality of living but could easily be mobilized for a war effort, with over 50 percent of economic activity directed to such. According to the report, a buildup of nonatomic weapons and military capability would reduce the need to threaten or use atomic bombs against the USSR, but the United States would make no such promise: "In our present situation of relative unpreparedness in conventional weapons, such a declaration would be interpreted by the USSR as an admission of great weakness and by our allies as a clear indication that we intend to abandon them."[83] While the report mentioned several times that preparing for war included a civilian defense program, the infrastructure to protect the public from nuclear attack was never fully funded, while funding was allocated to internal and external surveillance, war capacity, and propaganda for the American public as well as for allies of the United States. Individual protection from the nuclear option was ultimately left to the market to distribute resources and to the savvy purchasers to consume them wisely. Not incidentally, the NSC report defined the "free world" in liberal democratic terms.

SOWING THE HOMEFRONT IN TOTAL WAR

Bringing civilians into war predates the nuclear era and recalls the habits of mind from American industrialization. Mobilization during World War I included the "war garden" for civic efforts that supported and even mimicked the war front. "The war garden campaign officially began with Wilson's proclamation on April 15, 1917, which was printed on the cover of *Garden Magazine* in May of the same year."[84] The president's statement called upon women and men of all ages to do their part to supply the wartime nation with food. "Let every man and woman accept assume the duty of careful, provident use and expenditure as a public duty, as a dictate of patriotism which no one can now expect ever to be excused or forgiven from ignoring."[85] Wilson asked Americans to end their "wastefulness and extravagance," prefiguring the anxieties during the nuclear era that consumer society had reshaped hearty Americans into pleasure-seeking gluttons. A statement by the assistant secretary of agriculture in the August 1917 issue commended the American people for their great response to the "request to help win the War by growing food."[86] The June 1917 issue included a section entitled "The Patriotic Garden" that implored gardeners to "make your ground work for the family & nation."[87] The magazine called upon the Boy Scouts to help local gardeners distribute their excess harvest, and women were applauded for their domestic efforts in growing, canning, and drying. Articles throughout subsequent issues in 1917 and 1918 encouraged home gardeners to stop being "slackers" and to join the war effort, including by growing ornamental flowers to brighten spirits and to celebrate the bounty of God, and to do their part while their brothers were sacrificing themselves overseas. The magazine even called those who participated "war-gardeners" who had been drafted into service. The June 1918 issue cover states, "Can your vegetables, fruit and the Kaiser too," and featured an illustration of the head of Kaiser Wilhelm II in a glass jar labeled "Kaiser brand unsweetened."[88] The militarization of the humble garden is emphasized in the following passage from the June 1918 issue: "The past three years have seen the home gardens turned into 'munitions plants' each summer—for food is ammunition." The article takes an unexpectedly social turn, however, in calling for gardeners to work collectively rather than in their individual home plots. "Instead of making America a colossal vegetable farm of many different units, it should be made a gigantic cooperative enterprise in which each member works for one general big objective rather than to gratify individual desires."[89] The article suggested working with the National War Garden Commission to link efforts for community-scale canning, exchange, sales, and machinery shares. Although the article does not advocate socialism as such, it encourages more community-scale effort than did the later recommendations for every family to secure their own atomic age bunker.

World War II found the state calling for nationalist commitment to the war effort, including shifting industrial production to support military needs, pledging allegiance to the national wartime commitments, accepting rationed goods, and planting victory gardens. As Patrick Vitale argues, the national war effort united citizens to do their part through their work in factories and industry.[90] This effort and attitude not only strengthened national ties between citizens and the state but made the tightening linkages between industry, state, and war appear part of the necessary mobilization to protect freedom and the homeland. Victory gardens, renamed from the earlier "war garden" campaign, were an extension of the same efforts promoted by the federal government during World War I and encouraged citizens to join the fight from home, particularly women, by fortifying their bodies and the bodies of workers keeping the wartime economy running and to save meat consumption for soldiers. Victory gardens, promoted by the Office of Agricultural War Relations (renamed the War Food Administration in 1943), were well supported by agricultural corporations happy to sell seeds and promote their domestic goods.

Some scholars argue that the victory garden was a collective effort to reduce taxation on industrial food chains and resources so that those could be redirected to war capacity. Char Miller argues that the victory garden was a way for humans to assert themselves in the natural order, to shape their landscapes and establish order in a chaotic world of persistent war. The marketplace for victory gardens and home improvement emerged here too, just as the market for bunkers and bunkering supplies. "The promotion of consumption as a patriotic duty fostered gardening culture catalogs, encouraged price shopping, and increased demand for the latest varieties."[91] The victory garden as a civil defense activity relied on collective action (families and neighborhoods) and some degree of cooperation and sharing—you would not hide your garden from the neighbors or shoot them for pulling a carrot—and a more cooperative relationship with the natural environment on the level of cultivation, rather than an antagonistic relationship to the natural environment as a potentially life-ending set of conditions during a nuclear attack: "Victory gardens exemplified the organization of domestic life to the needs of industrial and national production during World War II. Organizing domestic space according to these needs extended the range of social demands for efficiency. Applying national goals of efficiency to the household increased the range of social space in which citizens were to find value and meaning by aligning their work to the needs of the nation."[92] Yet the victory garden was also a statement of American abundance and ability to serve as a world leader in agricultural production and food security:

> The food campaign of the Second World War differed from those of the First World War when nations focused on conservation and agricultural labor as necessities for survival. In the Second World War, President Roosevelt's ideology of food as an essential freedom to fight for not only influenced the way nations promoted wartime agricultural production, but also metaphorically put food on the front lines as both ammunition and as a symbol of postwar democracy and abundance. This metaphor identified agricultural laborers, whether rural or urban, as "soldiers of the soil."[93]

The victory garden was heavily promoted by the War Food Administration as a means to support the troops from home, especially for women, who were encouraged to continue their domestic responsibilities. Advertising oscillated between asking American families to take individual responsibility to support the war effort and encouraging communities to help educate and support cultivation and food preservation efforts. These efforts included training women on childrearing, eating to improve their beauty, and their proper place in the household. "In this way, the promotion of the home demonstration was, at its core, Americanization."[94] Victory gardens, while decidedly more community minded than the armed bunker, do not stand as a departure point between a good and bad civic engagement with a hostile outside world. Rather, it is possible to see, between the good-natured flower gardens and the prudent canning efforts, a citizen prepared for ongoing war and who readies their home for perpetual threat of attack from above. While the state encouraged the garden as civic duty and called on neighbors and the organizations of civil society to work cooperatively, the habits of mind about self-reliance and a frontiersman ethic meant everyday people were still left to their own efforts to survive a war waged by the state and to see themselves as part of the economy of war.

Americans were drawn into the total war conditions of the world wars as civilian soldiers. While "total war" often refers to the world wars that drew civilians into campaigns as targets, mobilized labor, and patriotic spies, it took a more serious turn after the atomic bomb was no longer an American monopoly. Now total war meant mutually assured destruction, and as such the United States had to be on alert, with everyone prepared to do their part. War industries from chemical production to weapons production began a federally led effort of dispersal across geographic space as lessons from Nazi Germany's efforts to hide airplane production facilities and the staggering effects of the atomic bombs on Japan were considered by American policy makers and industrialists.[95] The effort to distribute war industries across the landscape instead of centering them in cities was a tactical decision to make it more difficult for American enemies to disable the United States and its fighting infrastructure with just a few strategic bomb drops. The federal government issued guidelines to help major metropolitan areas determine their "target hot spots" and dispersion plans. To do so, employees needed to relocate away from city centers and into suburbs, and suburban populations were increasingly asked to be self-reliant in their preparation for atomic bomb impact in their region. Municipal planning was influenced by the federal approach to these concerns through information theory:

> But in the atomic rubble, as the analysts interviewed hundreds of blast survivors and canvassed the broken structures, as they methodically noted which kinds of concrete walls still stood at various radii of destruction, they began, quite explicitly, to see themselves, to see America, through the bombardier's eye. They began to wonder what an American city would look like after the bomb had fallen. . . . They began to see themselves, their towns and factories, on the crosshairs of radial targeting maps.[96]

Peter Galison argues that Americans were trained to see themselves as targets in an "atomic imaginary," that is, a "state of vigilance both proximately apocalyptic (at any moment the 'all-out' could come) and yet full of the banalities of the institutions of everyday business: profit margins for the long term, plans for market regions and economic tributaries."[97]

Organizing domestic life around the threat of atomic attack meant creating a domestic space underground, excluding people from use, and contributing to national production needs by remaining alive to support the bunkered businesses that likewise survived. While victory gardens could be tended year-round and perhaps be a welcome permanent feature of one's home landscape, it did not carry with it a sense of permanent wartime mobilization or represent the natural environment as an extension of the enemy's atomic weapons to wipe out the free world. The bunker, however, could be buried underground and, with regular necessary maintenance, always be ready for the fact of nuclear weapons as part of the world. Nuclear disarmament has not eliminated these weapons, and they now exist in other nations outside of Russia and the United States. We now live in a permanent state of readiness for potential nuclear attack. Prepping is not rendered obsolete during times of relative peace; peacetime can be used to permanently mobilize the family for the next nuclear threat. Likewise, climate change is a permanent feature of our lives. The effects of climate change will only intensify, and it will not spare any part of the globe. The new permanent state of emergency, the threat of atomic bomb use either accidentally or purposefully, prepared Americans to think of their survival as an individual endeavor that, when carried out effectively, would also support their nation. Although the bunker market sputtered, the impact of atomic war preparation on a public already imprinted with possessive individualism made it possible to think about bunkers beyond the A-bomb and to consider what it meant to fortify one's homeland not just on international borders but within the limits of one's home. Permanent crisis means permanent vigilance to preserve the institutions of an American way of life.

PERMANENT CRISIS

Just as the Cold War and nuclear weapon proliferation has made the threat of atomic attack a relatively new permanent crisis for which we all must be individually prepared, climate change operates in a similar way in the twenty-first century, although it is worth noting that climate change and the threat of nuclear annihilation coexist. Climate change is a long-term feature of our social and biophysical environment. Even if we managed a global consensus to radically cut carbon and greenhouse gas emissions, we have still passed crucial tipping points that will now play out in cascades of climatic changes. Atomic bomb tests have contributed to a long-term environmental disaster that continues to haunt mainland downwinders and Pacific Island nations. The United States has made poor provisions for both, denying claims by downwinders that their health crises are caused by exposure to lingering nuclear fallout and telling the Marshall Islands that their radioactive reefs and leaking Runit Dome on Enewetak Atoll are their responsibility, one of the gifts of sovereignty granted by the United States in the Compact of Free Association signed in 1983. Conveniently, the compact allows for U.S. military use of their missile test range until at least 2066, and the "Compact provides for settlement of all claims arising from the U.S. nuclear tests conducted at Bikini and Enewetak Atolls from 1946 to 1958."[98] The Marshall Islands are an important example of the convergence point between the eternal preparation for Cold War hostilities and the near-eternal presence of environmental disaster, in this case directly linked to the atomic bombs tested for the Cold War and the life-and-death calculations made by policy makers and brinkmanship experts to determine the losses acceptable in the efforts to fortify American superpower status.

The institutionalization of the bunker mentality firmly established during the Cold War smoothed the road toward the neoliberal approach to climate change. During the Cold War, the state abdicated responsibility for its citizens and discouraged collective action among citizens while taking action to protect itself and its representatives through networks of bunkers for essential government employees and military operations. In confronting climate change, collective action proposals like the Green New Deal are considered too radical and dangerously close to socialism, while individuals are instead encouraged to "buy green," "go green," invest in solar panels for their homes, buy electric cars, buy "clean, green" subscription services for food and cosmetics, and live an increasingly digital life to save the trees and cut down on material waste, all while trading it for different but less visible environmental demands (energy used and carbon emitted for warehouses full of servers, etc.). In short, individualizing life in a perpetual state of disaster and disaster anticipation is a hallmark of a neoliberal state. "The assault on society and social justice over the neoliberal decades is most familiar in the project of dismantling and disparaging the social state in the name of free, responsibilized citizens."[99] Bunkering itself has not fallen out of favor, either, as wealthy preppers make luxury bunkers for a number of anticipated crises, climate change impacts included, while others retrofit their basements as extreme weather events increase in intensity and show up geographically differently than they have in the past. One of the legacies of the Cold War persists in the neoliberal, highly individualized, and undemocratic approach to surviving climate change. The free society the United States sought to protect through the proliferation of weapons of mass destruction hardly exists.

4

PREPPING IN THE SHADOW
OF THE VALLEY

THE NEW state of permanent crisis and the institutionalization of bunker mentality that emerged from the nuclear standoff found traction in the antigovernment prepper movements of the rural Pacific Northwest in the 1980s and 1990s and again in the contemporary crisis of climate change. As climate change and related signs of global instability prompt deep concern for the viability of planetary life, people across socioeconomic classes in the United States have turned to doomsday prepping as a way to manage their anxiety and consider life after the collapse of the state, the environment, or the varying degrees of social disruption caused by both. In lieu of collectively organizing for these instabilities, most people are routed toward the market to answer their call for protection from changing natural, social, and economic environments. In a neoliberal society, market forces are the only ones that matter and that can provide relief and security. One such product on the market, Preppi, is a line of high-end doomsday preparation products designed for the stylish and upwardly mobile middle classes who eschew the paranoid style of the typical doomsday prepper but who cannot afford to escape to a private location by helicopter like the superrich. Products like Preppi, an invention of a California-based startup company, assume that (1) the democratic safeguards against natural and social disasters are tenuous, (2) these disasters are easier to prepare for individually than to address collectively, and (3) the most viable way to survive political and climactic upheaval is through individual consumption and preparation—and that in so doing, one's class status can be preserved. These assumptions are not just promoted by Preppi but by startup culture at large. Silicon Valley, the hub of neoliberal startup capital, not only responds to the desire to individually safeguard oneself; it encourages those anxieties and a neoliberal approach to survival, creating economic opportunity for the producers of doomsday goods. This chapter looks at the influential ideals and prescriptions from within Silicon Valley and how this encourages individual consumption in anticipation of climate change or other disasters, rather than collective democratic political action.

As prepping for disaster became less focused on the atomic bomb and dispersed into a generalized readiness for any kind of disaster, the market for bunkers likewise became a market for preparation in general. Silicon Valley plays a significant role in bunkerization, directly so as the critical production site for weapons components, including for atomic bombs. "Lockheed Missile and Space Corporation (LMSC) became the largest industrial employer in Silicon Valley during the Cold War."[1] Silicon Valley has for several decades been considered the engine of new products and new consumers, producing one and the other in disruptions to traditional industries with rideshare services, skilled taskers an app installation away, office share startups and office share crashes, the subscription economy, 3-D printing, and preparation for disaster, short-term and apocalyptic alike. The Santa Clara Valley after colonization, however, was a blanket of orchards on rolling hills, not a hub of self-styled tech gods and their nootropically enhanced foresight into the future of human life. To contextualize the development of the prepping startup market, a brief historical sketch of Silicon Valley helps draw a line from tinkering to industrialization to marketizing doomsday preparation.

FROM SWEET CHERRIES TO SILICON

Silicon Valley is, according to the historian Leslie Berlin, "the narrow stretch of the San Francisco Peninsula that is sandwiched between the bay to the east and the Coastal Range to the west."[2] Before Santa

Clara County and San Francisco became famous for the tech sector, native Ohlone had occupied this region since 500 CE. The Ohlone were forcibly put to work in the Spanish missions in the late 1700s, during which time they lost their land to the missions and were forced to Christianize. This period of Spanish colonization gave way to agriculture largely worked by Japanese and Chinese laborers, who were legally excluded from property ownership.[3] In the 1930s and '40s, tech companies and electronic components manufacturing began to replace agricultural land in the Santa Clara Valley. In 1951, Varian Associates became the first company to join the Stanford Industrial Park, a joint development between private companies and Stanford University. The park has hosted notables like Mark Zuckerberg's Meta and Elon Musk's Tesla and is credited as being part of the founding of the Silicon Valley we know today.[4] In 1955, William Shockley, one of the scientists from Bell Laboratories responsible for developing the transistor and for research on semiconductors, moved to Palo Alto and recruited scientists to join the Shockley Semiconductor Laboratory.[5] The inventive use of silicon pioneered by Shockley and later the "traitorous eight" employees who left Shockley's company inspired the nickname "Silicon Valley" in 1971, which has since dominated the identity of this geographic space.

Before the domination of silicon, the valley might have been more aptly described as Radio Valley. In the 1910s through 1930s, the local amateur radio community around San Francisco influenced the early founders of the tech sector, itself influenced by the U.S. Navy's presence on the peninsula and its extensive use of radio. As described in Christophe Lécuyer's history of Silicon Valley, the ham radio community was "characterized by camaraderie and intense sociability." This group of hobbyists helped found the reputation of the Bay Area as a new class of garage tinkerers who could repurpose basic industrially produced tools, like radio, to create physical and social networks: "radio amateurs built reputations among their brethren by innovating new circuitry, devising clever transmitter designs, and establishing contacts with faraway lands," and "ham culture was characterized by its mix of competitiveness and information sharing."[6] The early radio club culture provided an early blueprint for the ethos of Silicon Valley. As these engineers and tinkerers went on to start

Bay Area firms, they became producers of electronics components and the early corporations that would splinter and seed the valley with tech-sector startups. This fragmentation is consistent with tinkering because it is less concerned with understanding the entire process of production and more with how to intersect at certain points to "innovate" or "disrupt" along the way. By the 1970s, "Silicon Valley was, in particular, the main center for development and production of power-grid tubes, microwave tubes, and semiconductors. Local firms manufactured about half of the microwave tubes and more than a third of the silicon transistors and integrated circuits produced in the United States. Because these components were used in virtually every advanced weapon system and in a wide range of industrial goods, the Peninsula's electronics industry became central to the US defense effort and to the political economy of US manufacturing."[7]

The infusion of military funding was bolstered by research and financial support from Stanford University, which encouraged entrepreneurship in its engineering graduates. In comparison to their East Coast counterparts, Silicon Valley's technology manufacturing firms were relatively small and developed a distinctive business and management style in line with a tinkering habit of mind. "In industries where manufacturing processes were difficult to develop and to control, they needed to attract and retain a highly skilled and motivated workforce. This led them to develop innovative forms of management-employee relations. The entrepreneurs sought to involve their professional employees in the decision-making process." This gesture toward interdisciplinarity and networking made its way into the contemporary work style of Silicon Valley. In the 1960s, the Department of Defense scaled back purchasing, which forced tech companies to expand into the commercial market. Throughout the 1960s and 1970s, the companies that anchored the tech sector in the valley reorganized and spun out new companies. These startups were generously funded by venture capital: "Thirty new and reconstituted venture capital operations were formed on the Peninsula from 1968–1975 . . . by the early 1970s, the Bay Area was one of the largest centers for venture capital in the United States. The growth of the venture capital industry encouraged the formation of new semiconductor startups by assuring potential entrepreneurs that investment backing was available. . . . In short, the rise of the venture capital industry both facilitated and fostered entrepreneurship on the San Francisco Peninsula."[8] The presence of venture capital influenced the business management of tech startup firms, which had to maximize profit. Companies had to innovate rapidly, which encouraged closer relationships between engineers, manufacturing, and marketing to design products that would sell quickly. The push from capital coincided with the desire to run business differently from their East Coast predecessors and now competitors.

A combination of new business strategies, venture capital, and the countercultural movement coalesced into what would become Silicon Valley. The beginning of the Santa Clara Valley as a tech sector did more than develop an industrial infrastructure; it also laid the groundwork for the political, economic, and cultural particularities of Silicon Valley. The Bay Area tech sector brings together a strange mix of capitalist libertarianism, neoliberalism, a belief in the supremacy of human consciousness, techno-optimism, and a desire to overcome the limits of nature on the human mind and human habitat. Not unlike the Boy Scouts and the handicraft movements, Silicon Valley entrepreneurs imagined themselves harnessing a certain American spirit to pioneer new economic and technological grounds and to safeguard themselves against the vague threats of the state and economic policies that would stifle creative production and market development and, by extension, the human spirit of innovation, independence, and resilience.

The arrival of personal computers and publicly available internet access in the 1990s gave a new set of promises and fears to the countercultural revolutionaries fearful of bureaucracy and hopeful about their new freedom from geographic boundaries. The internet and personal computing allowed for individuals to continue their research into what to fear and how to prepare and gave them access to marketplaces and discussion boards that would bring prepping into the new digital and networked world. The vision of the internet and digitization of the self as liberating for the individual and for the capitalist economy is shared by Silicon Valley's contemporary visionaries. Men like Elon Musk and Peter Thiel, however, recognize the very material threat of war and climate change—or a combination of the two—as pressing down on the promise of accelerated human development. Musk worries that some catastrophic event, perhaps a third world war, will throw humans back into a dark age, leaving us bound by our bioregions and local economics once again. The fear of evolutionary regression is part of the anxiety over climate change. Unchecked greenhouse gas emissions threaten human existence and the gift of human consciousness. According to the titans of Silicon Valley, in order to ensure that human relations—economic and social in particular—remain liberated from the tyranny of regulations and the limits of industrial-era travel and communication, the species should not be dependent on a single planet for life. The solution to climate change becomes addressing inefficiencies in Earth's economics while creating information redundancy by building sustainable cities on other planets and sending our "data," encoded in humans who will, presumably, reproduce, to innovate with the help of private funding. Going multiplanetary is one such defense against a terrifying and unstable world and one of many approaches to prepping for an uncertain future. The approaches to protecting against substantial future losses and guaranteeing one's personal survival are built into the missions of various startups and their fast capitalization on old fears and new markets. This is not an approach that values democratic participation or leveraging public resources distributed primarily to everyday people and grassroots organizing to protect against climate change. Instead, this dark vision entails a redistribution of public resources into the private sector to secure the means for survival for just the wealthy worthy minority who should survive and thrive in the new world technologically optimized to endure the various existential threats. Not all preppers are antidemocratic, but many are attracted to consuming safeguards against disaster, where those safeguards are available on the market and at different price points, rather than distributed on a different organizing principle, such as socialized according to need. Some preppers anticipate resuming their socioeconomic class lifestyles after weathering a given disaster and take great pains to ensure that their survival strategies reflect their leisure-class status, including the quality of bunker in which they plan to hide.

Preppi can be seen as just another example of finding solace in the market against environmental and economic uncertainty, but it is also the attractively packaged product of a Silicon Valley assemblage of ideals and investments that is rooted in antidemocratic, neoliberal sentiment. Silicon Valley survivalism is not born out of concern for humanity. The market for survival products reinforces the already existing desire to limit the power of the government and to "opt in" to putatively distinct autonomous and privately run societies. That gold bars were included in some of the original Preppi kits indicates the founders are prepared for the kind of economic collapse that would render global state-backed currencies obsolete. In this fantasy, gold still holds value, despite its limited utility. While Preppi is an attractive object for inquiry, this chapter explores the ideological underside of prepping in Silicon Valley. Beneath the rhetoric of democratizing the internet and improving the standard of living for global populations, Silicon Valley is preoccupied with replacing governments via disruptive technologies that promote a highly individualized way of living and connecting to one another, by producing habituated citizens for whom access to politics is through consumption. Citizens came prepared for these shifts in the "be prepared" era of skill building through the Boy Scouts and with the handicraft and tinkering movements that encouraged people to link their independence to consumer choices and always keep in mind that the imperative to go it alone is always around the corner.

This Silicon Valley version of prepping politics is buttressed and inspired by the Dark Enlightenment, or the Neo-Reactionary movement (NRx), largely championed by Nick Land, an independent philosopher and novelist, and Curtis Yarvin, who goes by Mencius Moldbug in his writings, a software developer and entrepreneur in Silicon Valley. Preppi is an object of a Silicon Valley fantasy that refuses to acknowledge the possibility of collective action, and it is useful to draw out the neoliberal inclinations of this approach to organizing society in response to looming disasters. Many of Silicon Valley's entrepreneurs, CEOs, and their boosters promote aspirational political and economic formations that preserve class stratification as a feature of a society that is correctly organized around free-market principles, with the state in service to protect the market from unreasonable interferences such as wealth redistribution and corporate taxation. NRx propositions similarly see a democratic government as a limitation on individual freedom but prefer the rule of law, albeit embodied by a nondemocratic state, as the means to keep global peace and preserve individual freedoms. These attitudes in Silicon Valley are evidenced in the growing startup markets for individual disaster preparation, which reroutes collective anxiety about (mostly) legitimate crises into market demands for security and mass consumption.

Wendy Brown situates the ideological tendencies of Silicon Valley in critiques of neoliberalism and concern for the state (and fate) of democracy. We use Brown's reading of Foucault's lectures on biopolitics to explore the linkages between neoliberalism and Silicon Valley. Brown's work in *Undoing the Demos* argues that neoliberalism erodes democracy and replaces it with an economic sphere of existence in which the democratic subject is reduced to *homo oeconomicus*.[9] In complement to Brown's concern over the loss of democratic possibility, the "Californian Ideology," written in 1995, outlines the ideologies that drive Silicon Valley and describes "dotcom neoliberalism" while the dotcom bubble was still whole.[10] Taken together, these critical works provide a general outline of neoliberalism as an ideology that threatens to absorb democracy and specifically identify how that tendency is reinforced by the particular ideologies found in Silicon Valley. To narrow the inquiry, we look at the way antidemocratic institutions and the associated production of goods discourage collective, democratic responses to environmental, political, and economic disasters and encourage an economic and individualized response instead. Disasters almost always disrupt the delivery of essential public services and expose socioeconomic inequities, and they typically require the intervention of governments that, historically, struggle to address the wide range of material needs in the context of racial, gendered, and economic stratification. Indeed, neoliberalism makes it nearly impossible for the state to respond to disaster properly:

> The proper scope of social calamity is also social, of course, but one of the hallmarks of neoliberal authoritarianism is that the state is in recess (even though this recess is artificed through authoritarian interventions) and market forces are all that citizens can appeal to

as they make their way through a risky world with no social protection. As a result, the collapse of society is not a public concern, and only private provisioning through market interactions offers protection.[11]

Individualistic options for survival and recovery may appear more appealing compared to the bumbling and unequal efforts of a state long mired in institutional inequalities. Neoliberalism, especially as it is run through Silicon Valley, discourages democratic organizing by promoting consumerism as an act of personal responsibility, all while suggesting that the market-based options for ensuring survival is the only reliable way to preserve humankind. Although this twenty-first-century iteration of the institutionalization of consuming as citizenship is not bounded by the same discourse of duty as its twentieth-century counterpart, they share an imperative to "do one's part" by responsibilizing oneself as a subject of the state.

A SMART BET AGAINST THE FUTURE

Preppi was launched in 2014 after its founding couple experienced an earthquake and felt unprepared for an emergency.[12] The company sells a range of emergency kits, ranging from a $65 first aid kit to a nearly $5,000 "Prepster Ultra Advanced—Fireproof Emergency Bag." The product promises: "By bringing design to the forefront of our emergency kits we hope to make emergency preparedness less daunting and maybe even a little fun." The company does not specify which disasters Preppi is suited for but instead offers that "extreme weather and unpredictable emergencies" are "commonplace globally," so "it is no longer an option to treat the topic of preparedness lightly."[13] The website implies that emergencies are more common now than they have been in the past, and with reference to extreme weather, it implies that climate change is among those threats for which we must now be vigilant. This is the consumer side of the dynamic, discussed in the previous chapter, of the commonplace emergencies that the state is vigilant about. Products like Preppi seek to fill the gap for what savvy consumers ought to do.

This line of products is advertised on Gwyneth Paltrow's wellness and lifestyle website, GOOP, which caters to the luxury new-age market and promotes controversial, nontraditional wellness remedies, products for one's "cosmic health," high-end clothing, and wellness retreats that run into the thousands of dollars. Preppi emergency kits seem to encourage serious consideration of one's survival during a crisis while also assuming that the crisis is survivable and that what is left after the crisis is the same economic and social schema as before. To make the task of survival less fearful, Preppi kits include "luxe amenities and extra life-saving gadgets," including necessities such as rain ponchos, waterproof matches, military-grade food rations, high-end practical goods like a solar phone charger and a satellite phone, and luxury goods like a flask ("Many consider a fine Scotch to be the ultimate life saver!"), boutique chocolate, and high-end Malin+Goetz toiletries. The *Wall Street Journal* calls it "a smart hedge against a not-so-bright future."[14] This endorsement suggests that Preppi is a safe investment for those who anticipate trouble on the horizon but do not want to sacrifice class amenities; this advice is couched in the language of financial planning and betting on financial risk rather than suggesting collective strategies for responding to crises.

Preppi is an understated testament to the power of the antidemocratic ideologies that reinforce an individualistic approach to thinking of one's position in relation to others and cast doubt on the ability of people to organize together for common purposes. The average consumer is unlikely to buy a Preppi bag in the hope this signals the end of democracy. Yet this consumer has already conceded that the institutions of democratic deliberation are unreliable and cannot guarantee a political environment for collectively organizing and mobilizing the public resources for equitable public distribution in the face of disaster. The only path to survival, and indeed to thriving afterward, is through one's personal preparation, ingenuity, and the ability to access a responsive marketplace that will persist beyond any environmental collapse. The fear of state failure is a legitimate one, just as worrying about the inability of the state to respond adequately to any number of disasters justifies some degree of preparation. However, preparing alone, or just within a family unit, is not one choice among various available but is instead a one-dimensional choice in a neoliberal ideology that champions individual responsibility and market responses to public needs. Silicon Valley models this institutional ideology in its labor practices, in the intellectual output of its advocates and funders, and in the products it pitches to everyday consumers conditioned to expect the market to care for them and to indicate what they should and should not be worried about.

Personal doomsday prepping has a long history in the United States, drawn into sharp relief during the height of the nuclear standoff between the USSR and the United States in the 1950s and 1960s and accelerated through the burgeoning of Silicon Valley. Average citizens were encouraged to buy underground bunkers for their suburban homes, stock up on shelf-stable foods, and cache enough weapons and security to keep out their friends and neighbors. While physical bunkers may have gone out of style, the institution of prepping is still a way of life for an untold number of Americans. Their fears range from the natural (earthquakes, volcanoes, pandemics, and magnetic pole shifts) to the social (economic collapse and terrorist attacks), to events somewhere in between, like the effects of climate change. The markets for doomsday prepping target people who imagine living in primitive but safe hideouts but also those with the financial resources to secure luxury bunkers with the hope of minimizing the loss of their lifestyle and class status even after apocalypse. The popular press has intermittently run stories about prepping for the upper class, including the tech investor Peter Thiel's New Zealand property (and citizenship), which involves retrofitted military bunkers that include theaters, spas, and swimming pools, in addition to high-end practical services like hydroponic gardens and space for medical professionals.[15] A CEO of a luxury bunker company points out that the typical customer owns a yacht and therefore understands how to design and appoint such a space.[16] Between the poles of super-rich prepping and primitivist prepping is a middle-class approach to preparing for challenging times during which careful individuals may assume that public services and infrastructure will be in disarray and that the private sector is best able to fill one's needs for survival. Naomi Klein famously referred to the opportunism of capital waiting for the next exploitable crisis as "disaster capitalism," forming part of the "neoliberal shock doctrine."[17]

Many of the environmental crises for which people prepare are exacerbated or created by the environmentally reckless production and distribution of corporate goods and services, which are marketed to a public increasingly skeptical of the public sector's ability to provide stability in a changing world. The rush to provide private services to allay public fear of disaster is in some sense an opportunity seized by the private sector, but it is also an opportunity produced by the private sector, and even more specifically part of an effort to put into motion the neoreactionary ideology that would not just rescue humans from acute harms but would liberate humans from the failures of democracy and regulation. Rather than organize to pressure the state to act responsibly, citizens are encouraged to embrace the neoliberal capitalist market as a firewall against disaster. Given this argument, a relatively benign product like Preppi is an interesting object through which to explore the prepping phenomenon as a movement to undermine democracy and promote a world of privately run enterprises with clients and customers, rather than citizens.

THE SLOW EROSION OF DEMOCRACY

THE NEOLIBERAL CRISIS

The highly individualistic ideologies that animate Silicon Valley are a strange hybrid of libertarianism and neoliberalism and are, in some cases, explicitly antidemocratic. While libertarianism aims to shrink the state in size and influence, neoliberalism is a loose set of strategies and discourses that remakes the state as the protector of the market economy. Brown makes the claim that neoliberalism is undoing democracy: "My argument is not merely that markets and money are corrupting or degrading democracy. . . . Rather, neoliberal reason, ubiquitous today in statecraft and the workplace, in jurisprudence, education, culture, and a vast range of quotidian activity, is converting the distinctly *political* character, meaning, and operation of democracy's constituent elements, into *economic* ones."[18]

Neoliberalism does not just encourage the privatization of public services; it encourages the use of the market model as the template for all political and social relations. In the analytic mode of Marcuse's *One-Dimensional Man*, social and civic movements are thus subsumed into the bureaucratic apparatus shaped by and through capitalism. The promises of liberalism become the domain of the market. "As liberty is relocated from political to economic life, it becomes subject to the inherent inequality of the latter and is part of what secures that inequality. . . . Liberty itself is narrowed to market conduct, divested of association with mastering the conditions of life, existential freedom, or securing the rule of the demos."[19] In these terms, liberty is the freedom to sell oneself on the market, to be free from the constraints to financially (and otherwise) support other members of one's community, and enjoy a freedom from political decisions that are not anchored in market logic. These institutional dictates are easily carried over from the Cold War worry about losing Americanness.

In Brown's reading, Foucault claims that "human capital replaces labor" and "entrepreneurship replaces production." The individual as its own enterprise is visible in the markets of Silicon Valley, where the entrepreneur is the engine of the market. The entrepreneur is the one willing to take the financial and personal risks to achieve greatness, to "disrupt" the way things are produced and consumed. Financial risk is an expected aspect of participation, and it is conflated with other kinds of risks that may be valued in a democratic society, like speaking freely or defending the oppressed. Brown notes that "productivity is prioritized over product; enterprise is prioritized over consumption and satisfaction. An enterprise society is not about trucking and bartering things (exchange), nor is it based on desires or appetites for things (consumption)."[20] Productivity is so valued that it has become an industry in itself. Silicon Valley disrupters are voracious consumers of nootropic supplements and advocates of microdosing psychedelic drugs to improve creative productivity. Steve Jobs's infamous call to "stay hungry, stay foolish," a phrase he found on the back of the *Whole Earth Catalog* and then shared in his 2005 commencement speech at Stanford University, appears to be broadly interpreted as a call to be perpetually competitive and always seeking to uncover, then capitalize on, the next big thing.[21] In this mode of creating a neoliberal subject, democratic issues and interests not captured by efficiency, profitability, and savvy are all but distant concerns. Prepping, then, is not run through a critical lens in contemplating the means and purposes of one's life but is part of the value that must be maximized as a good neoliberal subject. As prepping becomes an entrepreneurial market itself, prepping as consuming exceeds consuming and becomes a way of orienting oneself to work of making a life.[22] More than the prepping consumer, prepping is part of the institutional makeup of a neoliberal society. As Brown points out, this is a version of production not tied to specific consumer appetites, but rather it is production for its own sake, or production as a demonstration of one's capabilities as an entrepreneurial person. To exist as a subject of the state is to be an entrepreneur.

> *Homo oeconomicus* . . . operates in a context replete with risk, contingency, and potentially violent changes, from burst bubbles and capital or currency meltdowns to wholesale industry dissolution . . . rather than each individual pursuing his or her own interest and unwittingly generating collective benefit, today, it is the project of macroeconomic growth and credit enhancement to which neoliberal individuals are tethered and with which their existence as human capital must align if they are to thrive.[23]

If that passage were rewritten to fit the narrative style of National Geographic's television series *Doomsday Preppers*, it would not feel out of place. Much of the anxiety faced by the people featured on the show is in direct relation to the economic conditions described by Brown. Some preppers have survived the loss of jobs from offshoring production and downsizing. Rather than pin their legitimate crises to the neoliberal turns of the market and the state, the television subjects turn their experiences with a state indifferent to their needs into paranoid and conspiratorial thinking about internal and external enemies. The geologic and climatic events of the planet likewise exist as a context "replete with risk, contingency, and potentially violent changes."[24] The fears and precautionary actions taken by preppers are absorbed into the marketplace, reproducing preppers as consumers of the tools of survival but also as objects to be consumed as featured guests on cable television. The ability to consume and be consumed is part of the freedom afforded by a neoliberal state that reduces life to economic metrics.

Rather than view the government as a set of institutions and mechanisms for maintaining order and for distributing needed resources in uncertain or disastrous times, many everyday people who prepare for hard times see the government as inept at best and out to get them at worst. Advocates of neoliberalism claim that reorganizing the state as a framework for a thriving capitalist economy provides a necessary distance between individual choice and the restraints on freedom by the state. Even the less paranoid prepper seems to understand that in the end, the state is not there to look after their welfare, as codified in federal-level policy like the Gaither Report. Is it any wonder that a government primarily tasked with supporting the market rather than its citizens (and those who cannot claim citizenship status) is incapable of inspiring confidence? Safeguards against the loss of human life and of basic necessities, like the Federal Emergency Management Agency (FEMA) and the Environmental Protection Agency (EPA), are ritually gutted by presidential administrations and judicial activists and replaced with a private-sector "honor system" of self-regulation. In the vacuum of publicly available services that maintain human life, dignity, and flourishing, even in difficult times, there exist private-sector answers to these needs in the form of conspicuous consumption like luxury bunkers, private security forces, helipads, and transportation to and from secret locations for the rich. Others are enticed to emulate the leisure class by availing themselves of the affordable-by-comparison Preppi kits, to freeze-dried potato soup marketed by evangelical leaders, and wilderness survival courses. Neoliberalism as a way of governing is stretched to serving as a way to orient oneself socially and politically: "Subjects, liberated for the pursuit of their own enhancement of human capital, emancipated from all concerns with and regulation by the social, the political, the common, or the collective, are inserted into the norms, and imperatives of market conduct and integrated into the purposes of the firm, industry, region, nation, or postnational constellation to which their survival is tethered."[25]

Individuals not only look toward the market to satisfy needs that ought to be publicly met, but the products and services increasingly available as safeguards against disaster are celebrated as examples of the market liberating the individual from the tyranny of taxes and imposed inept political leadership in ways that continue to reify the myth of the self-made frontiersman. Free from government limitations, individuals can take care of their needs through the private market and even become the next great entrepreneur, thereby making new markets. Under this logic, the market is not out to get anyone, and it is not best managed via normative liberal guardrails. The neoliberalized state functions as a prop for such a market, which claims to afford people consumer freedoms they cannot achieve as democratic citizens. In line with neoliberalism, the ethos of Silicon Valley is a deep skepticism of the state and governing apparatuses, skepticism of the capacity of "the people" to make rational collective decisions, and skepticism of regulatory controls over the market that, when working properly, produce the truth about what we value. Silicon Valley flourishes in the neoliberalized state not only because of market opportunities but because of ideological alignment among the startups, disrupters, and investors that contribute so much to the private replacements for democratic and collective responses to the challenges of living well. The Silicon Valley skepticism is echoed in the National Geographic Channel's prepper anxieties about our dependence on systems that may not hold.

THE CALIFORNIAN IDEOLOGY

In 1996, Richard Barbrook and Andy Cameron introduced the "Californian Ideology" in *Science as Culture*, with an abridged version published digitally in *Mute* magazine. The long version of the essay tries to make sense of the seemingly disparate parts of the guiding ideology of Silicon Valley as the digital technology age and economic bubble took hold. "The Californian Ideology promiscuously combines the free-wheeling spirit of the hippies and the entrepreneurial zeal of the yuppies." Entrepreneurialism is, just as in Brown's analysis, the energy behind and the purpose of work. Entrepreneurial zeal in the tech sector was assumed to produce a vast network of digital opportunities for social and economic connection that could sidestep public spaces, laws, and the slow pace of change associated with an enormously populated democratic state. "Above all, they are passionate advocates of what appears to be an impeccably libertarian form of politics—they want information technologies to be used to create a new 'Jeffersonian democracy' where all individuals will be able to express themselves freely within cyberspace."[26] This zeal reanimates the American myths of the prepping institutions of the twentieth century. Notable figures in the digital revolution, from Esther Dyson to Marshall McLuhan, championed this new frontier of connectivity and productivity, with Dyson even claiming that she no longer lived at a physical address but instead lived almost entirely digitally in the World Wide Web.[27] Barbrook and Cameron argue that the Californian Ideology embraced both the New Left and the New Right, including Newt Gingrich and his support for funding the newly emerging digital marketplace: "In this version of the Californian Ideology, each member of the 'virtual class' is promised the opportunity to become a successful hi-tech entrepreneur. Information technologies, so the argument goes, empower the individual, enhance personal freedom, and radically reduce the power of the nation-state. Existing social, political and legal power structures will wither away to be replaced by unfettered interactions between autonomous individuals and their software."[28]

The nation-state and its conservative pace of institutional change, its limitations on individual freedom, and its ability to track and manage people through bureaucratic data collection will lose its purpose as the digital revolution unleashes the entrepreneurial power of risk-taking engineers, hackers, and even corporations nimble and well funded enough to challenge the world as it is. At least so goes the promise of a world made in Silicon Valley's image. The authors point out that this explosion in digital entrepreneurship was made possible by public defense funding to the technology companies in the valley, an observation that challenges the bold claim that the digital revolution will render the government obsolete. These digital radicals embrace the "liberal ideal of the self-sufficient individual" and the need to turn the liberated productive energy into private property.[29]

The government remains essential, however, for acknowledging the very existence of private property and by providing legal cover for its protection, which runs against the libertarianism prevalent in Silicon Valley. To return to Brown, the neoliberalization of the commons means more than prioritizing the marketplace over the public square; it involves remaking our relations to fit a neoliberal template of what it means to live and interact with one another. It also means that everyday life itself becomes neoliberalized, regardless of any reconfigurations of the broader global order.

Over a decade after this article was written, some prominent Silicon Valley entrepreneurs and ideologues produced a darker dream of what the technological revolution could do. Rather than imagine a digital Jeffersonian democracy, venture capitalists, engineers, and their disciples articulated an antidemocratic vision of what their entrepreneurial power could unleash. Theirs was a narrative of an uncertain world made less free by ineffective democratic states that bound people together under the auspices of democracy while limiting individual freedoms and the ability to find one's freedom and security in a flourishing marketplace hemmed in only by consumer choices and producer innovation. The neoreactionary movement, in drawing together individual freedom and antidemocratic sentiment, helped create a political and economic environment for rejecting democratic organization and the socialization of goods, services, labor, and security, including protection from disasters.

THE DARK ENLIGHTENMENT AND THE NEOREACTIONARY MOVEMENT

Neoliberalism and the neoreactionary ideology do not perfectly map onto each other. Silicon Valley embraces both, and this is reflected in the way Silicon Valley encourages consumption patterns that align with these values. Neoliberalism promotes running the government as a corporation, but it does not necessarily advocate turning the government into a corporation, as does the Dark Enlightenment. Yet both wish to see any kind of governance, whether from a private or public entity, focus its power on creating a "propitious market milieu" where "competition, the agency of control, can function effectively." Neoliberalism attempts to "reengineer the state from within,"[30] while the neoreactionary prescription is to replace the state entirely with a corporation-as-state. In either case, radically remaking the state would emphasize rule by the laws of science and market logic, not through political participation. Democracy would no longer be a fundamental goal of good governance. People would find freedom for and within the market, and citizens as consumers would "vote" with their dollars. Transactions, not democratic participation, would make a state function. Like neoliberalism, NRx does not advance a liberal version of human nature. NRx attempts to make something of human nature out of poorly interpreted theories of Darwinian evolution and Richard Dawkins's work on genetics, but it lacks a coherent approach and conclusion. Both NRx and neoliberal thought argue that science and data analysis are yoked to the state but that both can and should be liberated and put to better use in support of a well-run governing machine in support of the capitalist market economy and a smoothly operating state in competition with others. Finally, both NRx and neoliberalism are skeptical of state attempts to rectify inequalities, particularly those stemming from supposed intolerance or historical mistreatment. Nick Land's "Dark Enlightenment Manifesto" suggests that the democratic liberal commitment to toleration allows "political forces" to legitimize silencing or stifling anything opposed to tolerance. Toleration begets more poor behavior "because grievance status is awarded as political compensation for economic incompetence."[31] Similarly, neoliberalism takes no issue with economic inequality and wishes to exclude politics from trying to right these perceived wrongs and interfere with the workings of the market.

THE DARK ENLIGHTENMENT'S SHADOW OVER THE VALLEY

While Silicon Valley's tech sector boom may have been born from public defense investment, the new torchbearers of the digital revolution are decidedly against state intervention and the promotion of democracy. According to Aikin, "what is needed, by the neo-reactionary's lights, is a Dark Enlightenment, one that systematically undoes and deprograms the ideology of the liberal-progressive Cathedral and the

Enlightenment norms it purports to promote."[32] The collection of ideas, ideologies, screeds, manifestos, and demands that together constitute the corpus of the Dark Enlightenment are scattered and disharmonious. Timothy W. Luke points out in his essay on the subject that "the writings of these thinkers are often contradictory, convoluted, and confusing. But one should not ignore the remarkable number of elective affinities between their strange political agendas and old ideological alliances at the advent of the Anthropocene." Luke rightly notes that their identity as "radical libertarian anti-statists" is sprung from a country "without an established church, a feudal aristocracy, or a once well-entrenched peasant economy." Yet, Dark Enlightenment types fit in from the perspective of American institutional development and the habits of mind of self-sufficient yeomen who are responsible only to themselves and their families. The loudest voices of the neoreactionary Dark Enlightenment movement are Nick Land and Curtis Yarvin. Both promote an antidemocratic accelerationist ideology to replace liberalism in the United States and even to replace the United States itself with a better, lighter, undemocratic system that would presumably function like a corporation while also protecting the free market, since "governments espousing liberty, equality, and fraternity, then, are fraudulent scams. Neo-cameralist states, however, should be regarded as exemplars of managerial perfection in which governance would whip up efficient, effective, and entrepreneurial miracles."[33]

The neocameralist state is in contrast to the current state, dubbed "the Cathedral." The Cathedral is a dense network of actors beholden to the state, including bureaucracies, universities, and the media. These institutions do not necessarily add up to a conspiratorial cabal, but they generally work in concert to promote liberal democracy, brainwash the masses, and maintain power within its own circuits. Democracy is a doomed project that rests on shaky, liberal premises of equality, natural rights, and the inherent goodness of political involvement for the everyday person, most directly and frequently exercised through voting. The critiques of democracy and liberalism are woven throughout complicated and logically unsound arguments, resting on untrue premises and misaligned comparisons. However, these sorts of issues have not stopped the popularity of these ideas or their circulation among Silicon Valley's funders, CEOs, and would-be disrupters. The Dark Enlightenment project is incoherent but influential, and it exceeds the limits of typical liberalism pitted against conservatism; it even looks beyond the promises of libertarianism. Instead, neoreactionary thought sits fairly comfortably alongside neoliberalism.

While libertarianism emphasizes fundamental negative liberties and the right to as much autonomy as is possible while still living in a barebones state, Land's and Moldbug's neoreactionary thinking does not share the enthusiasm for self-governance and doubts that most people are capable of such a thing. Some tenets of neoliberalism, however, fit the bill with a state designed to support and protect the market, a skeptical view of democracy, the conflation of living within a liberal state with living under conditions of slavery, and protecting the inequality that naturally follows from such freedoms. Land argues that promoting democracy is merely a means to expand the state, which is the goal of the left, an unfortunate but immutable fact for the right, and disagreeable for libertarians.[34] Democracy is a worst-case scenario for a society: it is the unwanted promise of progressivism and the reckless optimism of the Enlightenment period. In Land's words:

> For the hardcore neo-reactionaries, democracy is not merely doomed, it is doom itself. Fleeing it approaches an ultimate imperative. The subterranean current that propels such anti-politics is recognizably Hobbesian, a coherent dark enlightenment, devoid from its beginning of any Rousseauistic enthusiasm for popular expression. Predisposed, in any case, to perceive the politically awakened masses as a howling irrational mob, it conceives the dynamics of democratization as fundamentally degenerative: systematically consolidating and exacerbating private vices, resentments, and deficiencies until they reach the level of collective criminality and comprehensive social corruption.

Land's fear of the "howling irrational mob" chimes with Peterson's caution about panic turning ordinary Americans into panicked masses. While Peterson and other Cold Warriors were decidedly more sympathetic to liberalism than the NRx, they both imagined doom as a people out of control, driven by irrationalities and unable to rule themselves. Democracy must be contained, whether through anticommunist liberalism or corporate authoritarianism. Even the tepid and superficial democracy of Cold War America did not allow for popular interference in matters of national defense. In Masco's recounting of a tour of the Titan Missile Museum in Arizona, "We learn early in the presentation that crew members carried a pistol at all times while on duty, marked as a necessity for site security but also to ensure that a reluctant crewman 'did his job properly in case of a launch order.' "[35] The authoritarian approach to ensuring democracy is preserved is decidedly draconian and exists at the end of a gun. In the neocameral fantasy and the Cold War power structure, only the national "CEO" can make the order to launch nuclear weapons, with only the pretense of democratic permission when this is carried out by a popularly elected president. However, the Schmittian dynamics of political exceptionalism that operate in both liberal democracy and NRx authoritarianism only ask for their political subjects to play their part in serving as foils for legitimacy and vehicles for productivity. The argument here is not that the Dark Enlightenment can be retroactively applied to the atomic age of politics or that the atomic age of politics is the genesis of the Dark Enlightenment but rather that these affinities are instructive and not coincidental. They are outcroppings of institutional developments in American life and show different habits of mind. This example of Veblen's blind drift shows how different ideologies can result from some of the same premises. Prepping as an institutionalized mode of life contrary to democracy finds traction in both of these ideological branches, and in the Dark Enlightenment, prepping is collapsed into a exit politics of preparing, literally, to leave the Cathedral.

Land is not alone in his disdain for democracy and finds support from his fellow neoreactionary, Mencius Moldbug, to make his point: "If the state cannot be eliminated, Moldbug argues, at least it can be cured of democracy (or systematic and degenerative bad government), and the way to do that is to formalize it. This is an approach he calls 'neo-cameralism.' " The state CEO is finally free to rule without the pretense of democracy, which, in its current iteration, is useless at best and, as an ideal, dangerous and wrongheaded: "There is no longer any need for residents (clients) to take any interest in politics whatsoever. . . . If gov-corp doesn't deliver acceptable value for its taxes (sovereign rent), they can notify its customer service function, and if necessary take their custom elsewhere. Gov-corp would concentrate upon running an efficient, attractive, vital, clean, and secure country, of a kind that is able to draw customers. No voice, free exit."[36]

This sentiment is reiterated by Patri Friedman, the founder and former CEO of the Seasteading Institute, as well as the grandson of the famed economist Milton Friedman. He promotes seasteading as a means to experiment with a form of neocameralism. A seasteading community is a privately run society whose customer-members, if dissatisfied, a can opt out of and try their luck on another one.[37] This is a preferred alternative to the "noise" of democracy, which obscures the "signals" of the market. Forcing people into radically individualized relations with one another will force them to learn the tough lessons, although what those lessons are is a little opaque as they are run through confusing metaphors of zombie apocalypse, parasitism, doomsday prepping, and accelerationism. One of the few gifts of cursed modernity is technological, scientific, and business achievement and innovation, which Land wishes to rescue before throwing out the bathwater. Singling out these categories for special commendation and placing them in a vision of a good future presumably resonates with Silicon Valley. Not even libertarian conservatives are spared; they are criticized for accepting the natural rights enumerated in the U.S. Constitution, which keeps them tethered to the state as the rights-granting apparatus upon which they depend. The scattered potshots at conservatives and libertarians throughout NRx literature suggests that it is insufficient to collapse the Dark Enlightenment into libertarianism, and a closer read of Silicon Valley's gestures toward an ideology help bridge gaps between neoliberalism, libertarianism, and one version of their manifestation in the market through mainstream doomsday prepping. Beyond the particulars of prepping, the NRx literature bears the marks of bunkerization. Friedman wishes to muffle the noise of democratic static by walling himself off from the mess of everyday politics and everyday people. "Learning tough lessons" through forced individualization is in alignment with the bunker mentality, which states that everyone is responsible for themselves and that those who do not prepare adequately when the bomb strikes are deservedly exposed. The life-and-death lessons politics are meant to distribute are part of the freedom afforded by the liberated living offered through the Dark Enlightenment.

FREEDOM FROM DEMOCRACY IN SILICON VALLEY

Silicon Valley is driven by the efforts of venture capitalists, some well-known internationally and others who operate less frequently in the public eye but wield considerable financial and political influence. One such actor is Peter Thiel, who cofounded PayPal with Elon Musk; owns Palantir, which provides big data analytics for the Central Intelligence Agency (CIA); and was part of the transition team for President Trump. *Forbes* magazine consistently ranks him among the richest and most influential people in the tech sector. Peter Thiel wrote in his 2009 essay "The Education of a Libertarian" that freedom requires an escape from politics. "In our time, the great task for libertarians is to find an escape from politics in all its forms—from the totalitarian and fundamentalist catastrophes to the unthinking demos that guides so-called 'social democracy.'"[38] Thiel somewhat inexplicably sees libertarianism as distinct from politics and politics as a useless endeavor in the pursuit of meaningful human emancipation. Rather than following this logic to anarchism, he follows it to privately funded technology as an alternative to politics and as a means to build a better world. He specifies which technologies he has staked the future on: the internet, outer space, and seasteading—the design and construction of autonomous city-states floating in the ocean. Each of these extensions of frontiersmanship and citizenship as consumer choice presents an opportunity for private currency not dependent on state legitimacy and life beyond the control of democratic politics. Commercializing each of these frontiers, in his language, is a way to claim space for building a new world in a libertarian image.

These experiments in free living are not to be confused with collective action or a politics of care for shared living conditions. Thiel's commitment to individualism includes a vision of a great man who will rescue the future, an archaic habit of mind that persists in this vision of modern society: "The fate of our world may depend on the effort of a single person who builds or propagates the machinery of freedom that makes the world safe for capitalism."[39] Thiel claims capitalism is at risk and must be liberated from public constraints. The progress of the human species presumably rests on the ability of capital to flow freely toward worthy projects and away from compulsory ones directed by public taxes. This vision moves beyond a general conservative call to shrink the government and push back on public spending. Instead, it calls for a network of private actors behaving like sovereign states that will be free to produce technologies that will advance human evolution, whether or not there is democratic agreement on the means and ends.

Thiel and various voices that have joined the loose network of the neoreactionary movement move well beyond the preference for individual decision making in the market found in classical liberalism. In an essay, Patri Friedman asserts in a series of unfounded anthropological claims that humans are instinctively driven toward coalition-building politics to reform existing policies but that this instinct is ill-suited for the modern world of large populations and complex, corrupt politics. For Friedman, these are futile political activities, and energy is better spent building the new world in which he wants to live. The bunkerized world of the atomic age sought to preserve a fantasy of America in its windowless chambers, victory gardens, and blast-proof missile silos. Here, the prophets of the Dark Enlightenment want to make the world if not anew, then at least markedly different. A step toward realizing this new world is to abandon democratic approaches to change:

> Democracy is the current industry standard political system, but unfortunately it is ill-suited for a libertarian state. It has substantial systemic flaws, which are well-covered elsewhere, and it poses major problems specifically for libertarians. . . . Democracy is rigged against libertarians. Candidates bid for electoral victory partly by selling future political favors to raise funds and votes for their campaigns. Libertarians (and other honest candidates) who will not

abuse their office can't sell favors, thus have fewer resources to campaign with.[40]

According to Friedman, because all people, politicians included, respond to incentives, democracy and democratic debate is ineffective. Friedman's position is anchored in the Chicago School of economics, which broadly posits that humans are self-interested utility seekers and that as a result markets are the best way to coordinate human action. "Politicians, it was claimed, were just trying to maximize their own utility, as were voters."[41] This perspective is well supported by Land's manifesto, since "democracy under these conditions, then, must be, for the neo-reactionary, not the height of the exercise of human freedom, but the depth of its uncriticizable depravity. Those in elected office are tied to the electorate, and the electorate to each other, in an endless cycle of promises, incitement, recrimination, and resentment. And that's when they win elections."[42] Friedman frames government and state in market terms, arguing that the real challenge for a libertarian state is to defeat the old one, which has a monopoly on land and resources. Citizens are replaced with customers who can try different governments to see which suits their desires the best. Friedman also lends support to cryptocurrency and seasteading as opportunities to frustrate government regulation, which, in his view, necessarily means improved human freedom. For example, seasteading purports to address the loss of livable land under the pressures of climate change and could be a home of last resort for displaced peoples, but it is primarily an experiment in exiting a nation-state and opting into a privately run voluntary association of likeminded consumers. If someone is unhappy with their seastead, they could vote with their feet and their wallet and move to a different one.[43] Seasteading is appealing not just as a retreat from disaster-struck cities or states but also as an opportunity to prepare for reshaping the world to come. In his footnotes, Friedman endorses the work of Mencius Moldbug, who is generously regarded as a political theorist on Wikipedia.

In a 2012 talk given at a BIL conference (this is not an acronym, and it is an unaffiliated conference akin to TED talks), Yarvin proposes a first step in "rebooting" the U.S. government as "RAGE," which stands for "remove all government employees." In a slow build toward explaining the RAGE plan, Yarvin argues that since World War II, we have witnessed the rise of global leadership that supersedes national sovereignty and that "politics" and "democracy" may have "different emotional connotations" are essentially the same thing. He then asks why we regard "racism and fascism as nasty," positing that it is because Hitler is associated with both. To answer his own question, "what do we do about racists and fascists?," he asserts that we have an "extremely elaborate mechanism for persecuting racists and fascists . . . for firing them, for destroying their lives," and "then there's communism and socialism, which really killed a lot more people . . . if you're imagining an America that persecutes communists and socialists the way it persecutes racists and fascists, you're imagining a very different country." He continues to suggest that the U.S. Constitution has not been "entirely enforced" and that we are, perhaps, living in a state of force. After eliding his own questions, he concludes that the government is "crap" and that we need to start over, premised on new beliefs. He asks, "Is democracy an engineering device that produces good government? Is it a moral necessity?" From these brain teasers, he argues that to really change the political system, people have to quit participation in it altogether and to acknowledge one has neither the right to power nor the capacity to govern. He concludes that "a government is just a corporation that owns the country," but when a corporation has failed, you simply "delete them." He includes nongovernmental organizations and universities as part of the failed corporation that "needs to be destroyed." Instead, you need a "CEO, and a national CEO is called a dictator. . . . If Americans want to change their government they're going to have to get over their dictatorphobia."[44]

Disassembling Yarvin's eighteen-minute ramble through politics would not be difficult, but his points have been well taken by his contemporaries. However, what Yarvin is describing is less of a commitment to libertarianism than it is to neoliberalism and the fully economic subject. In writing about the impact of benchmarking on the public sector, Brown argues that the use of best practices implies that "politics appears as a combination of dicta or commands where there should be expertise . . . as partisanship where there should be neutrality and objectivity in both knowledge and practices, as provincialism where there should be the open doors and the lingua franca of the market." This observation fits nicely with the vision Yarvin has for the meddling role of politics in organizing social life. Politics ought to be replaced with experts and strong leadership built on the market model of successful enterprises. Again referring to best practices, Brown raises this concern, which can just as easily speak to Yarvin, Friedman, and Thiel's vision of an opt-in, privately run state: if best practices "are neoliberalism's alternative to the state that it officially abjures, proof that we can be both ethical and efficient without external interference, they can also be the Trojan horse through which law and the political order it secures may be transformed for and by neoliberal reason."[45] Neoliberalism with "dark" libertarian characteristics is visible in Silicon Valley attitudes about labor and market failure and in Silicon Valley leader's personal and professional approaches to disaster preparedness.

PREPPING AT THE END OF DEMOCRACY

Lurking behind the fears of economic collapse, electromagnetic pulses, and widespread environmental disaster are assumptions about the political generators of such events. Silicon Valley "thought leaders" argue that our system of governance cannot be trusted to make good decisions on behalf of an illusory "public good" and that it is not designed well enough to provide security for a healthy capitalist market system that can more effectively allocate resources, burdens, and benefits than a democracy can. The public has legitimate fears of a failed state tasked with managing global climate change, and working people face real crises, from outrageous medical bills to poor economic prospects. These deep issues make attractive the neoreactionary critiques of systems of governance, and their traction as one of the great engines of the economy makes opting out of trust in the government and opting into private options for one's safety and well-being not entirely the stuff of dreams. Perhaps investing in seasteading like the leisure class is too strange or cost prohibitive for the average American consumer, but buying security in emulative entrepreneurial outputs like Preppi is within reach. Having a plan for earthquakes, fires, and floods is not a bad idea, but the ability to plan for disaster does not have to run through the logic of neoliberalism and its darker antidemocratic tendencies, particularly as manifest in Silicon Valley, which churns out self-help products in exchange for money and data collection. To return to the initial premise of this chapter, the state remains central to maintaining a neoliberal operating environment by providing the capitalist market with legal and security support. The state is not pared down to a minimally powerful structure but rather strengthened to buttress the mechanisms of neoliberal habits of mind and enable this logic to penetrate beyond the marketplace, *pace* Brown.

Preppi provides a window into the policy suggestions for addressing public crises. The leisure class continues to frame crisis in personal terms (the individual is unable to meet the demands of a healthy and competitive market), in economic terms (a regulated market does not permit creative solutions to vexing problems), and in political terms (these very crises underscore the problem with democracy and show why alternatives, perhaps even private-sector dictatorships, are desirable). The poor can consume their way toward economic stability by accepting precarious labor with no guarantee of employment stability, and those in risky climatic regions can purchase mass-produced preparation goods. With these neoliberal and libertarian approaches to public crises as the standard within Silicon Valley, it should come as little surprise that similar ideological thinking is applied to environmental crises, too, from massive earthquakes to raging fires. Preparing for disaster becomes a personal responsibility, and the crises themselves are manifestations of a poorly run state relying on antiquated ideals of liberalism and democracy that strangle the market and, by extension, limit personal freedom.

There is ample evidence of state failure both to provide safeguards against future disasters and to respond to them when they do happen. Hurricane Katrina is one of the most widely criticized state responses to public disaster, for good reason. Not only did government support arrive late and disorganized and in its implementation reaffirm class and race segregation in New Orleans, but the state took no responsibility for contributing to the rise in powerful storms by addressing its role in fostering the Gulf of Mexico as a major economic zone for the oil and gas industries, as well as by denying the seriousness of climate change.[46] That some people take preparation into their own hands is neither surprising nor inadvisable. Rather, the trouble is that the twin forces of neoliberalism and Silicon Valley–driven NRx provide dangerous but appealing alternatives to a faltering state that cannot live up to its basic task of protecting its citizenry. These supposedly better possible worlds are not just promoted in blog-posted screeds; they are quietly modeled in a marketplace that enables people to sidestep political activism and democratic participation to pressure the state to respond well and instead to, as Andrew Szasz puts it, shop their way to safety.[47] Prepping is growing in popularity and social acceptability; it no longer lives on the fringes in the remote Mountain West. Products like Preppi make individualized preparation aesthetically palatable for the middle class, and they weave connections between legitimate concerns about the functioning the state with the market-driven, "vote with your dollar," antipolitical social formations promoted by the NRx and neoliberals in the heart of startup culture. The NRx right produces a politics that offers an exit ramp off of the standard liberal democracy of the United States and wishes to replace it wholesale with an entirely new configuration of ideology and institutional arrangements that prioritize individual sovereignty within a privatized authoritarian or monarchical structure. If this does not sound coherent, it is likely because the ideas contained within NRx are sprawling and not particularly well fitted together, but that does not make them less important to attend to.

Prepping and bunkering are part of a strategy to exit from the struggle of collective responsibility for collectively experienced (although differentially distributed) risks and crises. Accounting for oneself or immediate family unit provides a way to address the problem of survival individually and without the challenges of working together with others to face disaster, whether imminent or threatened. Likewise, Smith and Burrows describe the NRx fantasies of seasteading, cryptocurrency, and similar undertakings "mechanisms of 'exit' to develop a dynamic market for governance." Exit is less of a realistic alternative from the dictates of the state than a fantasy of radical sovereignty and self-control with the ability to leave a crashing system for one that best fits your consumer preferences. "The power to govern the conditions of exit, while likely futile in realizing any fantasy of fracturing the political status quo to restore a myth of sovereignty, nonetheless has a certain traction for neoreactionaries claiming to have access to some privileged, almost mythical, understanding of the contemporary social order ascertained only through red-pilling."[48] The NRx right is a different branch of the right, distinct from the alt-right, although there are compatibilities. NRx calls upon a feudal world order as a better alternative to liberalism, yet the ideology is often taken up with the language of corporate dictatorship that is not so absolute an individual could not opt out and try another society with another arrangement. Exiting liberalism should permit the opportunity to exit any other arrangement a person may live under. Here the individual is a sovereign unit, and the state is a sovereign unit that an individual must willingly commit to and have the option to voluntarily leave; there is no society, only a menu of societies and individuals with varying preferences. Those who patch together illiberal ideologies from the alt-right, NRx, versions of liberalism, libertarianism, and neoliberalism seek exits of their own as crises always loom: "For even greater peace of mind, others who fear the envious masses latch onto more secure assets: silver bullion, gold shares, blockchain currency, or New Zealand bolt holes. Immense wealth frequently is matched to libertarian values, but today's billionaires are deeply committed to their narrow self-interests, not unlike most robber barons during the Gilded Age before state trustbusting broke up big bank, oil, railway, and steel monopolies."[49]

Luke reminds us that for the NRx accelerationist, climate change is already pushing all systems—ecological, political, economic, and social—to their respective breaking points. Some members of the NRx right are not only holding onto survivalist resources but are also trying to establish a way to hold onto sovereign power at the expense of democratic organizing: "Many advocates of Dark Enlightenment naturalize cyberspace, accepting it as a given that can and will be accessed at will by anyone astute and equipped enough to gain entry through such Unablogger wisdom. Yet, for other NRx networks, it is an occult domain out-of-bounds for the 'normies,' who should never be granted the full access, authority, or acceptance already gained by the digiterati."[50]

The naturalization of cyberspace is part of the same naturalizing force of capitalism. As Luke explains:

> This salvation also sells itself with yet greater future revelations, putting consumers' and producers' trained incapacities into play in Vegas at the Consumer Electronics Show, in Gotham on the NASDAQ, or from Seattle through Amazon. Such technochauvinism reverberates at the established frequency and amplitude of today's commercial culture, which trusts in capital as a godly power. The deepest belief here remains rocksolid—corporations, markets, entrepreneurs of "the system" are always "the solution." Regardless, these commercial myths are nothing new, quite conservative, and very compatible with the wide range of retrogressive NRx thought.[51]

Regardless of how illiberal, implausible, and fringe the NRx belief system and its ideological cousins in libertarianism and strains of neoliberalism are, the bedrock of corporate capitalism remains the same, and this is still the foundation of whatever new world the reactionary right wishes to build. The exit ramps off of liberal democracy or, in their worst fears, socialist democracy, include seasteads, bunkers, neomonarchies, and corporate states, but none of this constitutes an exit from the institutional and ideological underpinnings of our current mode of life. As Marcuse has insisted in *One-Dimensional Man*, the counterculture, new religion, and the neoreactionary right are not building a brave new world out of the old but are instead trapped in the same preindustrial web of institutions that has produced prepared Americans to see after their own survival in the event of catastrophe—economic, ecological, or social.[52]

CONCLUSION

As card-carrying members of Land and Yarvin's "Media-Academic Complex," we are expected to defend the Cathedral, since we earn our living and legitimacy from it. Our position, however, is not to throw mud on the ideological and political musings of the Dark Enlighten-ment but rather to contextualize it within the broader tendencies of neoliberal thought and action within Silicon Valley. The product out-puts of CEOs and disruptors share at least some of these NRx visions in an already neoliberal environment. We have put forward the argument that neoliberalization of the public sphere is evident in ide-ologies popular in Silicon Valley, and it can be seen specifically in the products that emerge out of the entrepreneurial spirit of startups and their ideological funders, which shapes disaster preparedness as a market. Neoliberalism, when attached to the neoreactionary move-ment, produces a clearly antidemocratic, individualistic vision for the organization of society more appealing than a sluggish, unrepresen-tative democratic state that has consistently failed to meet the needs of its population. In the face of climate change, pandemics, and deep socioeconomic disparities, the collapse of the state and its reincarna-tion as the scaffolding to support a neoliberalized society may not look so bad both for those who stand to profit from crisis and those who seek security from crisis. Is there something between the fanta-sies of the neoreactionary right and the neoliberalization of U.S. lib-eral democracy since the 1970s? We answer yes, but how to disentan-gle ourselves from these antidemocratic ideologies, coupled with the legitimate (and some less legitimate) fears that drive people to buy their security from the private sector, is a little less clear. An impor-tant step toward thinking anew about the organization of society is to recognize the institutional drift toward the antidemocratic aims of the Silicon Valley ethos, which is often touted as the way of the future, and to take note of the ways in which people are encouraged to sidestep social organization as a response to political and environ-mental uncertainty. Looking critically at what ends up on our shelves is a window into interrogating the ideological pressures that drive us to those particular ways to orient ourselves to others and to our institutions.

5

BUGGING OUT IN OUTER SPACE

THIS CHAPTER traces aspects of the outer space efforts in the United States, particularly as they are aimed toward ameliorating the impacts of climate change on Earth and on the human species. This chapter focuses on outer space as unincorporated into the discourse of the environment, the destabilizing impact of fantasizing about preparedness for doomsday, and how outer space is already called into the politics of climate change apocalypse. Addressing the question of outer space—what it is for as run through the Anthropocene, who gets to access outer space and for what purposes, and what role outer space plays in the doomsday imaginary—is also a question of the role of technology in addressing climate crisis and other crises for which people prepare. For Herbert Marcuse, technology deserves skepticism but can also be part of a fundamentally better world. Andrew Feenberg explores this tension in his recent work *A Ruthless Critique of Everything That Exists*. He identifies three central theses of technology that Marcuse puts forward in his body of work, acknowledging that Marcuse did not fully work out a once-and-for-all position on the role of technology in society. To briefly summarize, these three positions are that technology takes the role of ideology in a society and is fully part of systems of oppression and domination, that technology is not value free or neutral, and that scientific rationality is "a priori adapted to maintenance of social domination."[1] Marcuse's positions, even if they do not together constitute a single precise argument, are instructive for thinking through the questions surrounding outer space and climate change beyond assessing whether a given piece of technology or mission is a good or bad endeavor. Could outer space be an outlet for industrial activity and for preserving some species if it were conceived in a qualitatively different society? Does the military genesis of outer space technologies (rockets, surveillance systems, and so forth) mean that spacefaring is only another manifestation of a violent and dominating social system? Marcuse's work helps turn questions about outer space toward more complex and compelling discussions offering potentially useful answers that push beyond space ethics, outer space environmentalism, antispace terrestrial environmentalism, and techno-optimism. Climate change, a third world war, or even an extinction event that wipes out humans may not rise to the level of apocalypse: end times for some species but not a world-ending event. Yet people prepare for these scenarios as if they were world ending or on the cusp of world building, or perhaps both. Outer space offers a way to think about doomsday as world building and world ending, regardless of the ideological context in which space technologies and programs are created. This chapter explores outer space development as a response to doomsday fears on Earth as a rationale for turning to the stars to meet one's prepping needs.

The designs and plans of commercial and leisure space travel are firmly embedded in the administrative and economic scheme of everyday life as organized within capitalism. Some people argue that commercializing and colonizing outer space can be bent toward good aims, like off-worlding pollution and ensuring that human life survives regardless of conditions on Earth. Yet a Marcuseian approach challenges the idea that within the current configuration of society space travel can be infused simply with good intentions:

What Marcuse calls the "technological rationality" of this society is indelibly marked by the presupposition that domination is the necessary condition for effective action. Formal social and economic concepts, the prevailing definitions of social objects, concepts of efficiency, progress, and so on all exhibit an a priori bias. Domination is already present in the very notion of means/ends rationality since the means are deployed in principle from above to control the labor force. This explains why capitalist economic and managerial theories appear "value free" and do not require constant reference to an explicit ideology to be serviceable under capitalism.[2]

Here, a superficial critique of a space program can suggest that the problem is the wrong actors but the right ideas, which can lend weight to arguments that claim that these same technologies, but in the hands of a leftist political movement, would be deployed for the right reasons without radically shifting the context in which these technologies are developed, produced, and deployed. If Musk, Bezos, and the other outer space capitalists were replaced with philanthropists, the state, or better democratic oversight within the existing frame of politics, then outer space exploration would be for the benefit of all. However, space programs are conceived within empires, from the USSR to the United States, and the American empire is still guided by imperialist institutions aimed at resource extraction, military power, and building wealth and power out of systems that cause suffering across humans and nonhumans alike. This position is not to suggest there can be no such thing as a good space program or that humans should not consider becoming multiplanetary. These decisions, however, are playing out in a political and social context that institutionally forecloses a humane space program. Outer space as the great "outside" to the Earth's environment is already claimed for military, scientific, and commercial uses; it is not a tabula rasa but a techno-scientific zone in service to imperial expansion.

As prepping for disaster remains a strongly encouraged activity, prepping for "the new normal" environment and inescapable weather patterns of climate change has driven some people to imagine outer space as the last remaining escape hatch for human life and a new frontier of industrial possibility, mimicking the treatment of the American West during westward expansion. The questions of where outer space fits into the prepping paradigm are part of existing and overlapping doomsday discourses: nuclear annihilation and living in the Anthropocene. The nuclear era and the Anthropocene are part of the same chronological period and overlap as part of the potential and already unfolding crises for which people prepare. Global warming has made the discursive shift to climate change, and climate change is an umbrella term for the suite of environmental and climatic changes associated with specific human interventions on the planet, particularly the production and combustion of fossil fuels, colonialism, and military activity. In tandem, the ever-present fear of nuclear war and the ever-present catastrophe of climate change present a bleak vision of the future and an anxiety-inducing state of the present. The two threats to human existence are connected beyond overlapping timelines; nuclear fallout from detonated test bombs, nuclear waste associated with bomb production, and irradiated landscapes and aquifers are part of the broader set of environmental concerns bound up with climate change. Arguably, the irradiated places and living beings in the sites affected by nuclear testing are already hot zones of war but are only recognized as test locations, not as war targets. As Masahide Kato argues, "Thus any nuclear explosions after World War II do not qualify as nuclear war in the cognitive grid of conventional nuclear discourse." Testing was largely conducted in the Global South and on land populated by and belonging to indigenous peoples, particularly in the American Southwest and the Marshall Islands in the South Pacific: "Thus, from the perspectives of the Fourth World and Indigenous Nations, the nuclear catastrophe has never been the 'unthinkable' single catastrophe but the real catastrophe of repetitive and ongoing nuclear explosions and exposure to radioactivity. Nevertheless, ongoing nuclear wars have been subordinated to the imaginary grand catastrophe by rendering them as mere preludes to the apocalypse."[3]

In recasting the ongoing impacts of nuclear testing as an aspect of nuclear war, climate change and nuclear war are even more tightly bound up with each other. Kato raises another important issue in the emphasis on possible extinction as the defining feature of nuclear war, to the exclusion of ongoing "nuclear violence" aptly described in Rob Nixon's work on slow violence.[4] Likewise, climate change is often considered a future threat that will produce a cataclysmic event, edging out of frame the myriad ways in which climate change is already at work, already part of everyday life and the forces that shape the environment. The discourses of doom surrounding nuclear war and climate change help produce an urgent need to safeguard oneself against the events that would usher in end times.

Instead, climate change can be seen as a slow-moving, unequally distributed apocalypse. Its threat to render the planet uninhabitable to humans and many other species has not yet come to pass but is nearly guaranteed by the previous generations of human-driven activity. Anthropogenic change worthy of a new epoch is most apparent in the "golden spike" of human industrial and military technology in the middle of the twentieth century, evidence of which includes the production and use of petroleum-based products like plastics, a major uptick in the production and consumption of fossil fuels, and deposits from nuclear radiation.[5] "The Anthropocene" is one of the names proposed for the geological period of human activity that social scientists consider has succeeded the Holocene period because of the demonstrable impacts of human life on the planet's geological record. Additionally, the Anthropocene is the time during which the discourse of climate change grew from warnings about global warming in the 1980s and the loss of the ozone layer to a new, all-encompassing, impossible-to-avert, and totally annihilating threat to human life on the planet. In the face of eerie predictions and actually occurring climatic shifts, people are left to wonder what it would take to turn climate change around or at least to survive the changes as they wash over roads, homes, and crops. States mostly remain in gridlock at every Conference of the Parties to the United Nations Framework Convention on Climate Change to hash out new voluntary terms of global cooperation to reduce carbon emissions and to assume responsibility for contributing to our current predicament.

Many people have serious doubts about state-driven responses to climate change. An increasingly popular approach takes its institutional cue from the atomic age: bunkering. Bunkers in the United States are closely associated with the atomic age and threat of mutually assured destruction with the USSR. Rather than provide for communal or individual bunkers for an increasingly worried population, the United States offered suggestions for survival that each person and family were expected to take up as their patriotic duty. Although only a small percentage of Americans installed subterranean bunkers in their backyards, bunkers became an icon of the era. Now in the age of the Anthropocene and reanimated Cold War anxieties, bunkers and the logic of bunkerization are back in style, this time to accommodate many different price points and without requiring a backyard. Bunkers range from spartan shipping containers to underground silos stocked with creature comforts including in-home theaters, light therapy, and full kitchens. The super-rich are superinvested in safeguarding not just their own lives but their class status and social power. They do not imagine stepping out of the bunker compounds into a world that does not recognize their wealth and power. The bunker mentality established during the Cold War smoothed the road toward the neoliberal approach to climate change. During the Cold War, the state abdicated responsibility for its citizens and discouraged collective action among citizens while taking action to protect itself and its representatives via networks of bunkers for essential government employees and military operations. In short, individualizing life in a perpetual state of disaster and disaster anticipation is a hallmark of a neoliberal state. In such a formation, individual consumption choices are perceived as the proper way to ameliorate those disasters.

Bunkering itself has not fallen out of favor, either, as wealthy preppers construct luxury bunkers for a number of anticipated crises, climate change impacts included, while others retrofit their basements to prepare for extreme weather events. One of the institutional legacies of American industrialization and the Cold War persists in the neoliberal, highly individualized, and undemocratic approach to surviving climate change. We increasingly live in a bunkerized society, a logic of the bunker at a planetary scale. Beyond the physical bunker in the backyard, the bunker has become a mentality, a way of orienting ourselves to the world, to protect ourselves from threats and risks, to fortify our homes and lives, sometimes with actual bunkers but other times by turning the home into a fortress with surveillance cameras, emergency preparedness kits, and backup plans for several kinds of catastrophic events. Yet there is another way in which we can see a bunkerized mode of life at work: the new space race and the desire to rescue humanity from the perils of climate change and associated geopolitical instabilities on Earth by sending humankind and extractive activities skyward. In order to conceive of outer space as a place to both extend the bunker and escape the climate apocalypse, outer space must first be considered as exterior to Earth and to our environment. Taking to outer space to once and for all avoid the consequences of climate change, a major world war, or other catastrophic futures anticipated by those who prep shows the limits of prepping as well as the fantastical approach to end-running the end times. While the average person will find the upper reaches of the atmosphere to be the upper limit of their ability to escape terrestrial disasters, the super-rich can at least invest in the fantasy of outer space as the final bunkering habitat to dodge uninhabitable conditions on Earth and create a new multiplanetary world in their own neoreactionary image. Although outer space may not be a doomsday bolt hole any time soon or for many people at all, it still serves a powerful function in the preparation imaginary. Outer space, then, must remain an exterior space to planet Earth in order to so powerfully represent the ultimate survival plan.

OUTER SPACE AS OUTER SPACE

Outer space is not yet meaningfully integrated into environmentalism discourse, nor is it considered a potential casualty of climate change. Instead, outer space is conceived of by preppers as an escape into a different inhospitable environment, one humans feel more confident about shaping to our climatic needs than we do about shaping the trajectory of climate change on planet Earth. The current approach to thinking about outer space and environmentalism picks up from policy-driven mainstream conservation and is focused on various types of outer space pollution and thinking about outer space as wilderness. Astroenvironmentalism makes an effort to integrate terrestrial environmentalism to outer space, porting over concepts like wilderness, untouched nature, preservation, conservation, contamination, pollution, and sustainability, echoing and reifying the institutional concerns of the frontier during American industrialization. In an article making a case for outer space environmentalism, the authors argue that low-Earth orbit (LEO) constitutes an ecosystem: "Humans have carried out activities in outer space since 1957, and we have reached a point where these can have deleterious impacts both in space and on Earth's surface. This is therefore a strong case for extending the concept of environment to orbital space."[6] Acknowledging that outer space is part of the environment, at least from the planet up to LEO, would make LEO manageable through the National Environmental Protection Act and other relevant environmental policies that govern issues like pollution, ownership, and responsible use. This argument suggests that LEO would be considered part of the terrestrial environment. LEO has a finite carrying capacity for objects like satellites, which the authors argue are not responsibly deployed or managed and create severe orbital pollution, light pollution, radio pollution, and increased danger for further launches. The sheer volume of satellites in orbit could alter the view of the night sky, which is considered a publicly available resource. Satellites as pollution could also interfere with indigenous astronomy and the use of the night sky by mammals and birds for migration orientation.[7] These more holistic approaches to LEO are in the vein of astroenvironmentalism. Noriyoshi Takemura defines astroenvironmentalism as "a concept which applies the value of environmentalism and preservationism to developments in space exploration, commercialization, and militarization. The declaration of celestial bodies as pristine wildernesses which need to be protected rather than frontiers to conquer is listed among space environmentalism's goals. Outer space, a source of wonder and inspiration for centuries, deserves to be preserved in its original pristine state, for its own sake and for future generations to enjoy."[8] Outer space, for environmentalism, is conceptualized as wilderness and as a working landscape; advocates for astroenvironmentalism must then contend with protecting outer space as a pristine environment or through a conservation approach as a resource-rich voidscape that ought to be managed under environmental sustainability principles.

Others argue that astroenvironmentalism can be best addressed through a "polycentric governance of space debris" that approaches the problem of LEO pollution as a common-pool-resource challenge requiring a mix of public and private incentives to compel states to take responsibility for their contributions to the problem.[9] Further still, some argue that outer space legal regimes do not think of outer space, or at least LEO, as an extension of the Earth's environment and therefore in need of protective measures against its overuse and exploitation. However, simply invoking an environmental regime to extend existing protection policies into space may bring ideological baggage associated with environmental politics from the global north. Alessandra Marino and Thomas Cheney recognize that "environmentalism is a discourse that Western powers have used to strengthen their claims to territorial access and exploitation."[10] An extension of a policy-based approach to sending environmentalism skyward is in astro-green-criminology, a way of looking at human-caused environmental destruction through the lens of criminalizing acts of environmental harm and associated damages to humans. The criminological model looks at harms caused to outer space by humans and new and potential harms in future outer space activity through such a lens.[11] Environmental protection through the criminological lens shifts from pollution as collective harm exposure to pollution as a trespass or violation of property. These approaches to outer space environmentalism may yield interesting results in public policy but do not yet speak to how outer space does or does not fit into the discourse of the human/nature relationship, what constitutes a dangerous environment, and whether space is an environment into which humans can prepare to escape those dangers. How do preppers imagine outer space in their plans?

Outer space as an environment extends beyond mainstream environmentalism. Valerie Olson and Lisa Messeri identify an "inner environment" and "outer environment" of the Earth and in reviewing geology, social science, and humanities literature find that the Anthropocene is often used to demarcate the inner "earthly" world of human life and ecosystems from the cosmological world of the outer environment, or outer space. "Despite ways in which extraterrestrial science and technologies contribute to understandings of the environmental dynamics at enlarged spatial scales, the Anthropocene concept is being deployed in ways that privilege downward, inward, and spherically enclosed terra- and anthropocentric understandings of what counts as environment."[12] The Anthropocene's downward focus likewise makes it difficult to notice environmental problems in outer space, including our growing problem of space garbage encircling the planet. While conventional economics might write off space garbage as an "externality" or a side effect of industrial production that may or may not affect people on Earth, Julie Michelle Klinger writes that "there are no 'externalities' in geography: The very word 'externality' reflects a way of thinking that does not match reality. As residents in an integrated biophysical Earth system, there is no part of the Earth that is external to our affairs."[13] This may be true, but there are no externalities in outer space, either, at least within our solar system. This concern about externalities as glossing over our biophysical interconnectedness maintains the boundary between inner and outer space and positions outer space as the place where Earth may dump its waste in asteroid and moon mining and similar resource exploits harmlessly. While outer space often seems an alien environment and wholly apart from life on Earth, we are already interconnected through satellites, the International Space Station, and defense technologies.

Outer space is conventionally conceived as a tabula rasa upon which states and individuals can project their fantasies, fears, and hopes. It is a literal void and a metaphorical mirror. Outer space is also the retreat from a hostile planet. Outer space is treated as distinct from Earth's environment, which it sometimes intersects with but of which it is not fundamentally part. While Earth is considered somehow discrete from outer space and the outer space environment, it is also considered a blueprint for finding a livable planet with Earthlike conditions. Messeri points to the search for another Earthlike planet as one in which humans seek an Edenic condition that they have never experienced, a planet that humans can inhabit envisioned as ideal, somehow better than Earth has been or equal to some mythical "peak" of earthly conditions for human flourishing. "The search for a habitable exoplanet is the search for Earth as we have never known it."[14] Stepping out of a rocket would mean stepping into a purified, new, and ideal environment, a version of the pristine wilderness envisioned by preservationists, a postapocalyptic landscape made whole by the second coming of Christ or the first coming of Silicon Valley utopians. Claiming other planets as a new home for humans, particularly if that planet is essentially a duplicate of Earth, would release humans from their remaining obligations to address climate change through radical political and economic action on this planet. Those who remain on Earth could bunker and fortify to protect their livable spaces and their assets while others could pay to go off-planet and rebuild the species in a turnkey environment or, if all that was available was a terraformed planet, an adequate remodel. The search for habitable exoplanets and imagining outer space as a release from what one must prepare against on Earth positions outer space as an external environment to the one we live in, despite the vexing situation of our very existence as one entirely set in outer space. Imagining outer space and non-Earth celestial bodies as an extension of the bunker, a place to retreat to when threats on Earth make everyday life too risky or unthinkable, allows for outer space to take on the characteristics of the bunker mentality. Yet planning to use outer space as a retreat and as a commercial opportunity to slow the pace of planetary decline by offloading industrial production off-world carries with it the same neoliberal ideological commitments that make outer space bunkering appear to be a rational approach to addressing the apocalyptic threats of climate change, world war, and nuclear attack.

ESCAPE TO THE VOID

One of the stated reasons that both state space agencies and space capitalists want to make the species multiplanetary is to avoid the potential loss of humanity in the myriad catastrophes of climate change that may render the planet inhospitable to human life. What will humans face in the apocalyptic moment and in the postapocalyptic world? Which are the environmental tipping points that signal a point of no return from the road to ruin? In Jean-Luc Nancy's work reflecting on Fukushima, he asks, "But the 'after' we are speaking of here stems on the contrary not from succession but from rupture, and less from anticipation than from suspense, even stupor. It is an 'after' that means: Is there an after? Is there anything that follows? Are we still headed somewhere?" Nancy elaborates in his argument that the ability for nations to acquire nuclear arms is "the equivalence that annuls tension by keeping it equal and constant . . . and its power is such that it can almost no longer be thought of as depending on human wills that are supposed to command its use: A mere mistake or stroke of madness could set off its use and plunge us into the horror of an unspeakable devastation."[15] Perhaps states, and every-day people, ought to concede that climate change is upon us and that there is no longer merely the possibility of catastrophe but a matter of preparing for waves of disaster, literal and figurative, to wash over the planet. Indeed, global warming is no longer a set of conditions that could result in climate change that we can, under our collective power as humans, improve, stabilize, or worsen; we continually are falling further from reclaiming a world that can be directed by human control, for better or worse. Is there a future after the rupture caused by climate change and its fulfillment as a world-altering or -ending disaster? It is worth quoting Nancy at length:

> If this civilization turns out to be at the same time a civilization of war against ourselves and against the world, if mastery coils back on itself subjecting us to ever-increasing constraints as we try to escape the previous ones, replacing every kind of progress with an aggravation of our condition, and if what had been the power of the people—the power of their technologies but also of their abilities to resist them—finally sets about exercising an autonomous power over them and over the rest of beings, then we are faced with a task as urgent as the task of making the broken reactors of Fukushima and the substances that have escaped from them powerless to cause harm.[16]

Finally, he argues that nuclear postapocalypticism does not end in revelation, divine or otherwise: "What Fukushima adds to Hiroshima is that threat of an apocalypse that opens onto nothing, onto the nega-tion of the apocalypse itself."[17] Opening onto nothing is a wasted apocalypse, end times for its own sake without the fulfilled promise of a new world, even if that world is worse than the previous one, which many anticipate will happen once climate change tips the environ-ment into one wholly different from the one that characterized the Anthropocene. Does climate change open onto a new world or just sig-nal the end of humanity and a specific set of planetary conditions?

Nancy argues that the effects of a catastrophe like Fukushima are intensified through the multivariate challenges of our increasingly networked society, including interconnection with ecosystems and all of their inhabitants. Arguably, these tightening interrelations are not exclusive to this planet but instead mark a denser interweaving between inner (the Earth) and outer space. The effects of climate change and the ways in which humans prepare, including a bunkerized mode of life, signal an attempt to disentangle from these relations, particularly as they are mediated by the state, and to instead place more emphasis on those relations ordered through the market, guaranteeing one's survival through climate change upheaval and emergence on the other side by participating in the flows of commodities. Here the opportunity to leave the planet as a survival strategy is likewise one that depends on the market as much as it does the state to make these opportunities possible and available for those who can afford it. This assumes a market that persists during and after catastrophe and even apocalyptic conditions, a future that, in the face of great uncertainty, remains fixed in the imagination as one steadfastly capitalistic. This capitalistic mode reifies the neoliberal discourse about the moral worth of people: those who can escape catastrophic conditions are worthy because they can afford to and do make the proper preparations. The tautology strengthens the bond between markets and morals and reifies atavistic habits of mind of self-sufficiency.

Nancy concludes that "Fukushima forbids all present: It is the collapse of future goals that forces us to work with other futures—but under the conditions of the ever-renewed present."[18] Climate change may well not result in a final end with a clear revelation and new future, but it will continue unfolding into many futures, including futures that take place in the void of outer space in colonies and mining sites. Outer space as one of the unfolding futures of humanity is appealing partly because it appears to be a new, unspoiled environment with resources laying in wait, like the fantasies of the American West. It is also, finally, a consequence-free offload for the externalities of capitalism. Yet outer space is not just out there waiting to be claimed; it is already crossed over with international relations through treaties, public policies, and the orbiting International Space Station. The future of outer space is guided by the promise of the expansion of capital protected through political arrangements, and this commercialization of outer space makes room not only for sustaining production targets but for marketplace prepping, in such things as tickets for future outer space trips, investment in outer space development startups, and electing public officials who will protect outer space interests for the good of America and its universal claim to survive at all costs.

THE ROAD TO OUTER SPACE

Interest in outer space is immemorial, and the U.S. space program dates back well before NASA and its teams of adventurous boy scouts. However, transforming dreams of becoming spacefaring people into a reality is a story of the twentieth century. Following World War II, there was interest in space activity from the developments in German rocketry brought to the United States with the Nazi scientist Werner Von Braun and his team. The launch of *Sputnik*, alongside the growing tension between the United States and USSR, drew concerns about the legality of overflights of satellites. In the 1958 Starfish Prime atomic bomb test, the United States detonated a thermonuclear warhead in the upper atmosphere. NASA was established in the same year, one year after the USSR successfully launched *Sputnik*. Just before that historic launch in 1952, "a UN lawyer, Oscar Schachter, asked 'Who owns the universe?' He suggested that space and celestial bodies belong, like the high seas, to all mankind."[19] Space law over the last several decades has tried to walk the line between ownership and commons, drawing on maritime and air law to guide the effort toward international treaties and agreements largely overseen by the UN. One of the first such treaties was the Limited Test Ban Treaty in 1963, with the United States and USSR as the key signatories. The treaty prohibited nuclear testing in outer space, an important step in limiting the use of outer space for warfare. Not long after the test ban, the Outer Space Treaty (OST) was ratified in 1967. The OST continues to serve as a legal guidepost to sovereignty and the use of outer space and celestial bodies, although it is being increasingly challenged by developments in outer space commercialization. The first article of the OST states: "The exploration and use of outer space, including the moon and other celestial bodies, shall be carried out for the benefit and in the interest of all countries, irrespective of their degree of economic or scientific development, and shall be the province of all mankind." Outer space exploration should not be exclusive to whichever countries and their citizens can marshal the capital and technology to become spacefaring. The second article states: "Outer space, including the moon and other celestial bodies, is not subject to national appropriation by claims of sovereignty, by means of use or occupation, or by any other means."[20] This passage implies that states cannot claim sovereign control over the moon, asteroids, and other bodies or over "air" territory in outer space. The treaty is not clear about how private entities may or may not claim resources like minerals and water on these bodies.

The subsequent Moon Treaty brought these questions of resource access to the fore when it was drafted in 1979. The treaty sought to "prevent the moon from becoming an area of international conflict, bearing in mind the benefits which may be derived from the exploitation of the natural resources of the moon and other celestial bodies." Article 11 states that the surface and subsurface of the moon and its natural resources cannot become the property of any "state, international intergovernmental or non-governmental organization, national organization, or non-governmental entity or of any natural person" but later states that one of the purposes of the international regime dedicated to cooperative outer space activities is to maintain "(a) the orderly and safe development of the natural resources of the moon; (b) the rational management of those resources; (c) The expansion of those opportunities in the use of those resources."[21] Further,

In a letter for November 13, 1979, Senator Richard Stone, also a member of the Senate Committee on Foreign Relations, urged Secretary Vance to reevaluate the US position on the draft moon treaty, which he describes as having "extremely dangerous potentialities" because it appeared to decrease "the ability of the United States to advance in yet unexplored fields" and to "greatly inhibit the actions and desires of U.S. corporations in space, negate the notion of free enterprise, and . . . place the United States in a position subservient to the Soviet Union."[22]

The hesitancy to ratify the treaty rested on concern for commercial development and economic competition with the USSR and drew out the desire to ensure a free-market approach to outer space development, sending capitalism skyward as an extension of the economic forces of the Anthropocene. Neither the United States, the USSR, nor China signed the treaty; as such, it carries little weight in international space law. In 2015, with support from congressional Republicans, the 114th U.S. Congress passed the U.S. Commercial Space Launch Competitiveness Act, the purpose of which is to "facilitate a pro-growth environment for the developing commercial space industry by encouraging private sector investment and creating more stable and predictable regulatory conditions." The law moved to remove unwarranted constraints from the commercial space industry, facilitate commercial exploration for and recovery of space resources by U.S. citizens, and discourage government barriers to the development in the United States of economically viable industries for commercial exploration and space resource extraction. Section 51303 states: "A United States citizen engaged in commercial recovery of an asteroid resource or a space resource under this chapter shall be entitled to any asteroid resource or space resource obtained, including to possess, own, transport, use, and sell the asteroid resource or space resource obtained in accordance with applicable law, including the international obligations of the United States."[23] This act codifies in the law what the Moon Treaty failed to guarantee to signatories: the right to acquire property in outer space for private entities and the right to commercial exploitation of outer space resources. This act marks a pivot away from the OST and the pledge to consider outer space as a global commons that is nonexclusionary and instead focuses legal protection on private commercial enterprise. In the static prose of public policy, outer space slowly shifts from common-pool resources to space available for private claims on resources and, with that, market-based space management to answer the pressing questions of livability on Earth.

In 2020, President Trump and NASA Administrator James Bridenstine developed the Artemis Accords, which promise to land a man and a woman on the moon, to explore Mars and other planets, and to encourage and tighten the relationship between the private and public sectors to develop spacefaring technologies and space commerce. "The Signatories emphasize that the extraction and utilization of space resources, including any recovery from the surface or subsurface of the Moon, Mars, comets, or asteroids, should be executed in a manner that complies with the Outer Space Treaty and in support of safe and sustainable space activities."[24] The accords claim that this article does not run afoul of the OST. Australia, Canada, Italy, Japan, Luxembourg, the United Arab Emirates, and the United Kingdom joined the United States in signing this agreement. These signatories come as little surprise: each of these countries is developing robust public-private partnerships of their own.

Each successive treaty and accord produced by the United States emphasizes commercial activity driven by free-market principles. Interpreting these treaties is complicated by a fractured understanding of commons and common-pool resources. Legal and economic definitions of the commons vary and are often conflated, and each object in space, from satellites to celestial bodies, may be subject to different legal and economic regimes.[25] While outer space may not be considered part of the environment in the way "environment" is often invoked here on Earth, it is looped into the extractive industries operating in a neoliberal capitalist environment, which binds outer space to the terrestrial environment through the mass exploitation, or anticipated exploitation, of these spaces and objects as natural resources. Outer space objects are "naturalized" as resources, and space joins the environment, but on the terms of capital. Perhaps with little resistance from environmentalists, outer space will be the next ecomanaged environment monitored by engineering, mining, and geospace experts with public contracts to ensure the efficient extraction, transport, and sale of outer space resources, a new market for a dying planet with state-of-the-art technologies that may make extraction gentler here on Earth as ice recedes, melts, and exposes new commercial opportunities.

Finding commercial and security opportunities in outer space allows for the leisure class to fantasize how they might bunkerize beyond the upper limits of the atmosphere. Not only do rockets serve as mobile bunker units for those fleeing Earth's end times for better luck in the vacuum, but outer space can serve as another fortress wall, keeping U.S. production needs available by encircling new territory, offering new opportunities for security surveillance (not unlike cameras at home trained on the front door), and conducting these activities under the American flag to protect more than the person but the American way of life they execute. The efforts to become multiplanetary as an extension of bunker planet provide a new way to turn over the central contradiction of bunkerization: an event may produce a fundamentally different future, but the only imaginable future is the status quo with its class dynamics intact. Going to space to build industry, stake private sector and state claims to space resources, and establish colonies may sound fantastical, impossible—even exciting. Finally, a last hope to rocket away from doomsday, particularly a climate change doomsday; if one can escape the evangelical "rapture" by fleeing Earth is a question for theologians. But outer space exploration as a response to climate change and related disasters depends on alienating outer space from earthly environmentalism. Exploration requires an enormous market to sustain its efforts: markets in extractive industries and a market for tickets on tourist rockets and colonization efforts—and the requisite class stratification between those who provide labor, those who own the space travel companies, and those who can afford to relocate off-planet without committing to a life of hard labor. The market opportunities are posed as disruptions to the slow pace of state-sponsored space programs and their equally sluggish movement to address climate change and other threats to the planet. Silicon Valley's pace of change has made a case for itself as the right intervener in the space race.

This supposedly radical opportunity to save and make the world anew bears all the features of the world as it is: capitalism, a market-based approach to attending to collective needs, states that abdicate to the market responsibility for their citizens, and facing risk, disaster, and doom as opportunities to fortify a way of life and assume that whatever conditions the space bunker allows for your survival will also allow for those same modes of living to resume. After all, who can appreciate a well-appointed bunker, on Earth or in the heavens, if there are no clear class divisions? With no underlying class that can only aspire to one's luxuries? To attend to Nancy's suggestion that the apocalypse may open out into nothing, this may be frightening not because it signals an end to the future but because it signals an end to whatever was worth bunkering for.

QUANTIFYING PROGRESS, QUANTIFYING RISKS

From the individual to the planetary scale, risk assessment is easily quantified using new technologies available on the market. Risk assessment is bound up with self-optimization, or the obsession with tuning the body and mind toward some quantifiable peak performance, the achievement of which not only "unlocks" human potential but makes a case for protecting embodied human potential from apocalyptic conditions and subsequent loss. While for now we are still bound to our earthly bodies, Silicon Valley innovators seek to optimize themselves through various means, with the emergence of the market for nootropic supplements to maximize cognitive efficiency. Global consciousness and connection championed by the counterculture have turned neoliberal in competitive meditation events, with cognitive metrics displayed for the audience to watch the nootropic sphere projected as digital readouts of one's brain activity. Silicon Valley is a strange mix of heady ambitions to improve the species and to maximize profit with supposedly risk-taking ventures. Eric Matzner, the founder of the Nootroo line of supplements, makes the case: " 'Look to how you can optimize yourself,' Matzner said, using one of his favorite verbs. 'The body offers plenty of weaknesses that can potentially be overcome.' "[26] Matzner has tested supplements on himself, creating a living laboratory out of his body, using personal experience, wearable technology, and naturopathic medicine to measure and assess the effects of his tinkering. Matzner, among many others who have created their own lines of nootropic supplements and those who subscribe to their delivery services, hope to push human evolution into overdrive, toward goals that are not clearly articulated. Matzner—a self-professed fan of Elon Musk—engages in the same affinities for science, self-control, and domination over nature that is emblematic of the Silicon Valley ethos. Training oneself to be the best at meditation (a dubious use of metrics, to be sure) is an effort to control the limits of nature, transcend them, and then use this supernatural superiority to overcome the rest of the barriers to human evolution, like the existential threats of climate change and the inefficiencies of democratic government. One of the strategies of biohackers and futurists like Matzner is to render in quantitative terms what is at stake for letting nature take its course. These sites of training and prepping the body for maximum efficiency in a variety of conditions are other vectors of prepping as a mode of life. The fetish for nootropics maps on to the same worries that scouting outfits were confronting during industrialization and mass migration: it takes a person disciplined enough to achieve and maintain peak performance to carry the American torch into an uncertain future.

Technological developments that open new possibilities for self-optimization are still based on surveillance, monitoring metrics, and making visible bodily functions that are either "only" felt or do not register consciously at all. The pioneers of human greatness are, in the final assessment, technocrats of the body using visual data to tweak, adapt, and consciously manipulate the outputs of their bodies and minds. Likewise, Timothy W. Luke writes that the science of climate change has been aestheticized in such a way as to give the impression that teams of experts are studying Earth-system data outputs and then finely tuning public policy to address these, as though they appear from out of a neutral space of politics and economics. He problematizes the efforts to illustrate the challenges with stalled human development:

> Climate change science, then, has worked to stabilize and legitimize these depictions of a systemic, if not essentially mechanic, set of environmental exchanges between "Earth" and "humanity." Despite all of the arrows, boxes, clusters, and delimitations so depicted, their actual interoperation over time in context and dispersed across space arguably is still now not being adequately measured, accurately understood, or aptly mitigated. Consequently, the imagination of a rapid global climate change being "better understood" in this fashion serves as a convenient *illusio* for individual experts, groups of decision makers, and segments of the public to believe they know what is happening and how to respond.[27]

Elon Musk, Jeff Bezos, and other "space disruptors" are the independent experts, backed by venture capital, who use their well-funded pulpits to speak technocratically about the practical solutions that Mars colonization and space travel offer for the emergent climate crises. The current limits imposed on us by our industrial past are mitigated by the plan to become multiplanetary. These plans are projected on enormous screens behind them: images of rockets of various sizes, graphs about fuel usage and payload, and photos of engineering feats at SpaceX headquarters. Humankind is in the hands of benevolent capitalists who also happen to be technologists, and they can toggle between those identities as necessary to advance their project. Whether the presentations show soaring carbon emissions, brain activity, or rocket power, they all render in technical imagery the plan to transcend natural limits and unbind ourselves from the problems of industrial minds producing industrial problems. Of course, the material costs of these cosmic projects to send humans away from the polluted soil and irradiated waters of the San Francisco Bay are felt in the bodies of rare-metal miners and factory workers. These projects are firmly industrial, a symptom of cultural lag between the industrial world we still occupy and the fantasy of a world that can avoid certain collapse if only we pivot toward outer space as an opportunity for survival.

Out of the new space race, well-funded through Silicon Valley, comes a more technologically sophisticated approach to bunkering and prepping, one that gives the impression that never have the stakes been so high, yet never have the pending and in-process disasters been so well rendered in data. Bunkerization is also a way to protect those who are prepared to optimize themselves and their lives, even if that optimization permits a return to traditional values of home, hearth, personal property, and a eugenicized vision of a healthy population that can and should make it through whatever dangers await us in the Anthropocene. To see this vision through, becoming multiplanetary is an essential extension of prepping. Prepping goes hand in hand with geoengineering. We can study risks and anticipate them, and we can surveil our territories, storms, threats, and opportunities with satellites, telescopes, GPS, drones, and streaming video. Both software and the wetware of the human mind will be put to use analyzing data and making predictions so that everyday people can anticipate various disasters and prepare for them. These same technologies also enable extractive activities that advance catastrophic climate change as well as assess the prospects of extraterrestrial industrialization. Members of the predatory leisure class like Elon Musk and Peter Thiel, however, recognize the very material threat of war and climate change—or a combination of the two—as pressing down on the promise of accelerated human development. The fear of evolutionary regression is part of the anxiety over climate change. Unchecked greenhouse gases will threaten human existence and the gift of human consciousness. To ensure that human relations—economic and social in particular—remain liberated from the tyranny of regulations and the limits of industrial-era travel and communications, the species should not be dependent on a single planet for life. The solution to climate change becomes addressing inefficiencies in Earth economics while creating information redundancy by building sustainable cities on other planets and sending our "data"—that is, the humans who will, presumably, reproduce, to innovate with the help of private funding.

During a presentation on climate change at the Sorbonne in 2015, Musk identified the redistribution of carbon that is sequestered underground into the carbon cycle as the driving cause of climate change. He claimed that in resisting the transition to renewable energy, humans are merely delaying the inevitable but that they are not going to be able to continue to depend on fossil fuels as an energy source. He did not identify capitalism, consumption, or production as problematic and in fact noted that "killing whales and cutting down trees" was good for a while but is not anymore.[28] He argued that unspecified "carbon producers" benefit from a carbon subsidy and rely on a small subset of scientists who deny climate change to sow public doubt. Musk then suggested a revenue-neutral carbon tax, which is neither "a left nor right issue," but he recommended reducing taxes in other places so only those using "high levels of carbon" would be affected by this tax. This is simply a version of the "triple bottom line" method of accounting that includes the environment in the calculus of profit and loss. In Musk's illustrated PowerPoint presentation of climate change and carbon emissions, he participates in the aestheticization of global warming, as put forward by Luke. As a fellow "PowerPointer" alongside Al Gore, one the subjects of Luke's article, Musk gathers up data on greenhouse gas (GHG) outputs and global impacts without differentiating between sources. "The complex systems of technology constructed out of consuming fossil fuels, and a more obtuse and obdurate structure for monitoring greenhouse gas gassing trends can be aggregated as national input/output tables with oil, gas, and coal consumption on one side and greenhouse gases on the other side. Images, then, may obfuscate as much as they illustrate." The impact of Musk's method of describing climate change is to make little distinction among polluters. "The moral calculus of this change, however, is quite problematic, because 'greenhouse gassers' basically are anyone, no one, and everyone. Those responsible are each individual, who engages directly or indirectly, in the combustion of hydrocarbon fuels. . . . In this manner, there can be an erasure of causal agency."[29] The erasure of causal agency is evident in the silence surrounding the Superfund sites and toxic dumps dotting Silicon Valley. The environmental cost of production in Silicon Valley is not attributed to anyone in particular, and the space-minded entrepreneurs concerned with climate change have nothing to say about the environmentally destructive legacy of Silicon Valley and the continued exploitation involved in producing electric cars and rockets.

In Musk's version of anthropogenic environmental crisis, "we" are all responsible, and "we" are all doomed, but only Silicon Valley's prophets of evolution can mobilize the capital, labor, and natural resources to produce alternative endings to the untimely demise of our species in outer space. In classic capitalist fashion, Musk bristles against government regulation. In his recent interview at SXSW by his friend the producer Jonathan Nolan, notable for the show *Westworld*, Musk notes that he is normally against regulation and prefers to minimize oversight. One assumes that the oversight of visionary thinkers like Musk should provide sufficient checks against inefficiency and a Martian version of totalitarianism. While space travel companies like Blue Origin are interested in providing services like space tourism for the rich, Musk believes his mission is philanthropic. At the forefront of market-based prepping are the startup companies and tech-sector entrepreneurs eager to fill the void of the state and provide another way to see the future through their disruptive dynamics of survival consumption.

DISRUPTION

When the state creates the conditions of harm exposure to everyday people and the market for prepping is bogged down in utilitarian supplies, the disruptive capitalists can find opportunities to turn prepping into a stylish class signifier and imperative for the reasonable person who is savvy about the threats to their personal safety and institutional stability. One of the oft-repeated boasts of Silicon Valley is its culture of disruption. In her work on disruption and mobile health technologies, Maria Levina provides a brief history of the concept of disruption: "Disruptive innovation—a term coined by Harvard Business School Professor Clayton M. Christensen—reinterprets creative destruction to describe a process through which a product or a service takes root in simpler, often poorer quality, application at the bottom of the market and then aggressively moves up the market, eventually displacing existing competition. . . . Disruptive technologies, in contrast, upend the traditional trajectory of steady improvement. . . . More often than not, these new technologies destroy established technologies."[30]

In Jill Lepore's analysis, disruption is a historically unbounded version of progress. It is the promise of Silicon Valley to move beyond producing goods to producing instability and a hypercompetitive environment of newness and progress for its own sake. "The idea of innovation is the idea of progress stripped of the aspirations of the Enlightenment, scrubbed clean of the horrors of the twentieth century, and relieved of its critics. Disruptive innovation goes further, holding out the hope of salvation against the very damnation it describes: disrupt, and you will be saved."[31] Disruptive technologies are the hallmark of Silicon Valley, where companies and startups pride themselves on making risky decisions to provide a good or service that not only undercuts an existing one but also radically changes how we, the consumer, socially and economically orient ourselves.

One of the features of disruptive technologies is to collectively pool and harvest data about the population while disassembling that collective so people are left to attend to their own health and safety as individual consumers. Levina describes disruptive mobile health technologies as a biopolitical move that extracts specialized information from individuals and enables them to manage their health independently of traditional health care services. "I have argued that in the Mobile Health (mHealth) industry, to disrupt often means to take bodies out of their socioeconomic context and to substitute the work of the communal body politic with the politics of data access, individualization, and personalization. In this way, mobile health and the disruptive innovation model disembodies and disregards our bodies as a source and potential for political and cultural change."[32] Mobile health technologies operate on a similar logic to Martian colonization, in imagining humans as "packages of information" who can provide data to computing applications to help them prolong their lives and manage their existences without state intervention. Becoming interplanetary disrupts the market that produces the conditions of climate change and presents an opportunity to move one's personal data—one's embodied genes and consciousness—for a better chance at surviving and improving the species, bypassing the sluggish pace of NASA and the public sector.

The unquestioned goodness of disruption in the tech sector has made it difficult to challenge the consequences of valuing disruption for its own sake. Disrupting or hacking health care, for example, may appear to empower the individual to track their own health metrics and to seek medical services facilitated by satisfaction ratings rather than by the insurance companies. But these innovative changes also contribute to turning health into a private matter and support a neoliberal logic of radical personal responsibility for one's surviving and thriving: this is part and parcel of a bunkerized prepping ethos. Disruptive technologies have even Westernized the Eastern religious practices of meditation and yoga, taking these already commodified practices from the studio to allow individuals to tinker with their brains in the privacy of their own home with wearables like Muse, "the brain sensing headband" that "gives you feedback about your meditation in real time by translating your brain signals into the sounds of wind." Muse offers incentives to improve one's meditation practice, as measured by its sensors. "After each session, you'll see how you did through a series of graphs and charts. Track your progress over time and earn points to unlock new features."[33] If meditation is not a good in and of itself, then app users can find external motivation through competition with oneself and in "unlocking" the potential of their economic investment in the app and the potential of their conscious minds.

These hacking technologies may be helpful or, more likely, inevitable, but they speak to a preoccupation in Silicon Valley with optimizing human evolution, forcing civilization to overcome barriers to progress such as climate change, and doing so through the market economy of device-driven products that will, presumably, prepare us to think beyond the confines of our Earth and earthly bodies. The interest in fusing technology to consciousness does not start with the Muse developers but can be seen as an extension of what Turner calls the "New Communalists" of the 1960s, who advocated class consciousness's replacement with a higher human consciousness straining to break free from bureaucratization, regulation, and rules. "Finally, if the self was the ultimate driver of social change, and if class was no more, then individual lifestyle choices become political acts, and both consumption and lifestyle technologies—including information technologies—would have to take on a newly political valence."[34] From the war rooms of MIT to the communes of Mill Valley in Northern California, status quo skeptics saw information feedback flows as liberating the self from government systems and argued that freedom meant one's being able to engage those systems as networked relations rather than as hierarchies. The leap from the commune to the startup brought with it the same promise of unbinding the individual from Evolution 1.0 and the public regulations that slow progress, unlocking the full potential of the self-made American.

The discourse of disruption has extended beyond Silicon Valley and its drive to reroute markets while still operating in a capitalist environment. Nicole Sunday Grove argues: "The desired result of disruption's critical productivity is the subject who no longer wishes for a sense of security and preparedness in the face of shocks, crises, and disasters, but who welcomes and even seeks to perpetuate such crises. . . . Disruption is limited in terms of its ability to capture a vision of an ethical and political response to the challenges of contemporary capitalism and global instability."[35]

Disruption may not usher in new possibilities to offer stability in a changing world through startups and innovative ideas; instead, it may encourage instability. Grove describes *"annihilative disruption,* or a form of feeling that organizes the world around disaster's insatiable appetite for itself." Annihilative disruption is different from other types of disruption that "offer capitalism as a permanent feature of life." Instead, annihilative disruption sees chaos as its own good, a sentiment shared by accelerationists and "annihilative technophiles who fancy themselves wizards that can perfectly surf the waves of chaos. They cannot, but when they get lucky it is neither because of virtuosity nor genius, but rather their vast cushion of immiserating capital accumulation which leaves them ready to leverage the aftermath of catastrophe for personal gain."[36] These technophiles of Silicon Valley, particularly the ones who imagine off-world opportunities as ones in which they can build their own empires stocked with freethinking libertarians, neomonarchists, and indentured laborers working off their ticket to a Martian colony, try to seize the tail of end times and, in the chaos, direct opportunities for their own new world. While the entrepreneurs of civilizational decline may claim worldsaving concern, love of human consciousness if not life, and philanthropic purpose, they thrive on sowing disruption and instability in their own business ventures based on precarious labor and in their visions of a world that needs to break before it can become something worth living in. Yet designing disruptive technologies and participating in a disruptive mood is not evidently a chaotic set of activities but rather perceptible in geoengineering projects, rocketry ventures, seeding the sky with satellites, making home surveillance technology as commonplace as a toaster oven in an average household, and discouraging collective action against inhumanity and inequality—or even thinking of ourselves in collective terms. Dealing with catastrophes to come and those already here, from climate change to the reinvigorated nuclear standoff between global superpowers, are individualized problems that indicate that the end is drawing nearer for our contemporary way of life. Mass consumption is one of the few options for surviving chaotic times, which requires releasing capitalism to meet the moment with markets. Consuming safety through bunkerizing is a way to bring the aesthetics of technocratic eco-managerialism to the home. The technologies, surveillance, and managerial decisions that take place on a global scale can reasonably be fitted to the home scale. Even the homeowner remote from their dwelling can make adjustments and real-time decisions about switching lights on and off, changing camera angles, and tinkering with sprinkler systems and climate control. At-home eco-managerialism takes the means of preparing, bunkering, and surviving out of the subterranean bunker and puts it into the home and marketplace of prepping. In so doing, the responsibilized subject can take account of their domain and manage it as part of their duty as good citizens. The market for prepping has moved beyond selling seeds, home garden equipment, bunkers, and shelf-stable food. The market for prepping is also a ripe opportunity for technological and consumer disruptions to the traditional modes of prepping, a hallmark of the Silicon Valley ethos that supports a technologically savvy way to route old-fashioned prepping and turn it into something sleek, smart, and ready for anything, even achieving escape velocity from the planet.

Disruption is a Silicon Valley trademark. Disrupting the market at the scale of business means challenging traditional corporations and corporate structures without challenging the fundamental structures of capitalism. Instead, disruption serves as an accelerant; it speeds the pace of service and product delivery, the pace of profit accumulation, and the pace of technological and commercial change that will support some social or biophysical evolution. Scaled further out still is "annihilative disruption," disrupting for its own sake as its own good, a disruption that opens onto nothing, perhaps the same nothing that Nancy speculated the apocalypse would reveal. This is not hastening toward a better world but instead the kind of institutional drift Veblen warned about. Prepping as an intervention and as a market interrupted by disruptive products like Preppi makes prepping a one-dimensional reflex within a bunker society, rather than a reaction to particular crises that, once survived, will unfold into a period of relative stability and institutional familiarity.

CONSUMING SURVIVAL

Taking to outer space as an extension of the bunker way of life is reflected in the reasons given by outer space entrepreneurs for investing in the technologies and infrastructure to make space adventurism and commercialization possible. While Musk does not explicitly argue that colonizing Mars is a reaction to climate change, he is concerned with ensuring human consciousness is not only located on Earth, and Bezos has drawn connections between climate change and his space efforts: "Blue Origin envisions a time when people can tap into the limitless resources of space and enable the movement of damaging industries into space to preserve Earth, humanity's blue origin."[37] Outer space is discursively styled as a limitless pool of resources lying in wait; environmental ethics cannot apply here, and outer space is firmly maintained as an "other" space apart from the home planet. Blue Origin and SpaceX have contracts with NASA, affirming their position as welcome disruptors to the space program, a planned absence by the state that the market is encouraged to fill. Working closely with corporate partnerships suggests state willingness to continue shaping outer space policy to permit private-sector claims and ownership schemes, effectively allowing bunkerization to extend beyond the atmospheric boundary and into outer space. In this iteration, bunkerization is covered in the language of philanthropy, that setting capital loose allows for more creative and timely responses to civilization's urgent needs. For example, Musk takes issue with the claim that establishing Mars and moon colonies would be "an escape hatch for rich people."[38] He counters that anyone is welcome to be among the first colonists, if they are willing to accept the statistical probability that the trip will be one-way.[39] The early stages of space exploration will require building a propellant factory, a power station, and glass domes to grow crops. After establishing the fundamentals of life, Musk claims there will be "an explosion of entrepreneurial activity" because "Mars will need everything from iron foundries, to pizza joints, to nightclubs. . . . I think Mars should have really great bars." He anticipated being able to send the first interplanetary ships on "up and down" flights by 2019, an ambitious but missed target. By making ships reusable, Musk can reduce the cost per flight, which, presumably, gets to the question of whether leaving Earth is only for rich people. Musk proposes that making breakthroughs in reusability in rocketry will enable humans to establish a city on Mars. This breakthrough, he claims, is akin to the dramatic industrial changes ushered in by the intercontinental railroad or the ocean liners. "So, we're going to do our best to get you there, and then make sure there's an environment in which entrepreneurs can flourish, and then I think it will be amazing."[40]

This largely unregulated environment for capitalism is part of Silicon Valley's interest in what Matthew Bishop calls philanthrocapitalism: "Philanthrocapitalism encompasses not just the application of modern business techniques to giving but also the effort by a new generation of entrepreneurial philanthropists and business leaders to drive social and environmental progress by changing how business and government operate."[41] Corporations have embraced the language of "doing well by doing good," which is echoed in Musk's motives for sinking his wealth into SpaceX and Tesla: " 'I try to do useful things,' he explains. 'That's a nice aspiration. And useful means it is of value to the rest of society. Are they useful things that work and make people's lives better, make the future seem better, and actually are better, too? I think we should try to make the future better.' "[42] In his SXSW interview, Musk considers the early stages of his Mars project a "philanthropic mission" to start greenhouses on Mars and use the photographs taken of the burgeoning colony as a beacon of hope to those still stranded on Earth, slowly drowning in carbon.

Even the production of popular culture helps prepare the public to see megarich capitalists as the great watchdogs of humanity and our potential losses in an unstable world. Jonathan Nolan produced a trailer about the recent launch of the Falcon Heavy rocket. Shot like a commercial for progress, the trailer featured multiple views of the rocket and launch, using footage from the Falcon itself and the dash cam of the now infamous red Tesla Roadster owned by Musk, currently orbiting the sun. While David Bowie's "Starman" played triumphantly in the background, the camera sought out the faces of excited, hopeful, and bemused men, women, and children gathered to watch history collide with their Martian future, recalling the sense of common public achievement in old footage of people watching the historic Apollo 11 mission. NASA has been replaced by SpaceX, and more specifically by the vision of Musk himself, wrapped up in a slick advertising campaign to sell to the broader public a mission not unlike the nineteenth-century imperative in the United States to "Go West!" The public remains the same, except their relationship to space exploration will be one of consumption and, perhaps less optimistically, of dire need.[43] Luke's description of Al Gore is just as apt for Musk as someone who has "deputized himself as a designated driver to defend the ecosphere."[44] Musk secured a dummy in a spacesuit to his spacefaring Roadster, giving a more literal interpretation to the "prophet as designated driver" imagery.

This capitalism with a humanitarian face pays lip service to concern for ecological sustainability and the survival of the species, but Mars is, in the end, an investment and a mode of entertainment. Musk is not concealing nefarious capitalist plans when he protests that his interest in Mars is about adventure first and survival second.[45] Musk trades on the frontiersman habits of mind as well as the legitimate fears of running out of habitable space on Earth and, for those living in advanced industrial societies, the loss of a comfortable standard of living and a presumed buffer from the effects of climate change. SpaceX and its fellow space-minded companies capitalize on these anxieties about climate change and loss of economic and cultural comfort by offering strategies to render nature controllable through scientific rationality while also creating new opportunities for the leisure class in the form of space tourism and experiments in Martian living. This chimes with Marcuse's critique of technological development as undertaken in a one-dimensional society: "Marcuse's (1964) ecological sensibilities move him to see how the technological means to conquer scarcity also turn into new tools for forestalling liberation. Obscene levels of overproduction and excessive consumption enjoyed by a few in many advanced industrial parts of the world cannot provide an acceptable model for the pacification of existence because they are accompanied by 'moronization, the perpetuation of toil, and the promotion of frustration.' "[46]

Luke aptly summarizes Marcuse's concerns with the modern capitalist strategy for pacifying nature to create a stable foundation for a thriving humanity. The ecological crisis as manifest in climate change is part of the conditions for "perpetual war" that Marcuse warns against: "To oppose one-dimensional society, which is marked by 'the increasing irrationality of the whole; waste and restriction of productivity; the need for aggressive expansion; the constant threat of war; intensified exploitation; dehumanization.' "[47] For Musk, climate change and a threat of the coming dark ages justify aggressive expansion into space. In Musk's view, humans will take up the necessary labor of city building on Mars and even the unnecessary labor of running pizza joints and bars. The production of culture and infantilizing entertainment is promised on trips to Mars and in the new Martian city.[48] Silicon Valley got its start as a production center for the U.S. military, so it is no surprise that its current entrepreneurs return to such a reliable source of credibility and support. Capitalism in space is meant to be a signal of hope, but a Marcuseian read reveals it is just another opportunity for capitalism, linked arm in arm with a public sector cooperating with private capital, to reiterate itself in a new atmosphere. The billionaires sell hope, but they are at the same time preparing for doomsday conditions. Peter Thiel notoriously bought New Zealand citizenship and a bunker compound, Douglas Rushkoff has chronicled the agonies faced by the prepping superrich, and becoming a multiplanetary species belies a fear that life-giving conditions on Earth are not going to remain hospitable for long.

CONCLUSION

DOOMSDAY PREPPING is evocative: it can arouse fear, anxiety, anticipation, exaltation, dread. Watching doomsday prepping from outside of the prepping world can turn into a type of gawking at its strange culture and behaviors, the extreme or outlandish beliefs that animate those practices, the ridiculous waste of wealth and time both the hoi polloi and the leisure class expend. Trying to understand doomsday prepping can lead to creating typologies of prepping movements, prepping psychologies, and even types of prepping objects, like what constitutes a bunker, a bug-out location, and so forth. While those are interesting approaches, we have chosen to theorize prepping as an institution, one that has historical roots in the industrial age of America. Prepping is not a fringe activity that has somehow migrated toward the center. Prepping has always been central to the American way of life, from "Be Prepared" to "duck and cover" to getting ahead of anticipated extinction by becoming a multiplanetary species. From this vantage point, prepping has moved out toward the fringes from the center, so the isolated doomsday communities in remote corners of western states are not the locus of prepping as a mode of life but instead now just a marginal example of such a mode. This approach to analyzing doomsday prepping inverts the standard entry into prepping as a strange but fascinating lifestyle and instead finds that prepping is as American as baseball and war crimes.

Creating an at-home fortress, whether with bunkers or other prepping technologies, allows for residents to withdraw from society and into a private and guarded world, one in which the things they needed to leave home to seek out are now built into the home itself. Depending on one's level of resources, this could include basement or garage bars to entertain friends, pool tables, playground equipment, at-home yoga studios and gyms, recording equipment for music production, storage for surplus goods to prolong gaps between visits to the store, hair and nail salons, personal doctors to provide basic medical care, on-demand medspa services that will come to the home with an array of injectable cosmetic treatments, spas, wine cellars, home movie theaters, bowling alleys, professional kitchens with restaurant-grade appliances and chefs for hire, and other services that members of the aspirationally middle class cannot even imagine. Those with the means to do so can hire people to venture out of the confines of the bunkerized home and into the hazards of the world to fetch groceries and run errands for them. Rowland Atkinson and Sarah Blandy note as much when they write, "Staying in, protecting the home base, has become part of an elaborate shift of social centrality. Fear of crime, home consumption of alcohol, televisions and home cinemas keep us more house-bound and entertained than previous generations." The home fortress does more than provide protection from the dangers and inconveniences of the world beyond the gate; it provides an opportunity to invest in the home as a "commodified financial asset." The fortified home is a smart bet: it provides for personal and psychological security while also offering a financial investment. "A declining sense of social support from the state and community form important background concerns within discussions about the role of the house and of home ownership, shaping the kinds of strategies many employ to manage these anxieties."[1] The fortress home is often filled with the latest consumer surveillance technologies, and the collected data is useful to the companies that own these technologies and, often, to law enforcement agencies. Not all preppers choose surveillance technologies that are connected to major technology companies; some seek a more "off the grid" approach to living in a state of readiness. Some prepping communities are part of various evangelical groups that have gathered in the Pacific Northwest to survive tribulation and make it to the rapture. In Crawford Gribben's study of evangelical prepper movements in the U.S. West, he cites a pamphlet from R. J. Rushdoony, one of the leading survivalist evangelical leaders of the religious right in the mid-twentieth century, who encouraged people to "invest in tangible assets, especially silver and gold, as well as in developing skills such as gardening and car mechanics."[2] Becoming a tinkerer, always being prepared, and planning survival around securing conservative Christian American values is just as comfortable in a right-wing religious political community as it was in the federal government's defense efforts during the atomic era.

Within the neoliberal worldview that dominates American politics, preppers still make and find community. That prepper communities exist does not negate the central argument that neoliberalism, in confluence with the history of prepping outlined in this book, produces a responsibilized subject impossibly expected to account for their own survival in an unstable world. Indeed, accounting for the loss of collectivized, public support for dangers associated with sea-level rise, weakening anti–nuclear weapons pacts between rival nations, and rising fear of civil unrest is part of the responsibility of the individual who realizes the state is not concerned with their well-being. In place of state support, people make use of market opportunities for prepper gear, survival guides, and survivalist real estate selling bug-out properties, fortified luxury homes, bunkers, and expertise to help build a self-sufficient compound. Some preppers prefer minimal intervention from the state, driven by their deep skepticism about state interference in their lives and the moral integrity of a state that may be run by "global elites," despite often feeling strongly about defending the U.S. Constitution and celebrating opportunities to buy bug-out property that shares property lines with state and federal land.[3] Cataloging different prepper movements will predictably yield a range of ideological orientations, visions of a fortified existence, contradistinct communities, and variant views on a post-doom world that is worth surviving in order to experience. One of the hallmarks of this project is precisely not creating a prepper taxonomy. There are many movements, and many psychological and sociological reasons people engage in survivalism. Some prepper movements align with leftist anarchism; others await the second coming of Christ. We pull examples from the various types of prepping movements to illuminate our arguments, but we are not establishing a set of boundary conditions for what counts and does not count as a bunker, prepper, or survivalist, nor are we adjudicating the ontological lines of what is a bunker or a prepper. Rather, the purpose of this project is to theorize the political context in which these social, psychological, economic, civic, and political arrangements exist, an institutional analysis of prepping that traverses the twentieth and twenty-first century of American political and social history. We set the parameters for a political analysis of prepping and establish the institutional development that sets the foundations for how these behaviors come to be legible, credible, and mainstream. The analysis extends beyond poor public policies and individual capitalists who, we argue, contribute to a worsening world and may themselves also prepare for disaster. Policies, the mechanisms of liberal democracy, and the actors that populate the capitalist hierarchies are all part of the arrangements of a world that allows for their existence and particular relations of power. As Marx and generations of people influenced by Marx have argued, removing individual capitalists from power does not fundamentally alter the systems that constitute capitalism, and in this spirit, we look behind institutional actors and at the ideological and material conditions that make prepping a rational and savvy thing to do for the average American.

THEMATIC OVERVIEW

We began the story of prepping in the United States by laying out how it has become an institution. This starting point is important because prepping behavior, as we have seen, is multifaceted, motivated by different ideological orientations, and too mainstream a practice to be reduced to a peculiar behavior by a particular demographic. As such, we begin by trying to chart out how this behavior became so accepted and widespread. Thorstein Veblen is an American theorist who developed institutional analysis, and he is especially useful to the study of prepping because he did not simply take institutions to mean only concretely formed social structures (such as the state) but to mean the ways in which behavior in groups is conditioned and how habits of mind are shaped. This adds an important historical dimension as well as an evolutionary one; it allows us to argue that prepping Americans did not simply emerge from nowhere during the Cold War or for the cable reality television cameras. Veblen's institutionalism argues that old habits of thought from bygone modes of life get smuggled into new machine processes of production. Historically, this provides a good basis for starting at the period of the rapid industrialization of the United States and for looking at what old habits of mind needed to be held onto, changed, or smuggled in to rationalize a new mode of life. Veblenian institutionalism also allows us to theorize how institutions, like prepping, evolve to become imbecilic and geared toward merely their own reproduction, not because they serve any socially useful purpose, as we see with the mass consumption of the prepping American. This complicates the too-easy narrative of whether prepping "works" or is somehow effective or efficient and instead moves the focus onto why this behavior persists, what ends it serves, and how these behaviors might preclude other ways of organizing our lives. In other words, it lets us cast the question of the politics of prepping as one in which prepping has become dominant and one-dimensional, crowding out alternatives. This institutionalist step is important because it refuses to simply gawk at the aberrant behavior of outré demographic groups but exposes how the rise of mass production and consumer culture necessitate an updated idea of what it means to be an American that smuggles in some archaic ideas but fulfills the needs of industrial production.

The second chapter takes up the institutional foundations of the prepping American that emerge during industrialization. We look at what makes up American identity, in particular, what it means for Americans to have a conception of themselves as self-sufficient frontier people able to work the land and fashion the ends of life from start to finish and who take full responsibility for their life outcomes. We focus on this conception because of how ubiquitous it is but also because these ideas of American identity are animated, changed, or deployed in novel ways when it comes to preparedness. To make this case we used the Boy Scouts of America, the Handicraft movement, and tinkering culture to show how ideas of the prepping American rationalize these romantic ideas of American identity, masculinity, and anxiety and are baked into industrialization itself, such that when Americans are asked to prep for nuclear conflict, the scout (who can identify, dominate, and manage nature), the crafter (who can build everything they need from start to finish), and the tinkerer (who can intervene in the production process to make products do things they were not designed to do or to serve their personal ends) easily can become prepping or bunkering Americans. If we assume that the directive to build personal fallout shelters is so fanciful as to be bizarre, then it is important to trace the institutional roots of how that request was legible and acceptable to Americans. Being prepared has been an institutional directive in the ways we detail in this nonexhaustive analysis and is wrapped up in archaic stories of American identity and how those stories are preserved. Whether the threat is the grime of urbanization that comes with industry, xenophobic concerns about immigrants befouling nature, or feeling helpless before hopelessly complex production systems and their rhythms, the idea of preparing for them by demonstrating personal mastery and discipline remains a distinct part of the narrative of the American character. By the time the Cold War emerges, these visions of American identity can be easily mobilized to propel Americans to become preppers. The question of whether this is effective, desirable, or intelligent behavior is less important than that it shows how institutionally these habits of mind are pulled into the Cold War and beyond, including into the contemporary period.

In the third chapter, we reach the atomic age and the threat of mutually assured destruction with the USSR. As doomsday prepping moves from the BSA into every American family, so too does doomsday prepping acquire the characteristics of an institution. During World War I and II, federal programs encouraged everyday people to grow "victory" or war gardens and, during the Cold War, to make provisions for themselves to survive a nuclear attack from the Soviet Union. Prepping helped draw people into a state of permanent guard against ongoing war and threats to American hegemonic supremacy. Although the state told Americans that surviving and prepping were part of their due diligence as good American citizens, prepping exists in contrast to serious democratic engagement with the political decisions that necessitated prepping. Prepping was, and still is, largely a market-based activity to buy the means of survival and then to buy the expertise to assemble and fortify a place to survive. You could also take inspiration from the BSA and acquire those handicraft skills to do it yourself. Meanwhile, the U.S. government dropped bombs in U.S. desert states, warned citizens about the perils of not prepping through bomb demonstrations on model suburbs, and funded state security initiatives and the military while claiming a public bunkering project would be cost prohibitive. The U.S. state's approach to preparing Americans to meet the communist threat on American soil helped institutionalize prepping as a way of life, suggesting that in undertaking preparations one would also become the good American who should and would survive whatever may come. Being and maintaining this American life would require regular vigilance, even beyond the bomb and into the second half of the twentieth century, when the threats only mounted but did not disappear and a growing neoliberal political project became a dominating organizing principle in the U.S. government and its private sector.

The fourth chapter explores another manifestation of the prepping mentality as it increasingly merges with an antidemocratic ethos in Silicon Valley. Prepping in the nuclear age was inextricable from military tension between the two superpowers. Likewise, prepping as it has intersected with the startup culture and paranoid politics of Silicon Valley continues its tight link to military action by the state. Silicon Valley's ascent as a technological and economic hub was seeded with military funding and projects, often funneled through Stanford University in the Santa Clara Valley. Both the space program and tech sector have been developed within the military-industrial complex under various historical iterations. As such, they are colored through with the violent and repressive cultural and ideological institutions in which they were created. In a social formation marked by militarism, rationalized violence, and competitive ideologies of total domination, outer space exploration and preparing for crisis, catastrophe, and cataclysm necessarily operate within the confines of the reality principle. What does preparing for survival on the one hand and

technological development on the other look like in a modern iteration of a dominating society? Drawing attention to the reality principle is to draw attention to the limits of remaking prepping as a
good rather than bad habit (although, to be clear, we do not draw these
distinctions in this book). Prepping, including developing a space program as a species-saving opportunity, cannot simply be remade as a
form of survivalism that reflects the right ethics, liberal democratic
principles, and national character. To think about the means of life
and how to live in a world of climate change we need to radically
shift the operating principles of our institutional arrangements.

The context of the startup and tech sectors provides a set of limit
conditions that reflect hostility toward democracy and collective
response to shared vulnerabilities. Even within the neoliberalism of
the modern American institutional formation, Silicon Valley has
developed a distinctive ideology called the Dark Enlightenment, which
is explicitly antidemocratic and often promonarchy and sees the market as the best vector for ideal communication in a given society.
Working as a complement to the neoliberal state as we have described
it, there is little room for collective action, collective care, and democratic approaches to managing risks, disasters, and climate change.
As such, prepping is an attractive market space, especially for the disruptive ethos of Silicon Valley, which is bent on repackaging existing
products and services as challenges to conventional markets offering
more or less the same thing. For example, rideshare companies are
meant to displace traditional taxis, even though they both offer chauf-
feured cars for hire operating on a similar rate of distance and time.
Disruption does not meaningfully change the reality principle; it
simply adjusts the temporal scale of market changes in a capitalist
economy. Prepping is part of the disruptive economy, with startups
intervening in the nuclear-era prepping market of subterranean bunkers and sleekly packaged, freeze-dried rations and survival gear,
bespoke panic rooms that match an interior design sensibility, and
various technologies to help monitor conditions of potential violence,
adverse weather events, and cosmic shifts like electromagnetic pulses.
This chapter weaves together the neoliberalism of the postwar period,
the dark ideology of Silicon Valley, and the prepper movement as it
adapts to these new conditions.

The final chapter approaches outer space as the ultimate escape opportunity from doomed conditions on the home planet. Prepping reaches its limits in the face of current catastrophes and future potentially apocalyptic conditions associated with climate change. If the planet itself may no longer host human life, what good is prepping, bunkering, and bugging out? Prepping is more than collecting surplus provisions and making survival plans; prepping is part of the phenomenon we call bunkerization, in which the acts associated with bunkering down to survive is part of a mode of life that exceeds those specific prepping behaviors and becomes an organizing principle. Bunkerization of life is to confront life as a risk that needs assessing, to proceed as a responsibilized subject that knows better than to depend on the state to provide for their security and indeed, takes a measure of pride in their self-sufficiency as a product of their nationalism. The bunkerized subject undertakes the means of living through a defensive posture and assumes that a collective, democratic life is one that must be guarded against in order to secure survival. Bunkerization is manifest in the multiple space programs and rationalizations for being a spacefaring people (and, in this context, America as a spacefaring nation), which are bound up in national security, extending the empire to include new colonizable resources and space in the vacuum of outer space, and as an escape from the possibility that a third world war, multiple nuclear bomb drops, and climate change will usher in the extinction of the human species and end of human consciousness. The spaceship may functionally be a bunker, and future lunar or Mars colonies may likewise be bunker compounds, but outer space as a new frontier of survivalism is intelligible as a version of bunkerization.

PREPPING TO BUNKERIZATION

SECURITY, MODERNITY, AND BUNKERIZATION

The bunker is emblematic of prepping more than it is the specific object of study. The bunker became an important metaphor during the height of the atomic age. The advent of nuclear war required a constant state of preparation to attack and to be attacked and to think about infrastructure in terms of mobilization of materials and machines for survival. "The countryside, the earth is henceforth given over, definitively consecrated to war by the cosmopolitan mass of workers, an army of laborers speaking every language, the Babel of logistics."[4] During the atomic age, the federal government prepared the U.S. citizen for this state of ongoing mobilization and preparation. Likewise, the Boy Scouts of America's motto to "Be Prepared" serves as a reminder that disaster of any sort, planned (a dropped bomb that hits its target) or accidental (a dropped bomb that misses its target, a storm event, and so forth), is imminent and requires ongoing surveillance and planning in order to ensure one's survival. Earth itself becomes part of the theater of war. Paul Virilio connects this to the medieval fortress, which, "with its entrances and exits, is a primary schema of the strategic calculator. . . . Social conflicts arise from rivalries between those who occupy and preserve an eco-system as the place that specifies them as a family or group, and that therefore deserves every sacrifice, including sudden death." The defense of this territory is necessary for survival. "In short, the fortresses of the Middle Ages replaced primitive welcomes and sacred ancient hospitality with permanent social rejection as the primary necessity for the workings of the war machine."[5] Claiming and strategically defending territory, as well as enforcing rejection from the territory, become essential features of the state of permanent defense. What does this mean when considering bunkerization and the sociopolitical response to ongoing and compounding threats to security? Virilio thinks about this problem in the 1970s era of living with nuclear threat as a multinational reality and as a mechanism that concentrates power. "The speed of the political decision depends on the sophistication of the vectors: how to transport the bomb? how fast? The bomb is political, we like to repeat—political not because of an explosion that should never happen, but because it is the ultimate form of military surveillance." The very existence of unending security threats to multiple environments encourages the transformation of civic engagement into individualized responsibility for securing the nation by securing the family unit. The doomsday bunker in the United States was specifically designed for the family unit rather than the community. Virilio argues that "civil and social protection in this type of affair is no longer contemporary with the catastrophe; it precedes it and, if need be, invents it."[6] The threat of a nuclear attack may always linger over the absence of a nuclear attack, but preparation is necessary just the same. The threat of climate change–induced disaster, while perhaps more of a sure thing than atomic bomb detonation, likewise requires preemptive securitization. Again, this approach to transforming the state into a fortress came of age during the Cold War. To quote Virilio:

> In fact, the government's deliberately terroristic manipulation of the need for security is the perfect answer to all the new questions now being put to democracies by nuclear strategy—the new isolationism of the nuclear State that, in the U.S., for example, is totally revamping political strategy. They are trying to recreate Union through a new unanimity of need. . . . We will see the creation of a common feeling of insecurity that will lead to a new kind of consumption, the consumption of protection; this latter will progressively come to the fore and become the target of the whole merchandising system. . . . The individual promotion of the need for security already composes a new composite portrait of the citizen—no longer the one who enriches the nation by consuming, by the one who invests first and foremost in security, manages his own protection as best he can, and finally pays more to consume less.[7]

This "unanimity of need" for security is a serious characteristic of the bunker state, which bases citizenship on the need to attend to one's security against future threats, which are increasingly unmoored from specific conflict and instead part of ongoing, nebulous threats like terrorism and climate change. Virilio highlights speed as the factor that radically changes the nature of war and threat from one dependent upon distance to one in which distance is dissolved by supersonic speed through air, land, and sea, mirrored in the nuclear triad. This analysis can be extended to the acceleration of climate change, which by most metrics is steadily increasing in intensity of consequences and speed of their arrival at various planetary points, ecosystems, and peoples. Likewise, cutting-edge capitalists tinker with speed on their rocketry and spacefaring technologies to hasten the process of making the human species multiplanetary, partly as a response to the rapid deterioration of livable conditions on Earth as climate change's effects pick up speed from above and below. Virilio believes that the speed of destructive capacity has rendered political decisions automatic: there is quite literally no time to deliberate, only time for strategic calculations and action. Not only are people robbed of democratic influence, but even the decisive state actors are no longer deciding on the exceptional case.

The bunker itself promotes imaginary doomsday scenarios and acting out preparation in anticipation of some postdisaster world that is radically changed. "The bunker fantasy promises shelter from the apocalyptic forces of nuclear war. But it also affords an opportunity to reorganize the world as it *could be* rather than as it is: the act of sheltering requires stripping one's life down to the bare essentials to rebuild from scratch and it provides a space for reckoning with everyone and everything sacrificed or left outside the bunker."[8] In Virilio's tour of the Atlantic Wall, he described being inside one of the abandoned bunkers as "being in the grips of that cadaveric rigidity from which the shelter was designed to protect him."[9] The modern doomsday shelter, as it developed out of the fortress, must attend to the changes in weaponry and threat. "Today the technological conjunction of the vehicle and the projectile concentrates both movements of reduction: with the supersonic jet with a nuclear payload, for example, the whole planet becomes 'a defensive redoubt.' . . . The conquest of the earth thus appears above all the conquest of energy's violence." As the superpowers of the midcentury urgently engaged the race to conquer energy's violence, the same powers took seriously the need to fortify their populations in anticipation of the use of such harnessed violence. While the USSR developed urban networks of bunkers, the United States focused on making public demonstrations of the bomb's capacity to scare their citizens into taking personal responsibility for bunkering by buying their means of survival on the marketplace. A bunkerized planet takes on two valences: one in the form of physical bunkers that still dot landscapes, and the other as a

bunker mentality with attendant material manifestation and econo-
mies. Bunkerization comes as a necessity given that total and planetary war is a product of harnessing nuclear energy. "From now on the
military establishment will defend not so much 'national' territory
so much as that of energy, *the area of violence.*"[10] While the bunker and
national defense has not completely broken with the defense of traditional national territory, militaries increasingly take up proxy
wars, cyber warfare, and work hand in glove with private military
firms providing mercenary work across the globe, often for corporate
interests in national stakes.

As the threat of nuclear attack changed the nature of military
threat, the fortress wall increasingly gave way to the bunker. "It was
no longer in distance but rather in burial that the man of war found
the parry to the onslaught of his adversary; retreat was now into the
very thickness of the planet and no longer along its surface."[11] The
bunker responded to the new environment of war mobilization, with
the omnipresent threat of total annihilation and the scale of destabi-
lization promised in the atomic bomb. While Virilio is describing the
partially aboveground bunkers of the Atlantic Wall, which were meant
for military defense more than family living, he makes critical observations about the nature of modern bunkers that are apt for the family hideout from the atomic age onward: "Contemplating the half-
buried mass of a bunker . . . is like contemplating a mirror, the
reflection of our own power over death, the power of our mode of
destruction, of the industry of war. The function of this very special
structure is to assure survival, to be a shelter for man in a critical
period, the place where he buries himself to subsist. If it thus belongs
to the crypt that prefigures the resurrection, the bunker belongs too
to the ark that saves, to the vehicle that puts one out of danger by
crossing over mortal hazards."[12] The bunker in the American family
backyard forms a nodal point in a geography of subterranean survival
that is both highly individualized and centered on assuring the survival of both the people in it and the social and political values they
carry with them. Virilio understands emergence from the bunker as
a resurrection and a haven from the attempt of a superpower (or supernatural power, in biblical terms) to wipe clean and start anew. The
bunker as a refuge for those who wish to repopulate a stripped Earth

fits alongside existing millenarian beliefs about nuclear war as apocalyptic.

Virilio argues that the Oriental military "tends to increase the time of war by mobilizing the population around active or passive—direct or indirect—survival objectives, natural catastrophes, accidents, and restrained conflicts seen as part and parcel of the same war; class struggle extending in the end into all dimensions of everyday life."[13] Arguably this extension of wartime attention and energy is true of the Occident as well, when the federal government directed its nuclear standoff campaigns toward generalized threats, with the development of Federal Emergency Management Agency (FEMA) in 1979 and encouraging everyday people to stockpile and prepare for any number of disasters, military related or not, including present-day threats from climate change. Although they are not at the forefront, the class dimensions of doomsday prepping are critical to the development of this version of "total war" and the doomsday economy.

BUNKERING AMERICA AT HOME

Virilio notes the importance of new defense technologies, like anti-aircraft weapons, and the detection systems that allowed pilots to see their targets from above and weapons systems to see their targets from below. These changes were marked by "transparency, ubiquity, total and instantaneous knowledge—these are the ingredients for survival." This description of what is necessary in total war is apt to describe the growing landscape of the everyday life of bunker Americans, with home defense systems that likewise produce transparency, ubiquity, and total and instantaneous knowledge, networked with security companies on standby to respond to the varied emergencies and security breaches that a homeowner may encounter. In its own way, these home defense systems, making a bunker out of everyday life and dwellings, allows the mobilized citizen, not just the soldier, to "put yourself . . . everywhere and in all of the dimensions of combat."[14] The citizen at the center of combat is also now the homeowner with a smart house wirelessly crisscrossed with internet-enabled objects that monitor, detect, report, warn, and, using their own decision-making powers, set into motion security procedures as

considered warranted, including contacting fire and police depart-
ments, private security firms, and of course the parent companies
like Amazon and Google, to contribute valuable data to their collection streams. Turning the home into a security site is an extension of
state surveillance of the family units that require welfare services,
dating back to the Ford Company's home visits to ensure immigrant
employees were keeping clean homes in line with American family
values.[15] Mike Davis read apocalyptic preparation in the urban landscape of Los Angeles in his seminal work *City of Quartz*:

> The market provision of "security" generates its own paranoid
> demand. "Security" becomes a positional good defined by income
> access to private "protective services" and membership in some
> hardened residential enclave or restricted suburb. As a pres-
> tige symbol—and sometimes as the decisive borderline between
> the merely well-off and the "truly rich"—"security" has less to do
> with personal safety than with the degree of personal insulation, in
> residential work, consumption and travel environments, from
> "unsavory" groups and individuals, even crowds in general.[16]

While he most directly refers to fear of gang violence, people of
color, and homelessness on the part of the middle and upper classes,
the observation that the marketplace of security provides its own
paranoid justification holds for current iterations of residential
bunkering. The FIRE sector (finance, insurance, and real estate) likewise has a strong interest in monitoring devices that send real-time
data about household habits and risky behavior and in ensuring that
individuals take responsibility for their own safety by rewarding and
punishing behaviors that are preferred and discouraged by these
risk-pooling sectors. Anticipating risk is a hallmark of the bunkerized household.[17]

The bunkerized household can operate on two levels: One version
of bunkering at home is preparation for catastrophic end times, where
one can expect near-total or total state failure and cannot count on
even private-sector support, infrastructural, emergency, security, or
otherwise. The doomsday hideout anticipates such needs by bringing
survival into the subterranean space of a bunker on one's property or

at a secret bug-out location accessible by heavy duty all-terrain vehicles or on foot. Another level is the bunker to protect against potentially devastating but not radically destabilizing security breaches and events, from superstorms to attempted robberies to infrastructural failures, such as supply chain crises precipitated by a global pandemic. The American bunker society supports both levels of preparedness. Some people and families engage in both, while others focus their energy either on the everyday crisis or on the apocalyptic. The federal government of the 1950s and 1960s advised the general public to prepare for the worst-case scenario of nuclear bomb attack, in which case those who wished to survive would need to anticipate survival conditions with no support in an uncertain, postapocalyptic world to step into once the irradiated dust cleared. The federal government of the 1970s began preparing the American public for less apocalyptic but still extreme disasters, with recommendations for earthquake kits, how to hunker down through a tornado, and, particularly after the World Trade Center attacks of 9/11, what to do in the event of a terrorist attack. In all cases, the home becomes the center of security and survival and the state merely an informational resource but not a guarantor of safety. To forestall such future attacks and risks and to promote the survival of a quintessential American population, the state invests in military might; internal and external nationalistic propaganda; anti-Muslim, anticommunist, and antileftist violent and intellectual suppression; and strong relationships with the private sector to provide the consumer with a means of survival in the absence of state support. The tendency toward safeguarding the right population is evident in the interviews collected by Bradley Garrett in his study of bunkerism. Garrett interviews the CEO of Vivos Group Global Shelters Network, Robert Vicino, who is quoted warning that "a third of Swedish women have been raped by Muslims" and that the people whom the government provides bunkers for, presumably federal employees, are "their most intelligent, successful, necessary, and reliable people. . . . In the private sector, those people are wealthy."[18]

Preparing for disaster, doom, and dislocation extends beyond a specific threat and is a generalized, one-dimensional approach to living in the modern world. Prepping is so fully mainstream as a way of life, rather than as a specific response to a specific threat, that prepping communities refer to the moment that turns prepping from anticipation to action as WSHTF, "when shit hits the fan." The phrase is open enough to include anything that could trigger disaster. The atomic age of prepping was attached to the nuclear warhead and atomic bomb, but after the bomb did not drop the U.S. federal defense agencies disbanded and reemerged as the Federal Emergency Management Agency (FEMA), the organization tasked with preparing for and responding to disasters of all kinds, from dirty bombs to tornados. Threats could come from anywhere, nature and enemies alike, accidents and purposeful violence, train cars spilling toxic chemicals and Hurricane Katrina. For some preppers, the list includes electromagnetic pulses, solar flares, currency crashes and economic tailspins, the rise of the antichrist and powerful cabals threatening mind and body control. Prepping now exceeds the fallout shelter and backyard bunker. Prepping emerged from the Boy Scouts as an obligation to be prepared for just about anything through the acquisition of low-technology skills. Prepping has since grown to become a feature of everyday life. The home itself can become a bunker, monitored by surveillance technologies and residential security contractors, kept clean from outside contamination with water and air filters, fitted with sufficient in-home storage for surplus supplies, and protected with the legal right to own firearms and to use them against anyone who crosses a property boundary and thus becomes an intruder. Not only is the home reconceived as a fortress but the car as well, with sport utility vehicles and trucks the size of military tanks and trucks fitted with heavy-duty bull bars, push bars, and bumper guards to ensure they can cause more damage than they receive in an impact. The "everyday carry" for many Americans includes pepper spray, tasers with both feminine and masculine designs, knives, and handguns. "For survivalists who stockpile ammunition, grow their own food, practice escape routes, and spend austere periods in the wilderness, at some level this is not about overcoming resistance. It is about *encountering* resistance."[19] For many preppers, their efforts are only rewarded when they are tested. Office buildings must meet code not only for flood and earthquake protection but for its inhabitants to survive mass shooting events. Prepping is not just border walls, military surveillance, and a sense of impenetrability by our military and ideological enemies; it is also on the residential scale, on the scale of individual subjects who can take measures to bunkerize their lives in the absence of a physical bunker. Even anticipating climate change, by all measures a reasonable thing to do, is a project for the individual to find the right property, homeowners' or renters' insurance, and to account for their personal safety during an extreme weather event. Bunkerization finds its most recent and dramatic iteration in outer space exploration, which reimagines the rocket as a bug-out experiment to make the human species multiplanetary and ensure that loss of life will not be the final WSHTF on Earth.

CENTRAL PARADOX

As part of the institutional analysis of prepping, we take a hard look at the class dimensions of prepping in the marketplace and in the expectations of a postdoomsday or disaster world and its class orderings. Regardless of why different people prep, they all assume that it is better to survive a crisis or world-ending event than to die in it. Under this assumption, there must be something worth living for on the other side of catastrophe or that there will even be that other side. Just as there are a range of preppers, there are a range of postapocalyptic visions that animate prepper movements. Whether hoping to experience the second coming of Christ firsthand or wishing to be part of the select group of surviving humans to rebuild civilization, people who prep want to see the other side. Yet prepping takes place in the context of socioeconomic class. Peter Thiel does not prep with a modest bug-out bag and a used shipping container retrofitted as a bunker. Thiel and his socioeconomic peers have exclusive and expensive compounds designed to accommodate their preapocalypse lifestyle. Any given U.S. president has access to a White House bunker anytime they feel threatened; it most recently was used in 2020 by President Trump during the protests against the murder of George Floyd by Minneapolis police officers. The Presidential Emergency Operations Center is one of the military-staffed underground centers that allows for both the state and the president to survive; the president is likewise not hunkered down in a small room with merely the bare accommodations for life. Members of the political and economic elite, as well as the predatory leisure class, anticipate entering the new world outside of the bunker wielding their same power and status as when they entered the bunker, even as the new world is expected to have been radically transformed in the meantime. Even those who live below elite status still imagine a world in which their class status remains legible. In the line of well-designed preparedness kits by Preppi, survival includes upscale toiletries, artisanal chocolate, and optional monogramming on the bug-out bag. The chocolate and monogramming may be part of one's personal enjoyment and reassurance that they belong to a class that can afford to prep wisely but not look like a working-class prepper, but these are also signs that must be recognized by others to gain significance.

This paradox is part of our broad argument that prepping extends beyond a set of behaviors and is instead an institutionalized way of life. Preparing does not happen outside of our given mode of life, as somehow apart from neoliberalism and a society that pins its members to a class hierarchy. Prepping is embedded in everyday life, and therefore activity related to prepping is constrained by the ways in which prepping itself has become an institution. Even in the fantasies of a postdisaster world as a blighted, unrecognizable wasteland, the survivors will still emerge with homemade canned foods or monogrammed kits or in security convoys belonging to this or that wealthy survivor. Even a wasteland will provide an adequate context for reanimating the social order of the old world with enough American spirit and knowhow. While accelerationists of all political stripes hope for the opportunity to remake the world, preserved in their fantasies are hierarchies of race, sex, gender, and class. Prepping brings with it not just tools for survival but ideological stability for a one-dimensional society. Some preppers anticipate religious salvation if they are able to hold out during turbulent times, but they are likely to be just as interested in salvaging key institutional features of the old world to shape the new. An evangelical prepper may wish to see a world wiped clean of the sins and crimes that make the secular world unlivable, but they do not wish to see certain traditions overhauled for a radically new way of life, like a patriarchal social organization. The superrich are not likely eager for a new world to be egalitarian and for class status and social stratification to be eliminated. This paradox, preparing for a new world while retaining the features of the old, makes the imperative to shape the current world we live in as a humane, democratic one all the more pressing. Whether we like it or not, preparing for doomsday is not simply a matter of attempting survival through a trial, but it is a matter of world making. How we prep, that is, how we anticipate disasters and experience crises, also shapes what it looks like to live on the other side of these disasters.

END OF THE WORLD/BEGINNING OF THE WORLD

A world that seems to be always coming to an end is a world in turmoil. Climate change is both unavoidable and underway. Populist far-right leaders and political parties continue to gain footholds across the globe, and the American empire is waning. The context in which people prepare for violence, instability, and disaster is severely hemmed in by neoliberalization, the preeminence of capitalism, skepticism that people are capable of living democratically, the enduring legacies and current activities of colonialism, and the dogged persistence of multiple manifestations of racial, class, and gender hierarchies. In this social, political, and economic environment, rational irrationality is the expected approach to making a life. What people prepare for are collectively experienced harms, like climate change, nuclear attack, and earthquakes. Prepping does not refer to accounting for individual-scale crises like running out of groceries or getting into a car accident. Although people can and do prepare for these events, doing so does not constitute a prepper movement. Prepping may only account for oneself, but the dangers are always felt and experienced beyond the individual. Prepping anticipates personal harm caused by a crisis that affects more than one person. The events someone may prep for exceeds their individual ability to avoid this harm. One person cannot turn around climate change any more than one person can end nuclear weapon proliferation. Yet in a neoliberalized world of personal responsibility and managed state absence, these collectively experienced dangers become individual responsibilities to manage. Collectively experienced crises are ones in which multiple people are exposed, although the exposure and harms are unevenly distributed and felt. Prepping allows some people to guard against or opt out of exposure to harm while other people must remain exposed and suffer accordingly. In such a neoliberal regime of living, the responsibilized subject can only blame themself for their own exposure to harm, even if they are not personally responsible for the harm. Those who cannot protect themselves are therefore unwilling or unable to adequately prepare and get the fate they deserve. After all, the home fortress is not just a strategic armor against experiencing harms but a defensive posture against the unprepared. Calum Matheson argues that fantasizing about doomsday has the unexpected effect of provoking enjoyment: "A danger of lurid descriptions of potential climate catastrophe is that, rather than producing anxieties that lead to collective efforts to preserve the Earth, it may enable a fantasy of survival and rebuilding which serves to distance subjects from the urgency of these tasks."[20] Focusing on the self as the surviving subject of a crisis makes it difficult to imagine confronting and surviving collectively experienced harms together and to account for others across the differentiated impacts they may experience.

The prepping movement charted through the Boy Scouts reflects these neoliberal values. The BSA is a voluntary association, not compulsory for all young men. The crafting and tinkering movements appealed to those who enjoyed developing a savvy of everyday life and retaining a skill set that industrialization threatened to turn anachronistic; joining this movement signaled a certain awareness of the future and how to anticipate what will be lost and what should be retained to preserve a proper American identity. The recommendations by the U.S. government to Americans to bunker and prepare for nuclear attack was likewise voluntary, up to individual families, and concerned with protecting and salvaging a certain kind of conservative, Christian, white nuclear family that would embody, defend, and propagate good American values against the communist threat. Preparing for and dodging climate change disasters requires studying weather and tide patterns, making wise investments, acquiring survival skills, and looking after the integrity of your body and the spaces in which your body dwells. Becoming a multiplanetary species demands dependence on the ultrarich to fund and shape these projects and one's not standing in the way by electing officials who will demand state regulation over outer space industries. In all of these instances of prepping, the movement exceeds the individual; the goal is to preserve a way of life, something essentially American, the religiously righteous, and the socioeconomic regime that makes it all possible. Yet prepping also falls on the individual as a set of personal decisions and acts that make someone vulnerable or protected—it is up to you. The state moves out of the way for the market to provide the means of securing oneself if you are clever enough to anticipate the future and to provision for your survival into that future. The BSA may predate neoliberalism, but the trajectory of prepping in the United States demonstrates an ideological foundation that made the meeting of neoliberalism and prepping an easy fit. Politics, then, needs to overcome the institutional lock-in of prepping as a way of life.

Preppers often account for TEOTWAWKI, or "the end of the world as we know it." The "as we know it" is an important qualification. The end may not be the end of all existence in the present and future but the end of what is known and familiar. What comes at the end of the world as we know it? Only those who are prepared will know. The new world might be salvation through Jesus Christ and unification with God; it might be a wasteland in which those who were smart enough to prepare can rebuild the world; it might be the vision of tech CEOs and space entrepreneurs who seek a libertarian, market society with limited government or a secular monarchy and the liberty to develop an ideal world of eugenics, life-extension technologies, and outer space colonization. For however dismal the outlook has been in this book, the upshot is the unknowability of the future. The end of what we know may be the beginning of a world liberated from the oppressive systems we have discussed. The end may also be one that has no clear path forward, just a break from the past. The prepper version of TEOTWAWKI likely requires the hard skills of hunting, water system engineering, and defense that they have presumably honed in anticipation of reaching the end. This end would also signal the beginning of rebuilding based on the conservative religious values that they are meant to embody. Yet the prepper imaginary is not fated, and

TEOTWAWKI remains open, unscripted, and very hard to prepare for. For many indigenous groups, communities that have survived genocide, ethnic cleansing campaigns, and legacies of chattel slavery, the world as they knew it already ended, and the future continues to unfold. Perhaps, as Nancy suggested, the end of the world culminates into nothing. Here the futility of American-style prepping comes into relief. Aside from ensuring bare survival, prepping does not actually prepare people to live in a radically changed or new world. Prepping likewise limits the vision of entering a new world to one of fortification, outliving others, and looking for a future of competition over scarce resources. At the edge of what anyone or any algorithm can predict is the edge of what prepping can do discursively and materially. Prepping as an institution in the way we have characterized it cannot prepare people to rethink how we live and organize ourselves, and therefore it cannot prepare people to move into a future different from our current trajectory, which involves worsening conditions of exploitation, suffering, and climate catastrophe. Without endorsing an accelerationist perspective, we instead wonder what could happen if we look at how prepping has shaped our subjectivities and what new frames of thinking could emerge from such an effort.

NOTES

INTRODUCTION

1. "Current Time—2023," *Bulletin of the Atomic Scientists*, https://thebulletin.org /doomsday-clock/current-time/.
2. "A New Era," *Bulletin of the Atomic Scientists* (1991).
3. Helene Cooper, Julian E. Barnes, and Eric Schmitt, "Russian Military Leaders Discussed Use of Nuclear Weapons, U.S. Officials Say," *New York Times*, November 2, 2022, https://www.nytimes.com/2022/11/02/us/politics/russia-ukraine -nuclear-weapons.html.
4. Casey Ryan Kelly, *Apocalypse Man* (Columbus: Ohio State University Press, 2020).
5. Kelly, *Apocalypse Man*, 17.
6. Kelly, *Apocalypse Man*, 19.
7. Carlen Lavigne, "Making the End Times Great Again," in *The Routledge Companion to Gender and Science Fiction*, ed. Lisa Yaszek, Sonja Fritzsche, Keren Omry, and Wendy Gay Pearson (London: Routledge, 2023), 82.
8. Kelly, *Apocalypse Man*, 30.
9. Kelly, *Apocalypse Man*, 31.
10. Katherine Belew, *Bring the War Home* (Cambridge, MA: Harvard University Press, 2018).
11. Belew, *Bring the War Home*, 6.
12. Herbert Marcuse, *One-Dimensional Man* (Boston: Beacon, 1968).
13. Milton Friedman, "Neoliberalism and Its Prospects," https://miltonfriedman .hoover.org/internal/media/dispatcher/214957/full.
14. Philip Mirowski and Dieter Plehwe, *The Road from Mont Pèlerin* (Cambridge: Harvard University Press, 2009), 15.

15. Wendy Brown, *Undoing the Demos: Neoliberalism's Stealth Revolution* (Cambridge, MA: MIT Press, 2015); Adam Kotsko, *Neoliberalism's Demons* (Stanford, CA: Stanford University Press, 2018), 2.

16. Herbert Marcuse, *Eros and Civilization: Philosophical Inquiry Into Freud* (Boston: Beacon, 1992); Benjamin Fong, *Death and Mastery: Psychoanalytic Drive Theory and the Subject of Late Capitalism* (New York: Columbia University Press, 2018); Norman O. Brown and Christopher Lasch, *Life Against Death: The Psychoanalytical Meaning of History*, 2nd ed. (Middletown, CT: Wesleyan University Press, 1985).

17. Timothy W. Luke, "Beyond Prepper Culture as Right-Wing Extremism: Selling Preparedness to Everyday Consumers as How to Survive the End of the World on a Budget," *Fast Capitalism* 18, no. 1 (2021): 50–62.

18. "Astronauts Who Were Youth in the BSA," Glenn Research Center, NASA, n.d., https://www1.grc.nasa.gov/space/education-outreach/nasa-bsa-path-to-explo ration/astronauts-who-were-youth-in-the-bsa/.

19. This is the idea behind Veblen's famous notion of "conspicuous consumption." While this term is often taken up in economic or psychological discourses as a kind of shorthand that broadly means "keeping up with the Joneses," it is clear that Veblen has the deployment of leisure as a form of class domination in mind, not merely emulation for emulation's sake.

20. Amy Kaplan, "Manifest Domesticity," *American Literature* 70, no. 3 (1998): 581–606.

21. Kaplan, "Manifest Domesticity."

22. Joseph Masco, *The Future of Fallout, and Other Episodes in Radioactive World-Making* (Durham, NC: Duke University Press, 2021). For instance, Masco lays out the example of "the house in the middle" of Cold War propaganda, where the government told Americans that their house might literally withstand a nuclear blast better if they had a fresh coat of paint.

23. Paul Virilio, *Bunker Archeology* (Hudson, NY: Princeton Architectural Press, 1994), 15, 18, 33.

24. United States President's Science Advisory Committee Security Resources Panel and United States Congress Joint Committee on Defense Production, *Deterrence and Survival in the Nuclear Age (the "Gaither Report" of 1957)* (Washington, DC; U.S. Government Printing Office, 1976).

25. Luke, "Beyond Prepper Culture."

26. "Mission | Homeland Security," https://www.dhs.gov/mission.

27. "Mission | Homeland Security."

1. PREPPING AS AN AMERICAN INSTITUTION

1. Tom Vanderbilt, *Survival City: Adventures Among the Ruins of Atomic America* (Chicago: University of Chicago Press, 2010); Thomas Bishop, *Every Home a Fortress: Cold War Fatherhood and the Family Fallout Shelter* (Amherst: University

of Massachusetts Press, 2020); Tracy C. Davis, *Stages of Emergency : Cold War Nuclear Civil Defense* (Durham, NC: Duke University Press, 2007); Laura McEnaney, *Civil Defense Begins at Home: Militarization Meets Everyday Life in the Fifties* (Princeton, NJ: Princeton University Press, 2000); Guy Oakes, *The Imaginary War: Civil Defense and American Cold War Culture* (London: Oxford University Press, 1995).

2. Thomas Carlyle's *On Heroes, Hero-Worship, & the Heroic in History* is the usual touchstone for such a theory and is dependent on "born" leaders who have traits that are not available to the mass of people. While scientifically debated even at the time, such an approach to cultural, historical, and organizational change still persists, although without much empirical basis. In regards to prepping, this might look like analyzing the Eisenhower regime and its policy directives and what they were able to achieve.

3. Even still, individualistic, trait-based theories of heroic change persisted, not only in terms of social change but in organizational management. Banta notes that the "scientific management" movement of Frederick Winslow Taylor maintained that a certain type of person was dispositionally able to manage a rationalized production process. Martha Banta, *Taylored Lives: Narrative Productions in the Age of Taylor, Veblen, and Ford* (Chicago: University of Chicago Press, 1995).

4. Thorstein Veblen, "The Socialist Economics of Karl Marx and His Followers," *Quarterly Journal of Economics* 21, no. 2 (1907): 303; Emilie J. Raymer, "A Man of His Time: Thorstein Veblen and the University of Chicago Darwinists," *Journal of the History of Biology* 46, no. 4 (2013): 669–98.

5. Veblen uses the word "barbaric" in a very narrow way. The thrust of human development, according to Veblen, more or less looks like this: first, a peaceable savagery (close to Marx's notion of "primitive communism"), but with the introduction of honorifics and class divisions based on ownership emerges a barbarism based on subjugation (especially of women) and surplus extraction of underlying populations. As mass production takes hold, Veblen sees the dangers of "exploit" that barbaric habits of mind could wreak even in a "rationalized" industrialization process, even if formally held in check by laws or civil society institutions.

6. Rick Tilman, "Thorstein Veblen's Views on American 'Exceptionalism': An Interpretation," *Journal of Economic Issues* 39, no. 1 (2005): 177–204. Things are different in the rapidly growing cities, of course.

7. Geoffrey M. Hodgson, "On Fuzzy Frontiers and Fragmented Foundations: Some Reflections on the Original and New Institutional Economics," *Journal of Institutional Economics* 10, no. 4 (2014): 591–611.

8. Clare Virginia Eby, *Dreiser and Veblen, Saboteurs of the Status Quo*, 1st ed. (Columbia: University of Missouri, 1999), 2.

9. Jean Baudrillard, *For a Critique of the Political Economy of the Sign* (St. Louis, MO: Telos, 1981), 31.

10. Rick Tilman, "Thorstein Veblen: Science, Revolution and the Persistence of Atavistic Continuities," in *Institutional Economics and the Theory of Social Value: Essays in Honor of Marc R. Tool*, ed. Charles M. A. Clark (Boston: Springer, 1995), 241–48; Sidney Plotkin and Rick Tilman, *The Political Ideas of Thorstein Veblen* (New Haven, CT: Yale University Press, 2011).

11. Thorstein Veblen, *The Instinct of Workmanship: And the State of Industrial Arts* (Macmillan, 1914).

12. Eby, *Dreiser and Veblen, Saboteurs of the Status Quo*, 4.

13. Phillip O'Hara, "Veblen's Critique of Marx's Philosophical Preconceptions of Political Economy," *European Journal of the History of Economic Thought* 4, no. 1 (1997): 68.

14. Thorstein Veblen, *The Theory of the Leisure Class*, ed. Martha Banta (Oxford: Oxford University Press, 2009); Thorstein Veblen, *The Theory of Business Enterprise* (New York: C. Scribner's Sons, 1915); William Dugger and Howard Sherman, "Institutionalist and Marxist Theories of Evolution," *Journal of Economic Issues* 31, no. 4 (1997): 991–1009; Doug Brown, "Institutionalism, Critical Theory, and the Administered Society," *Journal of Economic Issues* 19, no. 2 (1985): 559–66; Gonzalo Caballero and David Soto-Onate, "The Diversity and Rapprochement of Theories of Institutional Change: Original Institutionalism and New Institutional Economics," *Journal of Economic Issues* 49, no. 4 (December 2015): 947–77; Christopher Kingston and Gonzalo Caballero, "Comparing Theories of Institutional Change," *Journal of Institutional Economics* 5, no. 2 (2009): 151–80; John Hall and Udo Ludwig, "Veblen, Myrdal, and the Convergence Hypothesis: Toward an Institutionalist Critique," *Journal of Economic Issues* 44, no. 4 (2010): 943–61; Floyd B. McFarland, "Thorstein Veblen Versus the Institutionalists," *Review of Radical Political Economics* 17, no. 4 (1985): 95–105; Rick Tilman, "Some Recent Interpretations of Thorstein Veblen's Theory of Institutional Change," *Journal of Economic Issues* 21, no. 2 (1987): 683–90; Roy Suddaby, "Can Institutional Theory Be Critical?," *Journal of Management Inquiry* 24, no. 1 (January 1, 2015): 93–95; Marc R. Tool, *Evolutionary Economics: Foundations of Institutional Thought* (M. E. Sharpe, 1988); Timothy Wunder and Thomas Kemp, "Institutionalism and the State: Founding Views Reexamined," *Forum for Social Economics* 37, no. 1 (2008): 27–42.

15. Thorstein Veblen, *Essays in Our Changing Order* (Transaction Publishers, 1997). In particular, see the essay in this volume "The Barbarian Status of Women," where Veblen makes the case that the origins of private property are based on the ownership and enslavement of women. Thus, the ornamental and wildly impractical aspects of women's dress were updated ways of displaying wasteful ownership that were emblematic of the cultural lag of a bygone era of owning humans.

16. Plotkin and Tilman, *The Political Ideas of Thorstein Veblen*.

17. Veblen, *The Theory of the Leisure Class*. Whether members of the leisure class have a job is beside the point because they are so highly paid that the idea of

wage for work becomes on its face ludicrous, but it does rationalize habit of thought about remuneration resulting from productivity from neoclassical economics.

18. Sidney Plotkin, *Veblen's America: The Conspicuous Case of Donald J. Trump* (New York: Anthem, 2018).

19. L. Randall Wray, "Veblen's 'Theory of Business Enterprise' and Keynes's Monetary Theory of Production," *Journal of Economic Issues* 41, no. 2 (2007): 617–24.

20. A recent example that emerged during the global financial crisis of 2008 that might starkly show this difference is between General Motors (GM), the manufacturer of automobiles, and its subsidiary General Motors Acceptance Corporation (GMAC), which claimed rent on financing the sale of automobiles through loans. GMAC, being solely a concern of pecuniary gain, reaped far more income than did the actual sale of automobiles. One might also look at home mortgage financing as opposed to the home-building industry. These things are, of course, related; after all, GMAC doesn't work unless GM makes cars, but it creates a layer of rent-seeking for intermediaries.

21. Alison Coleman, "Is Google's Model of the Creative Workplace the Future of the Office?" *The Guardian*, February 11, 2016, https://www.theguardian.com /careers/2016/feb/11/is-googles-model-of-the-creative-workplace-the-future-of -the-office.

22. Brown, "Institutionalism, Critical Theory, and the Administered Society."

23. The Frankfurt School theorist Herbert Marcuse noted that this process, while not explicitly referencing Veblen, is the pacification of the working class to neutralize its class potential. Meanwhile, John Kenneth Galbraith referred to this skimming as the "bezzle"—the undisclosed embezzlement that was the cost of doing business that enriches businesspeople.

24. Thorstein Veblen, *The Engineers and the Price System* (B. W. Huebsch, 1921), 14.

25. Dugger and Sherman, "Institutionalist and Marxist Theories of Evolution," 993.

26. Veblen, *The Theory of Business Enterprise.*

27. Plotkin and Tilman, *The Political Ideas of Thorstein Veblen*, 33. Whether this technological rationality was too easily assumed to be a critical rationality was a criticism from the left, in particular the Frankfurt School.

28. Plotkin and Tilman, *The Political Ideas of Thorstein Veblen*, 62, 35.

29. Sidney Plotkin, "The Critic as Quietist: Thorstein Veblen's Radical Realism," *Common Knowledge* 16, no. 1 (December 25, 2009): 79–94.

30. Ross E. Mitchell, "Learning from Veblen's Masterless Man for Grassroots Democratic Change," in *The Anthem Companion to Thorstein Veblen*, ed. Sidney Plotkin (New York: Anthem, 2016), 237–56.

31. The prevalence of mid-level marketing (MLM) schemes, as well as the crop of business literature about how participating in business enterprise is a kind of entrepreneurship of the self, points to the persistence of this myth of being masterless, but this is a masterlessness that is not based on being able to make a self-sufficient life but instead by exploiting other people.

32. Thorstein Veblen, *The Vested Interests and the Common Man: The Modern Point of View and the New Order* (New York: B. W. Huebsch, 1920), 36.

33. Clare Virginia Eby, "Babbitt as Veblenian Critique of Manliness," *American Studies* 34, no. 2 (1993): 8.

34. Benjamin René Jordan, *Modern Manhood and the Boy Scouts of America: Citizenship, Race, and the Environment, 1910–1930* (Chapel Hill: University of North Carolina Press, 2016).

35. Judith Butler, "Performative Acts and Gender Constitution: An Essay in Phenomenology and Feminist Theory," *Theatre Journal* 40, no. 4 (1988): 519–31.

36. Thorstein Veblen, *Absentee Ownership: Business Enterprise in Recent Times—the Case of America* (New Brunswick, NJ: Routledge, 1996).

37. "Soviet of Engineers" is surely emblematic of Veblen's sarcasm but is also coming from the person who earnestly reported to the American Farm Bureau to directly employ the tens of thousands of members of the Industrial Workers of the World to make up a projected labor shortage in the 1918 grain harvest caused by to World War I. Thorstein Veblen, "Using the I.W.W. to Harvest Grain," *Journal of Political Economy* 40, no. 6 (1932): 797–807. He also wrote an article entitled "Bolshevism Is a Menace—to Whom?" (1919), where he caustically remarked that the urge to bring democracy into the workplace is only a problem for the vested interests who extract profit from workers. This is all to say that Veblen uses these needling terms consciously to skewer the archaic habits of mind that infect the business industry and make it geared toward private profit rather than toward the public production of the ends of life.

38. Mark Cowling and James Martin, eds., *Marx's "Eighteenth Brumaire": (Post)Modern Interpretations* (London: Pluto, 2002), 19.

39. Caballero and Soto-Onate, "The Diversity and Rapprochement of Theories of Institutional Change"; Hodgson, "On Fuzzy Frontiers and Fragmented Foundations"; Kingston and Caballero, "Comparing Theories of Institutional Change." In political science, institutionalism since the 1990s has arguably branched into three different kinds of "new" institutionalisms—historical, rational choice, and sociological, and perhaps a fourth, discursive institutionalism. Historical institutionalism focuses on always already existing institutions that are structural determinants that shape the scope of agentic behavior. Rational choice institutionalism tries to quantitatively unveil the strategic calculus between individual behavior and institutions. Finally, sociological institutionalism uses the culturally embedded practices that shape the agents before they enter a decision-making arena. Regardless of the daylight between these three institutionalisms, it is not clear what makes these "new" or what distinguishes them from the "old" institutionalisms. We hark back to Veblen because his institutionalism does not assume already existing institutions, nor does it posit individuals finding themselves in confrontation with institutions and deciding what to do (this might be a weakness of American political science—they may indeed recognize that institutions like the state are not

neutral arbiters among competing interests but are instead constellations of bureaucracy, interest groups, etc. Still, in this story, individuals confront institutions that are clearly defined [like Congress], have structural roles, and shape parameters of action). This still keeps institutions as static, whereas Veblen's institutionalism is dynamic, where individuals do not confront institutions but shape them, and where institutions are not monoliths that streamline behavior but instead condition the habits of mind of agents. While this book is less interested in the problems of the various "new" institutionalisms, it is important to at least justify why Veblen and his "old" institutionalism fits the bill for the task at hand.

40. This can work in conjunction with, or apart from, the Marxian idea of "false consciousness." A Veblenian analysis would not adopt this framework because it assumes too much of a teleological thrust, that there is a true consciousness that is being occluded. That is, by assuming that the working class must recognize itself as the motor of history and the class-for-itself and that anything else is aberrant places too much in the basket of the final cause of the proletariat. Veblen, absolutely a socialist, definitely thought that the working class *should* be in charge of production to better rationalize making the ends of life and to provide a better foundation for human flourishing, but he would not admit that this was its historical *destiny*. Things could always go otherwise (and perhaps do, and perhaps for the worse).

41. Anne Mayhew, "Culture: Core Concept Under Attack," *Journal of Economic Issues* 21, no. 2 (1987): 586–603.

42. Not all of which are new. Nationalism was a chief concern of Veblen's and remains so now because of its atavistic impulses, which preclude international cooperation. Even still, consider something like privacy in an ongoing evolution of digitalization. The atavistic impulse here of deference to authority causes the cultural lag of the following kind of habit of mind: that one has nothing to fear if one has done nothing wrong. In the level of surveillance from both public and private organizations, such an attitude fails to come to grips with the scope of the technology and defaults to the kind of attitude Foucault detailed from the eighteenth century, where privacy was a matter of making legible a certain kind of citizen to a state apparatus, whose governmentality was centered around identification, criminality, and punishment.

43. Tilman, "Thorstein Veblen."

44. This is not linear, of course. Institutions might string along, and a confluence of events might cause them to be reanimated. Veblen thought patriotism functioned this way, lying in wait, ready to be reanimated in the run-up to a war—in his contemporaneous case, World War I.

45. This is not dissimilar from institutionalisms in other radical strains, though with perhaps different political impacts. Ernesto Laclau discusses "sedimentation" in his 1990 text *New Reflections on the Revolution of Our Time*. Using a stratigraphical metaphor, institutions become layers of sediment whose origins

are forgotten but that are a result of, as well as distinct from, the preceding institutional arrangements. The idea of forgetting maps onto Veblen's notion of imbecility. Still, there are some important differences. Sedimentation only makes sense in a backward-looking register. That is, it is only definable when the next layer has started. For Veblen, this makes it inadequate as a scientific theory, because it cannot account for the immanent developments as they happen. Veblen savaged the disciplines of economics for not being scientific and being content merely to taxonomize economic phenomena or insist on the niceties of teleological equilibrium.

46. Veblen made this critique of "Coxey's Army." In the 1890s, Jacob Coxey founded a movement for unemployed people to petition the federal government to hire them directly. Veblen fully supported the ends of the movement (see also note 37 in this chapter), but he noted that Jacob Coxey was a businessman whose enterprise stood to gain from direct employment and that the movement was not about changing the relations of labor and capital per se but about using the power of the federal government to maintain a status quo for the institution of the business enterprise. Veblen's critique of the "Army of the Commonweal" presaged many of the radical critiques of what can broadly be summed up in FDR's New Deal suite of policy implementations. Basically, Veblen was concerned that "cephalization," or centralization, would be an accelerant for an institution becoming aloof and (more) imbecilic.

47. William Waller, "Public Policy Adrift: Veblen's Blind Drift and Neoliberalism," *Forum for Social Economics* 46, no. 3 (2017): 223–33.

48. This might give a whole new cast to the idea of "resilience."

49. Veblen, *Absentee Ownership*, 19.

50. Waller, "Public Policy Adrift," 226.

51. Plotkin and Tilman, *The Political Ideas of Thorstein Veblen*, 44.

52. Timothy W. Luke, *Ecocritique: Contesting the Politics of Nature, Economy, and Culture* (Minneapolis: University of Minnesota Press, 1997).

53. Ann Jennings and William Waller, "Evolutionary Economics and Cultural Hermeneutics: Veblen, Cultural Relativism, and Blind Drift," *Journal of Economic Issues* 28, no. 4 (1994): 997–1030.

54. Waller, "Public Policy Adrift," 226.

55. John D. Kelly, "Reigniting the Anthropology of Capitalism: Returning to Veblen, After Postmodernism, After Postcoloniality," in *The Anthem Companion to Thorstein Veblen*, ed. Sidney Plotkin (New York: Anthem, 2016), 178.

56. Waller, "Public Policy Adrift," 224.

57. William Dugger and Howard Sherman, "Institutionalist and Marxist Theories of Evolution," *Journal of Economic Issues* 31, no. 4 (1997): 992.

58. Philip Mirowski and Dieter Plehwe, eds., *The Road from Mont Pèlerin: The Making of the Neoliberal Thought Collective* (Cambridge, MA: Harvard University Press, 2009).

59. As Mirowski and Plehwe have shown in *The Road from Mont Pèlerin*, the drift of institutions toward neoliberalism was a conscious effort that has since become blindly accepted. In other words, there is no reason to think that just because institutions might be wrested toward a certain end that it is a socially desirable end.

60. Dugger and Sherman, "Institutionalist and Marxist Theories of Evolution," 992.

61. Luke, "Beyond Prepper Culture as Right-Wing Extremism."

62. Tony Lawson, "Process, Order and Stability in Veblen," *Cambridge Journal of Economics* 39, no. 4 (2015): 8.

63. Max Weber, *Max Weber on the Methodology of the Social Sciences* (Free Press, 1949), 88–89.

64. Timothy W. Luke, *Ideology and Soviet Industrialization* (Westport, CT: Greenwood, 1985), 18.

65. Lawson, "Process, Order, and Stability in Veblen," 10.

66. McFarland, "Thorstein Veblen Versus the Institutionalists," 98.

67. Tilman, "Some Recent Interpretations of Thorstein Veblen's Theory of Institutional Change," 688.

2. CRAFTING A PREPPING AMERICAN

1. In fact, internal government documents such as the infamous "Gaither Report" indicate that the US federal government was well aware that "passive" defenses such as homemade fallout shelters were not adequate to the threat of nuclear war and that they would lead to "probably unacceptable" numbers of casualties.

2. Mischa Honeck, *Our Frontier Is the World: The Boy Scouts in the Age of American Ascendancy*, Illustrated ed. (Ithaca, NY: Cornell University Press, 2018), 25–28.

3. Jordan, *Modern Manhood and the Boy Scouts of America*, 18.

4. Jordan, *Modern Manhood and the Boy Scouts of America*, 6–7.

5. Jordan, *Modern Manhood and the Boy Scouts of America*, 5.

6. Martha Banta, *Taylored Lives: Narrative Productions in the Age of Taylor, Veblen, and Ford* (Chicago: University of Chicago Press, 1995), 17.

7. Jordan, *Modern Manhood and the Boy Scouts of America*, 5.

8. Jordan, *Modern Manhood and the Boy Scouts of America*, 45–46.

9. Banta, *Taylored Lives*.

10. Banta, *Taylored Lives*.

11. Jordan, *Modern Manhood and the Boy Scouts of America*, 99–100.

12. Thorstein Veblen, *Imperial Germany and the Industrial Revolution* (London: Macmillan, 1915).

13. Honeck, *Our Frontier Is the World*, 5–6.

14. Honeck, *Our Frontier Is the World*.

15. Honeck, *Our Frontier Is the World*, 8–9.
16. Sarah Mills, "'An Instruction in Good Citizenship': Scouting and the Historical Geographies of Citizenship Education," *Transactions—Institute of British Geographers (1965)* 38, no. 1 (2013): 120–34.
17. David Macleod, "Original Intent: Establishing the Creed and Control of Boy Scouting in the United States," in *Scouting Frontiers: Youth and the Scout Movement's First Century*, ed. Nelson R. Block and Tammy M. Proctor (Newcastle-upon-Tyne: Cambridge Scholars, 2009), 16.
18. Honeck, *Our Frontier Is the World*. This would also change with World War II, where the BSA not only was an openly pro-military organization, but many scouting troops also spent time various American bases afterward, as youthful Cold Warriors. Honeck, *Our Frontier Is the World*, 245.
19. Kaplan, "Manifest Domesticity."
20. Dugger and Sherman, "Institutionalist and Marxist Theories of Evolution."
21. Robert H. MacDonald, *Sons of the Empire: The Frontier and the Boy Scout Movement, 1890–1918* (Toronto, CA: University of Toronto Press, 1993).
22. Honeck, *Our Frontier Is the World*.
23. Joy Schulz, "Making Men Into Boys: How the Boy Scouts of America Put on the Uniform of U.S. Imperialism and Became the Face of Twentieth-Century Masculinity," *Diplomatic History* 43, no. 5 (2019): 956–58.
24. Jordan, *Modern Manhood and the Boy Scouts of America*, 100.
25. William H. Whyte Jr., *The Organization Man* (Doubleday Anchor, 1957).
26. "What Are the Scout Oath and Scout Law?," Boy Scouts of America, n.d., https://www.scouting.org/about/faq/question10/.
27. Honeck, *Our Frontier Is the World*.
28. Jordan, *Modern Manhood and the Boy Scouts of America*.
29. Thorstein Veblen, *The Higher Learning in America: A Memorandum on the Conduct of Universities by Business Men* (Baltimore, MD: Johns Hopkins University Press, 1926).
30. Consider the fictional world of HBO's *Succession*, where doing business is often referred to as a battle or something to be "won," and, in so doing, businesspeople "kill" their rivals by outmaneuvering them.
31. "History of the BSA Fact Sheet," Boy Scouts of America Innovation and Research, n.d., https://filestore.scouting.org/filestore/pdf/210–531_WB.pdf.
32. Honeck, *Our Frontier Is the World*.
33. Anna Westberg Brostrom, "'Wild Scouts': Swedish Scouting Preparing Responsible Citizens for the Twenty-First Century," *Child & Youth Services* 34, no. 1 (2013): 9–22.
34. Westberg Brostrom, "'Wild Scouts.'"
35. Jordan, *Modern Manhood and the Boy Scouts of America*.
36. "The Conservation Legacy of Theodore Roosevelt," October 25, 2016, https://www.doi.gov/blog/conservation-legacy-theodore-roosevelt.

37. Max Oelschlaeger, *The Idea of Wilderness from Prehistory to the Age of Ecology* (New Haven, CT: Yale University Press, 1991).

38. Jordan, *Modern Manhood and the Boy Scouts of America.*

39. Jordan, *Modern Manhood and the Boy Scouts of America*, 125–26.

40. Honeck, *Our Frontier Is the World*, 131.

41. Honeck, *Our Frontier Is the World*, 31, 32.

42. Anson Rabinbach, *The Human Motor* (Berkeley: University of California Press, 1992).

43. Jordan, *Modern Manhood and the Boy Scouts of America*, 141.

44. Honeck, *Our Frontier Is the World*, 36.

45. Honeck, *Our Frontier Is the World*, 12.

46. Jordan, *Modern Manhood and the Boy Scouts of America*, 9.

47. We again note that whether this is a historically accurate formulation of how Americans lived is beside the point. Certainly, this conception of Americanness ignores the very recent history of chattel slavery, Indian removal, and imperial expansionism. The rural yeoman farmer is simply an extension of the atavism of Veblen's "masterless men" who strode out and conquered the land, mastering nature and themselves. As we will argue, this same impulse animates prepping behavior in and beyond the nuclear age.

48. Lorne W. Barclay, *Educational Work of the Boy Scouts*, Bulletin, 1919, no. 24 (Washington, DC: ERIC Clearinghouse, 1919), 15.

49. "SEE IN SCOUT WORK END OF THE BAD BOY: Students of Juvenile Delinquency Blame Misdirected Energy for Most Cases," *New York Times*, December 5, 1915.

50. Adam Smith, *An Inquiry Into the Nature and Causes of the Wealth of Nations* (Simon & Brown, 2012), 654.

51. Veblen, *Essays in Our Changing Order.*

52. Veblen was not a Marxist, but this insight invites a Marxist synthesis with Veblen. For the less Marxian-inclined, Sraffa's *Production of Commodities by Means of Commodities* tries to capture this from an economic standpoint.

53. Evgeny Morozov, "Making It," *New Yorker*, January 13, 2014, https://www.newyorker.com/magazine/2014/01/13/making-it-2Morozov. Morozov also looks ahead and recasts "hacking" as a kind of handicraft for the digital age but notes many of the same limitations that Veblen does.

54. Veblen, *Essays in Our Changing Order.*

55. Peter Betjemann, *Talking Shop: The Language of Craft in an Age of Consumption* (Charlottesville: University of Virginia Press, 2011).

56. Peter Betjemann, "Craft and the Limits of Skill: Handicrafts Revivalism and the Problem of Technique," *Journal of Design History* 21, no. 2 (July 1, 2008): 186.

57. Betjemann, *Talking Shop*, 120.

58. While it goes beyond the scope of this chapter, Veblen's conception of "instincts" are not necessarily biological imperatives but cultural ends that humanity sets

for itself given a certain set of material facts that can be empowered or frustrated.

59. Veblen, *The Instinct of Workmanship*, 256, 276.

60. Max Horkheimer and Theodor W. Adorno, *Dialectic of Enlightenment* (Palo Alto, CA: Stanford University Press, 2002).

61. Veblen, *The Instinct of Workmanship*.

62. Paul Virilio, *Speed and Politics*, Semiotext(e) Foreign Agent Series (South Pasadena, CA: Semiotext(e), 2006).

63. Mitchell, "Learning from Veblen's Masterless Man for Grassroots Democratic Change," 239.

64. Veblen, *The Instinct of Workmanship*.

65. Plotkin and Tilman, *The Political Ideas of Thorstein Veblen*, 182.

66. Virilio, *Bunker Archeology*.

67. While Veblen was known for building his own furniture, it is likely that his upbringing in rural Minnesota was enough to shape his own habits of thought that handicrafting an agricultural existence was grueling and that there was much to be said about the release from the drudgery that industrial production represented.

68. Oscar Lovell Triggs, *Chapters in the History of the Arts and Crafts Movement* (Bohemia Guild of the Industrial Art League, 1902), 58.

69. Walter Benjamin, *Illuminations: Essays and Reflections*, ed. Hannah Arendt (New York: Schocken, 1969).

70. Veblen, *Essays in Our Changing Order*, 195.

71. Veblen, *The Theory of Business Enterprise*.

72. Veblen, *Essays in Our Changing Order*, 197.

73. Betjemann, "Craft and the Limits of Skill," 186.

74. Veblen, *Essays in Our Changing Order*, 198, 196.

75. Veblen, *The Theory of the Leisure Class*.

76. Mark Richardson, "Pre-Hacked: Open Design and the Democratisation of Product Development," *New Media & Society* 18, no. 4 (April 1, 2016): 653–66.

77. Jake Greear, "Walking, Working, and Tinkering: Perception and Practice in Environmentalism," PhD. diss., Johns Hopkins University, 2013, https://jscholar ship.library.jhu.edu/bitstream/handle/1774.2/36971/GREEAR-DISSERTATION -2013.pdf.

78. Kathleen Franz, *Tinkering: Consumers Reinvent the Early Automobile* (Philadelphia: University of Pennsylvania Press, 2011), 4, 3.

79. Franz, *Tinkering*.

80. Franz, *Tinkering*, 17.

81. Franz, *Tinkering*, 81. In the current context, this remains relevant—the myth in the late 1990s of the "killer app" or plucky dropouts making computers in the garage, as well as the "learn to code" mantra of making a living on iOS or Android, all point to a similar but, as will be shown, qualitatively different version of this phenomenon.

82. While it was once not unknown for people to build cars from start to finish, few smelt their own pig iron. In any event, consider that an automotive enthusiast does not necessarily need to know how to make an intake manifold to know how to diagnose or repair a malfunctioning one.

83. Franz, *Tinkering*.

84. Elizabeth Guffey, "Crafting Yesterday's Tomorrows: Retro-Futurism, Steampunk, and the Problem of Making in the Twenty-First Century," *Journal of Modern Craft* 7, no. 3 (November 1, 2014): 254.

85. Timothy W. Luke, "Kanban Capitalism: Power, Identity, and the Exchange in Cyberspace," 1998.

86. John M. Gross and Kenneth R. McInnis, *Kanban Made Simple: Demystifying and Applying Toyota's Legendary Manufacturing Process* (Nashville, TN: American Management Association, 2003).

87. Andreas Folkers, "Freezing Time, Preparing for the Future: The Stockpile as a Temporal Matter of Security," *Security Dialogue* 50, no. 6 (2019): 493–511.

88. The *Ever Given* fiasco in the Suez Canal, which interrupted seafaring commerce; the ongoing chip shortage for cars; the lack of toilet paper during the first phases of the coronavirus pandemic; and the labor shortages that are decimating the service industry are all top-of-the-head examples of JIT production falling apart.

89. Jackie Charniga, "Dealers Go with Their Gut Amid Price Surge; Valuation Guides Can't Keep Up with Impact of Demand, Chip Shortage," *Automotive News* 95, no. 6990 (2021): 22.

90. Here it is easy to poke fun at Elon Musk, the plucky CEO of the upstart Tesla, which is only dubiously profitable and required an infusion of venture capital in part from his own fortune of founding PayPal (and the family fortune preceding that of even more alarming origin). But even looking at Lordstown Motors in Ohio (which engaged in securities fraud to avoid being short sold out of existence, on top of having automobiles that were susceptible to go up in flames) or Rivian in California (which optimistically hopes to have a fleet of ten thousand of its vehicles on the road by 2030), among others, shows that knowing how to make a car is different than navigating the exigencies of a JIT machine process, which heavily disfavors late entrants into this highly developed market.

91. Luke, "Kanban Capitalism."

92. Josh McHugh, "For the Love of Hacking," *Forbes*, https://www.forbes.com/forbes/1998/0810/6203094a.html.

93. Timothy W. Luke, "What Is Information? The Neoliberal Turn, Digitalization, and Interdisciplinarity," in *Transforming Higher Education: Economy, Democracy, and the University*, ed. Stephen J. Rosow and Thomas Kriger (Lanham, MD: Lexington, 2010).

94. Ricardo Antunes, *The Meanings of Work: Essay on the Affirmation and Negation of Work* (Leiden: Brill, 2012).

95. "FEMA Grants Management—OneGlobe, LLC," http://www.oneglobeit.com /?page_id=543.

96. Scott Mitchell, "Narratives of Resistance and Repair in Consumer Society," *Third Text* 32, no. 1 (January 2, 2018): 61.

97. "Motor Vehicle Owners' Right to Repair Act," 109 H.R. 2048 § (2005).

98. Nicholas A. Mirr, "Defending the Right to Repair: An Argument for Federal Legislation Guaranteeing the Right to Repair," *Iowa Law Review* 105, 110. 5 (July 2020): 2393–2424.

99. Mitchell, "Narratives of Resistance and Repair in Consumer Society," 61.

100. Michael F. Mills, "Preparing for the Unknown . . . Unknowns: 'Doomsday' Prepping and Disaster Risk Anxiety in the United States," *Journal of Risk Research* 22, no. 10 (October 3, 2019): 1267–79.

101. Gwendolyn Audrey Foster, "Consuming the Apocalypse, Marketing Bunker Materiality," *Quarterly Review of Film and Video* 33, no. 4 (May 18, 2016): 285–302.

102. Casey R. Lynch, " 'Vote with Your Feet': Neoliberalism, the Democratic Nation-State, and Utopian Enclave Libertarianism," *Political Geography* 59 (2017): 82–91.

103. Mihir Zaveri et al., "How the Storm Turned Basement Apartments Into Death Traps," *New York Times*, September 2, 2021, https://www.nytimes.com/2021/09 /02/nyregion/basement-apartment-floods-deaths.html; CAL FIRE, "2021 Fire Season Outlook," https://www.fire.ca.gov/incidents/; Andrew Weber, "Texas Winter Storm Death Toll Goes up to 210, Including 43 Deaths in Harris County," *Houston Public Media*, July 14, 2021, https://www.houstonpublicmedia.org /articles/news/energy-environment/2021/07/14/403191/texas-winter-storm -death-toll-goes-up-to-210-including-43-deaths-in-harris-county/.

104. Cynthia Belmont and Angela Stroud, "Bugging Out: Apocalyptic Masculinity and Disaster Consumerism in *Offgrid* Magazine," *Feminist Studies* 46, no. 2 (2020): 431–58; Jordan, *Modern Manhood and the Boy Scouts of America*.

105. Mitchell, "Narratives of Resistance and Repair in Consumer Society."

106. Jeremy Hunsinger and Andrew Schrock, eds., *Making Our World: The Hacker and Maker Movements in Context* (New York: Peter Lang, 2018).

107. Mills, "Preparing for the Unknown . . . Unknowns."

108. Barclay, *Educational Work of the Boy Scouts*, 15.

109. Executive Office of the President: Office of Civil and Defense Mobilization, "Annual Report of the Federal Civil Defense Administration for Fiscal Year 1958" (Washington, DC: U.S. Government Printing Office, 1959), 9.

110. Executive Office of the President: Office of Civil and Defense Mobilization, 9.

3. FROM THE BUNKER FAMILY TO BUNKERIZATION

1. Ian Angus, *Facing the Anthropocene: Fossil Capitalism and the Crisis of the Earth System* (New York: New York University Press, 2016).

2. Jan Zalasiewicz et al., "When Did the Anthropocene Begin? A Mid-Twentieth-Century Boundary Level Is Stratigraphically Optimal," *Quaternary International* 383 (October 5, 2015): 196–203; Colin N. Waters et al., "Can Nuclear Weapons Fallout Mark the Beginning of the Anthropocene Epoch?," *Bulletin of the Atomic Scientists* 71, no. 3 (May 1, 2015): 46–57.

3. "Current Time—2023," *Bulletin of the Atomic Scientists*, 2023, https://thebulletin.org/doomsday-clock/current-time/.

4. "Nuclear Testing," n.d., https://www.atomicarchive.com/almanac/test-sites/index.html.

5. Joseph Masco, *The Future of Fallout, and Other Episodes in Radioactive World-Making* (Durham, NC: Duke University Press, 2021), 2.

6. Masco, *The Future of Fallout*, 5, 7.

7. Philip Mirowski and Dieter Plehwe, *The Road from Mont Pèlerin* (Cambridge, MA: Harvard University Press, 2009).

8. Carl Schmitt, *Political Theology* (Chicago: University of Chicago Press, 2005), 5.

9. James S. Lay, "A Report to the National Security Council—NSC 68," Truman Papers (Charlottesville, VA: The Miller Center, April 12, 1950), 8, http://web1.millercenter.org/cpc/brownell/mod5-doc1-NSC-68.pdf.

10. Guy Oakes, *The Imaginary War: Civil Defense and American Cold War Culture* (London: Oxford University Press, 1995), 49, 105.

11. Harry S. Truman, "Statement by the President Upon Signing the Federal Civil Defense Act of 1950" (National Archives, Harry S. Truman Library and Museum, January 12, 1951), https://www.trumanlibrary.gov/library/public-papers/10/statement-president-upon-signing-federal-civil-defense-act-1950.

12. Kenneth Rose, *One Nation Underground: The Fallout Shelter in American Culture* (New York: New York University Press, 2004), 32–33.

13. Brett Spencer, "From Atomic Shelters to Arms Control: Libraries, Civil Defense, and American Militarism during the Cold War," *Information and Culture* 49, no. 3 (2014): 358, 364.

14. "An Underground Elementary School That Doubled as an Advanced Cold War Fallout Shelter," *Slate*, July 4, 2014, http://www.slate.com/blogs/the_eye/2014/07/04/abo_elementary_school_in_artesia_new_mexico_was_built_to_double_as_a_cold.html.

15. Oakes, *The Imaginary War*, 105.

16. Rose, *One Nation Underground*, 119.

17. This practice is still relevant in the twenty-first century. After the attacks of September 11, 2001, major Wall Street firms duplicated their services in places other than lower Manhattan.

18. Laura McEnaney, *Civil Defense Begins at Home: Militarization Meets Everyday Life in the Fifties* (Princeton, NJ: Princeton University Press, 2000), 41.

19. Masco, *The Future of Fallout*, 21.

20. Tracy C. Davis, *Stages of Emergency: Cold War Nuclear Civil Defense* (Durham, NC: Duke University Press, 2007), 24.

21. Davis, *Stages of Emergency*, 27, 35.

22. Jenny Barker-Divine, " 'Mightier Than Missiles': The Rhetoric of Civil Defense for Rural American Families, 1950–1970," *Agricultural History* 80, no. 4 (Autumn 2006): 425; Davis, *Stages of Emergency*.

23. "Nevada National Security Site," n.d., https://www.nnss.gov/pages/about.html.

24. Liam J. S. Powell, "America's Nuclear Wasteland: Conflict Landscape, Simulation, and 'Nonplace' at the Nevada Test Site," in *Beyond the Dead Horizon: Studies in Modern Conflict Archaeology* (Oxford: Oxbow, 2012), 217.

25. Andrew G. Kirk and Kristian Purcell, *Doom Towns: The People and Landscapes of Atomic Testing, A Graphic History* (Oxford: Oxford University Press, 2016).

26. "Civil Test Effects," U.S. Department of Energy, August 2013, https://nnss.gov/wp-content/uploads/2023/04/NNSS-CIVI-U-0048-Rev01.pdf.

27. Andrew G. Kirk, "Rereading the Nature of Atomic Doom Towns," *Environmental History* 17, no. 3 (July 2012): 639, 637.

28. Taylor N. Johnson, " 'The Most Bombed Nation on Earth': Western Shoshone Resistance to the Nevada National Security Site," *Atlantic Journal of Communication* 26, no. 4 (October 9, 2018): 224–39.

29. Rob Nixon, *Slow Violence and the Environmentalism of the Poor* (Cambridge, MA: Harvard University Press, 2013).

30. Powell, "America's Nuclear Wasteland," 220.

31. John Wills, "Exploding the 1950s Consumer Dream," *Pacific Historical Review* 88, no. 3 (2019): 411, 413.

32. Wills, "Exploding the 1950s Consumer Dream," 414.

33. Kylie Kinley, "Flashback Friday: When Behlen Manufacturing in Columbus Tested Shed with Atomic Bomb," *History Nebraska*, 2016, https://history.nebraska.gov/blog/flashback-friday-when-behlen-manufacturing-columbus-tested-shed-atomic-bomb.

34. Masco, *The Future of Fallout*, 170–71.

35. Wills, "Exploding the 1950s Consumer Dream."

36. Oakes, *The Imaginary War*.

37. Rose, *One Nation Underground*.

38. "Civil Defense: Boom to Bust," *Time*, May 18, 1962, http://content.time.com/time/subscriber/article/0,33009,896157,00.html.

39. "Atlas Survival Shelters—Best Underground Steel Fallout Shelters & Bomb Shelters in The Industry," n.d., https://www.atlassurvivalshelters.com/.

40. Bruce Watson, "We Couldn't Run, So We Hoped We Could Hide," *Smithsonian Magazine*, 1994.

41. Thomas Bishop, " 'The Struggle to Sell Survival': Family Fallout Shelters and the Limits of Consumer Citizenship," *Modern American History* 2 (2019): 119.

42. "Shelter Boom," *Newsweek*, 1961.
43. Bishop, " 'The Struggle to Sell Survival,' " 129.
44. Rose, *One Nation Underground*, 191.
45. "Civil Defense."
46. "Civil Defense."
47. "Would-Be Shelter Mogul Folds Up," *New York Times*, September 11, 1951, http://timesmachine.nytimes.com/timesmachine/1951/09/11/84860869.html.
48. Rose, *One Nation Underground*, 187.
49. David K. Berlo et al., "The Fallout Protection Booklet: A Report of Public Attitudes Toward and Information About Civil Defense" (Alexandria: Defense Documentation Center for Scientific and Technical Information, 1963), 7, 9, 10, https://apps.dtic.mil/sti/citations/AD0404511.
50. Berlo et al., "The Fallout Protection Booklet," 13–14, 16.
51. Berlo et al., "The Fallout Protection Booklet," 21, 23–24.
52. Rose, *One Nation Underground*, 201–2.
53. "Religion: Gun Thy Neighbor?" *Time*, August 18, 1961, http://content.time.com/time/subscriber/article/0,33009,872694-1,00.html.
54. "Religion: Gun Thy Neighbor?"
55. Oakes, *The Imaginary War*, 32.
56. Oakes, *The Imaginary War*, 25.
57. Oakes, *The Imaginary War*.
58. Sheldon S. Wolin, *Fugitive Democracy and Other Essays* (Princeton, NJ: Princeton University Press, 2016).
59. Val Peterson, "Panic: The Ultimate Weapon?," *Colliers*, August 21, 1953, 100.
60. Peterson, "Panic: The Ultimate Weapon?"
61. Corey Robin, *Fear: The History of a Political Idea* (London: Oxford University Press, 2006), 4.
62. Robin, *Fear*, 44.
63. Robin, *Fear*, 45.
64. Robin, *Fear*, 47, 87.
65. Robin, *Fear*.
66. Lay, "A Report to the National Security Council—NSC 68."
67. Char Miller, "In the Sweat of Our Brow: Citizenship in American Domestic Practice During WWII—Victory Gardens," *Journal of American Culture* 26, no. 3 (2003): 5.
68. Wendy Brown, *Undoing the Demos: Neoliberalism's Stealth Revolution* (Cambridge, MA: MIT Press, 2015), 26.
69. Brown, *Undoing the Demos*, 27.
70. Brown, *Undoing the Demos*, 28.
71. "House Un-American Activities Committee | Harry S. Truman," n.d., https://www.trumanlibrary.gov/education/presidential-inquiries/house-un-american-activities-committee.

72. "EXECUTIVE ORDER 9835 | Harry S. Truman," n.d., https://www.trumanlibrary .gov/library/executive-orders/9835/executive-order-9835.

73. Davis, *Stages of Emergency*, 20.

74. Robert Scheer, *With Enough Shovels: Reagan, Bush, and Nuclear War* (New York: Vintage, 1982), 18.

75. Scheer, *With Enough Shovels*, 23.

76. Scheer, *With Enough Shovels*, 22.

77. Jodi Dean, *Democracy and Other Neoliberal Fantasies* (Durham, NC: Duke University Press, 2009), 4, 11–12.

78. Dean, *Democracy and Other Neoliberal Fantasies*, 91.

79. Dean, *Democracy and Other Neoliberal Fantasies*, 94.

80. Wolin, *Fugitive Democracy and Other Essays*, 100–2.

81. Wolin, *Fugitive Democracy and Other Essays*, 102.

82. "The President and the National Security State During the Cold War | Miller Center," June 12, 2018, https://millercenter.org/the-presidency/teacher-resources /recasting-presidential-history/president-and-national-security-state-during -cold-war.

83. Lay, "A Report to the National Security Council—NSC 68," 44.

84. Joachim Wolschke-Bulmahn, "From the War-Garden to the Victory Garden: Political Aspects of Garden Culture in the United States During World War I," *Landscape Journal* 11, no. 1 (Spring 1992): 53.

85. Woodrow Wilson, "The President to the People," *Garden and Home Builder*, 1917, https://babel.hathitrust.org/cgi/pt?id=coo.31924094248956&view=1up&seq =230&q1=woodrow%20wilson.

86. Carl Vrooman, "The Patriotic Garden: Crop Conservation and Distribution," *Garden and Home Builder*, August 1917.

87. J. M. Patterson, "The Patriotic Garden: Somebody Has to Raise Everything You Eat," *The Garden Magazine*, June 1917.

88. National War Garden Commission, "Home Canning & Drying of Vegetables & Fruits" (Washington, DC, National War Garden Commission, 1919), https:// archive.org/details/homecanningdryino1nati/page/n1/mode/2up.

89. "Among Our Garden Neighbors," *Garden Magazine*, June 1918.

90. Patrick Vitale, "Wages of War: Manufacturing Nationalism During World War II," *Antipode* 43, no. 3 (2010): 783–819.

91. Miller, "In the Sweat of Our Brow," 406.

92. Miller, "In the Sweat of Our Brow," 406.

93. Cecelia Gowdy-Wygant, *Cultivating Victory: The Women's Land Army and the Victory Garden Movement* (Pittsburgh, PA: University of Pittsburgh Press, 2013), 133.

94. Gowdy-Wygant, *Cultivating Victory*, 139.

95. Peter Galison, "War Against the Center," *Grey Room* 4 (Summer 2001): 5–33.

96. Galison, "War Against the Center," 29–30.

97. Galison, "War Against the Center," 29–30.

98. *Background Notes, Marshall Islands* (U.S. Department of State, Bureau of Public Affairs, Office of Public Communication, 1994).

99. Brown, *Undoing the Demos: Neoliberalism's Stealth Revolution*, 29.

4. PREPPING IN THE SHADOW OF THE VALLEY

1. Thomas Heinrich, "Cold War Armory: Military Contracting in Silicon Valley," *Enterprise & Society* 3 (June 2002): 258.

2. Leslie Berlin, "Why Silicon Valley Will Continue to Rule," *Wired Magazine*, May 1, 2015, https://www.wired.com/2015/05/why-silicon-valley-will-continue-to-rule/.

3. Lisa Sun-Hee Park and David Naguib Pellow, *The Silicon Valley of Dreams: Environmental Justice, Immigrant Workers, and the High-Tech Global Economy* (New York: New York University Press, 2002).

4. "About," Stanford Research Park, https://stanfordresearchpark.netlify.app/about.

5. Berlin, "Why Silicon Valley Will Continue to Rule."

6. Christophe Lécuyer, *Making Silicon Valley: Innovation and the Growth of High Tech, 1930–1970* (Cambridge, MA: MIT Press, 2007), 17.

7. Lécuyer, *Making Silicon Valley*, 2.

8. Lécuyer, *Making Silicon Valley*, 5, 258.

9. Wendy Brown, *Undoing the Demos: Neoliberalism's Stealth Revolution* (Cambridge, MA: MIT Press, 2015).

10. Richard Barbrook and Andy Cameron, "The Californian Ideology," *Science as Culture*, January 1996.

11. Robert Kirsch, "You Can't Handicraft the Apocalypse: The Invidious Consequences of 'Opting Out,'" *New Political Science* 41, no. 4 (October 2, 2019): 1.

12. Jenna Schnuer, "This Startup Is Making Stylish Earthquake Survival Kits," *Entrepreneur*, March 13, 2015, https://www.entrepreneur.com/article/242518.

13. "About Preppi—Makers of the Best Emergency Preparedness Kits for Earthquakes, Hurricanes, Blizzards, and Fires.," Preppi, https://www.preppi.co/pages/about-us.

14. "The Prepster | Two-Person | 3-Day Emergency Kit Bag," Preppi, https://www.preppi.co/products/the-prepster.

15. Eleanor Ainge Roy, "New Zealand Gave Peter Thiel Citizenship After He Spent Just 12 Days There," *The Guardian*, June 29, 2017, https://www.theguardian.com/world/2017/jun/29/new-zealand-gave-peter-thiel-citizenship-after-spending-just-12-days-there.

16. Elizabeth Stamp, "Billionaire Bunkers: How the 1% Are Preparing for the Apocalypse," CNN, https://www.cnn.com/style/article/doomsday-luxury-bunkers/index.html.

17. Naomi Klein, *The Shock Doctrine: The Rise of Disaster Capitalism* (Picador USA, 2008).

18. Brown, *Undoing the Demos*, 17.
19. Brown, *Undoing the Demos*, 41.
20. Brown, *Undoing the Demos*, 65–66.
21. Stanford University, "Text of Steve Jobs' Commencement Address (2005)," *Stanford News*, June 14, 2005, https://news.stanford.edu/2005/06/14/jobs-061505/.
22. Jean Baudrillard, *For a Critique of the Political Economy of the Sign* (St. Louis, MO: Telos, 1981).
23. Brown, *Undoing the Demos*, 84.
24. Brown, *Undoing the Demos*, 84.
25. Brown, *Undoing the Demos*, 108.
26. Barbrook and Cameron, "The Californian Ideology," 1.
27. Fred Turner, *From Counterculture to Cyberculture* (Chicago: University of Chicago Press, 2006).
28. Barbrook and Cameron, "The Californian Ideology," 4.
29. Barbrook and Cameron, "The Californian Ideology," 7.
30. Barbrook and Cameron, "The Californian Ideology," 143, 163.
31. "The Dark Enlightenment, by Nick Land," *Dark Enlightenment* (blog), December 25, 2012, pt. 3, https://www.thedarkenlightenment.com/the-dark-enlightenment-by-nick-land/.
32. Scott F. Aikin, "Deep Disagreement, the Dark Enlightenment, and the Rhetoric of the Red Pill," *Journal of Applied Philosophy* 36, no. 3 (July 2019): 425.
33. Timothy W. Luke, *Anthropocene Alerts: Critical Theory of the Contemporary as Ecocritique* (Candor, NY: Telos, 2020), 267, 268.
34. "The Dark Enlightenment, by Nick Land," *Dark Enlightenment* (blog), December 25, 2012, pt. 1, https://www.thedarkenlightenment.com/the-dark-enlightenment-by-nick-land/.
35. Joseph Masco, *The Future of Fallout, and Other Episodes in Radioactive World-Making* (Durham, NC: Duke University Press, 2021), 130.
36. "The Dark Enlightenment, by Nick Land," pt. 1.
37. Patri Friedman, "Beyond Folk Activism," *Cato Unbound*, April 6, 2009, https://www.cato-unbound.org/2009/04/06/patri-friedman/beyond-folk-activism.
38. Peter Thiel, "The Education of a Libertarian," *Cato Unbound*, April 13, 2009, https://www.cato-unbound.org/2009/04/13/peter-thiel/education-libertarian.
39. Thiel, "The Education of a Libertarian."
40. Friedman, "Beyond Folk Activism."
41. Philip Mirowski and Dieter Plehwe, *The Road from Mont Pèlerin* (Cambridge, MA: Harvard University Press, 2009), 162.
42. Aikin, "Deep Disagreement."
43. "About Seasteading," *Seasteading Institute* (blog), April 6, 2020, https://www.seasteading.org/about/.
44. *BIL2012—Mencius Moldbug: How to Reboot the US Government*, https://www.youtube.com/watch?v=ZluMysK2B1E.
45. Brown, *Undoing the Demos*, 139, 141.

46. Sarah Marie Wiebe and Jennifer Lawrence, eds., *Biopolitical Disaster* (New York: Routledge, 2017).

47. Andrew Szasz, *Shopping Our Way to Safety* (Minneapolis: University of Minnesota Press, 2009).

48. Harrison Smith and Roger Burrows, "Software, Sovereignty, and the Post-Neoliberal Politics of Exit," *Theory, Culture, and Society* 38, no. 6 (2021): 145, 158.

49. Luke, *Anthropocene Alerts*, 48–49.

50. Luke, *Anthropocene Alerts*, 59.

51. Luke, *Anthropocene Alerts*, 64.

52. Herbert Marcuse, *One-Dimensional Man* (Boston: Beacon, 1968).

5. BUGGING OUT IN OUTER SPACE

1. Andrew Feenberg, *The Ruthless Critique of Everything Existing: Nature and Revolution in Marcuse's Philosophy of Praxis* (Brooklyn: Verso, 2023), 96.

2. Feenberg, *The Ruthless Critique of Everything Existing*, 102.

3. Masahide Kato, "Nuclear Globalism Traversing Rockets, Satellites, and Nuclear War Via the Strategic Gaze," *Alternatives: Global, Local, Political* 18, no. 3 (Summer 1993): 339, 348.

4. Rob Nixon, *Slow Violence and the Environmentalism of the Poor* (Cambridge, MA: Harvard University Press, 2013).

5. Ian Angus, *Facing the Anthropocene* (New York: Monthly Review Press, 2016).

6. Andy Lawrence et al., "The Case for Space Environmentalism," *Nature Astronomy* 6 (April 2022): 429.

7. Lawrence et al., "The Case for Space Environmentalism," 228–35.

8. Noriyoshi Takemura, "Astro-Green Criminology: A New Perspective Against Space Capitalism," *Toin University of Yokohama Research Bulletin* 40 (June 2019): 14.

9. Jean-Frederic Morin and Benjamin Richard, "Astro-Environmentalism: Towards a Polycentric Governance of Space Debris," *Global Policy* 12, no. 4 (September 2021): 568–73.

10. Alessandra Marino and Thomas Cheney, "Centering Environmentalism in Space Governance: Interrogating Dominance and Authority Through a Critical Legal Geography of Outer Space," *Space Policy* 63 (2023): 8.

11. Jack A. Lampkin, "Mapping the Terrain of an Astro-Green Criminology: A Case for Extending the Green Criminological Lens Outside of Planet Earth," *International Journal of Space Politics and Policy* 18, no. 3 (2020): 238–59.

12. Valerie Olson and Lisa Messeri, "Beyond the Anthropocene: Un-Earthing an Epoch," *Environment and Society* 6, no. 1 (January 1, 2015): 29.

13. Julie Michelle Klinger, *Rare Earth Frontiers* (Ithaca, NY: Cornell University Press, 2018), 8.

14. Lisa Messeri, "Gestures of Cosmic Relation and the Search for Another Earth," *Environmental Humanities* 9, no. 2 (November 2017): 332.

15. Jean-Luc Nancy, *After Fukushima* (New York: Fordham University Press, 2014), 14, 22.

16. Nancy, *After Fukushima*, 18.

17. Nancy, *After Fukushima*, 21.

18. Nancy, *After Fukushima*, 37.

19. Glenn H. Reynolds and Robert P. Merges, *Outer Space: Problems of Law and Policy*, 2nd ed. (Boulder, CO: Westview, 1997), 6.

20. "RES 2222 (XXI)," United Nations Office for Outer Space Affairs, 1996, https://www.unoosa.org/oosa/oosadoc/data/resolutions/1966/general_assembly_21st_session/res_2222_xxi.html.

21. Reynolds and Merges, *Outer Space*, 110, 105–6.

22. Reynolds and Merges, *Outer Space*, 112.

23. Kevin McCarthy, "Text—H.R.2262—114th Congress (2015–2016): U.S. Commercial Space Launch Competitiveness Act," November 25, 2015, https://www.congress.gov/bill/114th-congress/house-bill/2262/text.

24. James F. Bridenstine, "Artemis Accords," 2020.

25. Eytan Tepper, "Discourse on the Exploitation of Space Resources," *Space Policy* 59 (August 2019); Cassandra Steer, "Global Commons, Cosmic Commons: Implications of Military and Security Uses of Outer Space," *Georgetown Journal of International Affairs* 18, no. 1 (2017): 9–16.

26. Olga Khazan, "The Brain Bro," *The Atlantic*, September 13, 2016, https://www.theatlantic.com/magazine/archive/2016/10/the-brain-bro/497546/.

27. Timothy W. Luke, "The Climate Change Imaginary," *Current Sociology Monograph* 63, no. 2 (2015): 287.

28. "Elon Musk Gives a Talk at the Sorbonne, Paris—COP 21," 2015, https://www.youtube.com/watch?v=v3AmtjqqVvo.

29. Luke, "The Climate Change Imaginary," 289, 291.

30. Maria Levina, "Disrupt or Die: Mobile Health and Disruptive Innovation as Body Politics," *Television and New Media* 18, no. 6 (2017): 550.

31. Jill Lepore, "The Disruption Machine," *New Yorker*, June 16, 2014.

32. Levina, "Disrupt or Die," 560.

33. "Muse™ EEG-Powered Meditation & Sleep Headband," 2023, https://choosemuse.com/.

34. Fred Turner, *From Counterculture to Cyberculture* (Chicago: University of Chicago Press, 2006), 38.

35. Nicole Sunday Grove, "Receding Resilience: On the Planetary Moods of Disruption," *Review of International Studies* 49, no. 1 (2022): 8.

36. Grove, "Receding Resilience," 15, 18, 19.

37. "About Blue," Blue Origin, https://www.blueorigin.com/about-blue.

38. Elon Musk, "Elon Musk Answers Your Questions! | SXSW 2018," 2018, YouTube video, https://www.youtube.com/watch?v=kzlUyrccbos.

39. Elon Musk, "Elon Musk Reveals His Plan for Colonizing Mars," YouTube video, https://www.youtube.com/watch?v=W9olSzNOh8s.

40. Musk, "Elon Musk Answers Your Questions."

41. Matthew Bishop, "Philanthrocapitalism: Solving Public Problems Through Private Means," *Social Research* 80, no. 2 (Summer 2013): 474.

42. Neil Strauss, "Elon Musk: Inventor's Plans for Outer Space, Cars, Finding Love," *Rolling Stone*, November 15, 2017, https://www.rollingstone.com/culture/culture -features/elon-musk-the-architect-of-tomorrow-120850/.

43. Bryan Bishop, "Elon Musk and the Creator of *Westworld* Made an Inspirational Trailer for the Falcon Heavy Launch," *The Verge*, March 10, 2018, https://www .theverge.com/2018/3/10/17105322/elon-musk-spacex-falcon-heavy-westworld -jonathan-nolan-trailer-sxsw.

44. Luke, "The Climate Change Imaginary," 284.

45. Musk, "Elon Musk Reveals His Plan for Colonizing Mars."

46. Timothy W. Luke, "One-Dimensional Man: A Systematic Critique of Human Domination and Nature-Society Relations," *Organization and Environment* 13, no. 1 (March 2000): 99.

47. Luke, "One-Dimensional Man," 99.

48. Musk, "Elon Musk Reveals His Plan for Colonizing Mars."

CONCLUSION

1. Rowland Atkinson and Sarah Blandy, *Domestic Fortress: Fear and the New Home Front* (Manchester: Manchester University Press, 2016), 178, 23, 48.

2. Crawford Gribben, *Survival and Resistance in Evangelical America: Christian Reconstruction in the Pacific Northwest* (Oxford: Oxford University Press, 2021), 25.

3. "Rural, Sustainable, Off-Grid Property and Agents," SurvivalRealty.com, https:// www.survivalrealty.com/.

4. Paul Virilio, *Bunker Archeology* (Hudson, NY: Princeton Architectural Press, 1994), 85.

5. Paul Virilio, *Speed and Politics*, Semiotext(e) Foreign Agent Series (South Pasadena, CA: Semiotext(e), 2006), 99.

6. Virilio, *Speed and Politics*, 119, 139.

7. Virilio, *Speed and Politics*, 139.

8. David L. Pike, "Haunted Mountains, Supershelters, and the Afterlives of Cold War Infrastructure," *Journal for the Study of Religion, Nature and Culture* 13, no. 2 (2019): 16.

9. Virilio, *Bunker Archeology*, 16.

10. Virilio, *Bunker Archeology*, 21.

11. Virilio, *Bunker Archeology*, 38–39.

12. Virilio, *Bunker Archeology*, 46.

13. Virilio, *Bunker Archeology*, 22.
14. Virilio, *Bunker Archeology*, 32.
15. Sophia Maalsen and Jathan Sadowski, "The Smart Home on FIRE: Amplifying and Accelerating Domestic Surveillance," *Surveillance and Society* 17, no. 1/2 (2019): 118–24.
16. Mike Davis, *City of Quartz* (New York: Verso, 2006), 224.
17. Maalsen and Sadowski, "The Smart Home on FIRE."
18. Bradley Garrett, *Bunker* (New York: Scribner, 2020), 24–25.
19. Calum Matheson, "Enjoying the Heat: Anxiety, Fantasy, and Doomsday Prepping," in *Lacan and the Environment* (Cham: Palgrave, 2021), 140.
20. Matheson, "Enjoying the Heat," 137.

BIBLIOGRAPHY

Aikin, Scott F. "Deep Disagreement, the Dark Enlightenment, and the Rhetoric of the Red Pill." *Journal of Applied Philosophy* 36, no. 3 (July 2019): 425.

Angus, Ian. *Facing the Anthropocene: Fossil Capitalism and the Crisis of the Earth System*. New York: NYU Press, 2016.

Antunes, Ricardo. *The Meanings of Work: Essay on the Affirmation and Negation of Work*. Leiden: Brill, 2012.

Atkinson, Rowland, and Sarah Blandy. *Domestic Fortress: Fear and the New Home Front*. Manchester: Manchester University Press, 2016.

Banta, Martha. *Taylored Lives: Narrative Productions in the Age of Taylor, Veblen, and Ford*. Chicago: University of Chicago Press, 1995.

Barbrook, Richard, and Andy Cameron. "The Californian Ideology." *Science as Culture*, January 1996.

Barclay, Lorne W. *Educational Work of the Boy Scouts*. Bulletin, 1919, no. 24. Washington, DC: ERIC Clearinghouse, 1919.

Barker-Divine, Jenny. " 'Mightier Than Missiles': The Rhetoric of Civil Defense for Rural American Families, 1950–1970." *Agricultural History* 80, no. 4 (Autumn 2006): 415–35.

Baudrillard, Jean. *For a Critique of the Political Economy of the Sign*. St. Louis, MO: Telos, 1981.

Belew, Katherine. *Bring the War Home*. Cambridge, MA: Harvard University Press, 2018.

Belmont, Cynthia, and Angela Stroud. "Bugging Out: Apocalyptic Masculinity and Disaster Consumerism in *Offgrid* Magazine." *Feminist Studies* 46, no. 2 (2020): 431–58.

Benjamin, Walter. *Illuminations: Essays and Reflections*. Ed. Hannah Arendt. New York: Schocken, 1969.

Berlin, Leslie. "Why Silicon Valley Will Continue to Rule." *Wired*, May 1, 2015. https://www.wired.com/2015/05/why-silicon-valley-will-continue-to-rule/.

Berlo, David K., Erwin P. Bettinghaus, Dan Costley, and Robert Van. "The Fallout Protection Booklet: A Report of Public Attitudes Toward and Information About Civil Defense." Alexandria, VA: Defense Documentation Center for Scientific and Technical Information, 1963. https://apps.dtic.mil/sti/citations/AD0404511.

Betjemann, Peter. "Craft and the Limits of Skill: Handicrafts Revivalism and the Problem of Technique." *Journal of Design History* 21, no. 2 (July 1, 2008): 183–93.

——. *Talking Shop: The Language of Craft in an Age of Consumption*. Charlottesville: University of Virginia Press, 2011.

Bishop, Bryan. "Elon Musk and the Creator of Westworld Made an Inspirational Trailer for the Falcon Heavy Launch." *The Verge*, March 10, 2018. https://www.theverge.com/2018/3/10/17105322/elon-musk-spacex-falcon-heavy-westworld-jonathan-nolan-trailer-sxsw.

Bishop, Matthew. "Philanthrocapitalism: Solving Public Problems Through Private Means." *Social Research* 80, no. 2 (Summer 2013): 473–99.

Bishop, Thomas. *Every Home a Fortress: Cold War Fatherhood and the Family Fallout Shelter*. Amherst: University of Massachusetts Press, 2020.

——. "'The Struggle to Sell Survival': Family Fallout Shelters and the Limits of Consumer Citizenship." *Modern American History* 2 (2019): 117–38.

Brown, Doug. "Institutionalism, Critical Theory, and the Administered Society." *Journal of Economic Issues* 19, no. 2 (1985): 559–66.

Brown, Norman O., and Christopher Lasch. *Life Against Death: The Psychoanalytical Meaning of History*. 2nd ed. Middletown, CT: Wesleyan University Press, 1985.

Brown, Wendy. *Undoing the Demos: Neoliberalism's Stealth Revolution*. Cambridge, MA: MIT Press, 2015.

Butler, Judith. "Performative Acts and Gender Constitution: An Essay in Phenomenology and Feminist Theory." *Theatre Journal* 40, no. 4 (1988): 519–31.

Caballero, Gonzalo, and David Soto-Onate. "The Diversity and Rapprochement of Theories of Institutional Change: Original Institutionalism and New Institutional Economics." *Journal of Economic Issues* 49, no. 4 (December 2015): 947–77.

Charniga, Jackie. "Dealers Go with Their Gut Amid Price Surge; Valuation Guides Can't Keep Up with Impact of Demand, Chip Shortage." *Automotive News* 95, no. 6990 (2021): 22.

Coleman, Alison. "Is Google's Model of the Creative Workplace the Future of the Office?" *The Guardian*, February 11, 2016. https://www.theguardian.com/careers/2016/feb/11/is-googles-model-of-the-creative-workplace-the-future-of-the-office.

Cooper, Helene, Julian E. Barnes, and Eric Schmitt. "Russian Military Leaders Discussed Use of Nuclear Weapons, U.S. Officials Say." *New York Times*, November 2,

2022. https://www.nytimes.com/2022/11/02/us/politics/russia-ukraine-nuclear
-weapons.html.

Cowling, Mark, and James Martin, eds. *Marx's "Eighteenth Brumaire": (Post)Modern Interpretations*. London: Pluto, 2002.

Davis, Mike. *City of Quartz*. New York: Verso, 2006.

Davis, Tracy C. *Stages of Emergency: Cold War Nuclear Civil Defense*. Durham, NC: Duke University Press, 2007.

Dean, Jodi. *Democracy and Other Neoliberal Fantasies*. Durham, NC: Duke University Press, 2009.

Dugger, William, and Howard Sherman. "Institutionalist and Marxist Theories of Evolution." *Journal of Economic Issues* 31, no. 4 (1997): 991–1009.

Eby, Clare Virginia. "Babbitt as Veblenian Critique of Manliness." *American Studies (Lawrence)* 34, no. 2 (1993): 5–23.

——. *Dreiser and Veblen, Saboteurs of the Status Quo*. 1st ed. Columbia: University of Missouri, 1999.

Executive Office of the President: Office of Civil and Defense Mobilization. "Annual Report of the Federal Civil Defense Administration for Fiscal Year 1958." Washington, DC: U.S. Government Printing Office, 1959.

Eytan Tepper. "Discourse on the Exploitation of Space Resources." *Space Policy* 59 (August 2019).

Feenberg, Andrew. *The Ruthless Critique of Everything Existing: Nature and Revolution in Marcuse's Philosophy of Praxis*. Brooklyn: Verso, 2023.

Folkers, Andreas. "Freezing Time, Preparing for the Future: The Stockpile as a Temporal Matter of Security." *Security Dialogue* 50, no. 6 (2019): 493–511.

Fong, Benjamin. *Death and Mastery: Psychoanalytic Drive Theory and the Subject of Late Capitalism*. New York: Columbia University Press, 2018.

Foster, Gwendolyn Audrey. "Consuming the Apocalypse, Marketing Bunker Materiality." *Quarterly Review of Film and Video* 33, no. 4 (May 18, 2016): 285–302.

Franz, Kathleen. *Tinkering: Consumers Reinvent the Early Automobile*. Philadelphia: University of Pennsylvania Press, 2011.

Friedman, Milton. "Neoliberalism and Its Prospects." https://miltonfriedman.hoover
.org/internal/media/dispatcher/214957/full.

Friedman, Patri. "Beyond Folk Activism." *Cato Unbound*, April 6, 2009. https://www
.cato-unbound.org/2009/04/06/patri-friedman/beyond-folk-activism.

Galison, Peter. "War Against the Center." *Grey Room* 4 (Summer 2001): 5–33.

Garrett, Bradley. *Bunker*. New York: Scribner, 2020.

Gowdy-Wygant, Cecelia. *Cultivating Victory: The Women's Land Army and the Victory Garden Movement*. Pittsburgh, PA: University of Pittsburgh Press, 2013.

Greear, Jake. "Walking, Working, and Tinkering: Perception and Practice in Environmentalism." PhD diss., Johns Hopkins University, 2013. https://jscholarship
.library.jhu.edu/bitstream/handle/1774.2/36971/GREEAR-DISSERTATION-2013
.pdf.

Gribben, Crawford. *Survival and Resistance in Evangelical America: Christian Recon-struction in the Pacific Northwest.* Oxford: Oxford University Press, 2021.

Gross, John M., and Kenneth R. McInnis. *Kanban Made Simple: Demystifying and Applying Toyota's Legendary Manufacturing Process.* Nashville, TN: American Man-agement Association, 2003.

Grove, Nicole Sunday. "Receding Resilience: On the Planetary Moods of Disruption." *Review of International Studies* 49, no. 1 (2022): 3–19.

Guffey, Elizabeth. "Crafting Yesterday's Tomorrows: Retro-Futurism, Steampunk, and the Problem of Making in the Twenty-First Century." *Journal of Modern Craft* 7, no. 3 (November 1, 2014): 249–66.

Hall, John, and Udo Ludwig. "Veblen, Myrdal, and the Convergence Hypothesis: Toward an Institutionalist Critique." *Journal of Economic Issues* 44, no. 4 (2010): 943–61.

Heinrich, Thomas. "Cold War Armory: Military Contracting in Silicon Valley." *Enter-prise & Society* 3 (June 2002): 247–84.

Hodgson, Geoffrey M. "On Fuzzy Frontiers and Fragmented Foundations: Some Reflections on the Original and New Institutional Economics." *Journal of Institu-tional Economics* 10, no. 4 (2014): 591–611.

Honeck, Mischa. *Our Frontier Is the World: The Boy Scouts in the Age of American Ascen-dancy.* Illustrated ed. Ithaca, NY: Cornell University Press, 2018.

Horkheimer, Max, and Theodor W. Adorno. *Dialectic of Enlightenment.* Palo Alto, CA: Stanford University Press, 2002.

Hunsinger, Jeremy, and Andrew Schrock, eds. *Making Our World: The Hacker and Maker Movements in Context.* New York: Peter Lang, 2018.

Jennings, Ann, and William Waller. "Evolutionary Economics and Cultural Herme-neutics: Veblen, Cultural Relativism, and Blind Drift." *Journal of Economic Issues* 28, no. 4 (1994): 997–1030.

Johnson, Taylor N. " 'The Most Bombed Nation on Earth': Western Shoshone Resis-tance to the Nevada National Security Site." *Atlantic Journal of Communication* 26, no. 4 (October 9, 2018): 224–39.

Jordan, Benjamin René. *Modern Manhood and the Boy Scouts of America: Citizenship, Race, and the Environment, 1910–1930.* Chapel Hill: University of North Carolina Press, 2016.

Kaplan, Amy. "Manifest Domesticity." *American Literature* 70, no. 3 (1998): 581–606.

Kato, Masahide. "Nuclear Globalism Traversing Rockets, Satellites, and Nuclear War Via the Strategic Gaze." *Alternatives: Global, Local, Political* 18, no. 3 (Summer 1993): 339–60.

Kelly, Casey Ryan. *Apocalypse Man.* Columbus: Ohio State University Press, 2020.

Kelly, John D. "Reigniting the Anthropology of Capitalism: Returning to Veblen, After Postmodernism, After Postcoloniality." In *The Anthem Companion to Thorstein Veblen,* ed. Sidney Plotkin, 151–88. New York: Anthem, 2016.

Khazan, Olga. "The Brain Bro." *The Atlantic,* September 13, 2016. https://www.theatlantic.com/magazine/archive/2016/10/the-brain-bro/497546/.

Kingston, Christopher, and Gonzalo Caballero. "Comparing Theories of Institutional Change." *Journal of Institutional Economics* 5, no. 2 (2009): 151–80.

Kinley, Kylie. "Flashback Friday: When Behlen Manufacturing in Columbus Tested Shed with Atomic Bomb." *History Nebraska*, 2016. https://history.nebraska.gov/blog /flashback-friday-when-behlen-manufacturing-columbus-tested-shed-atomic -bomb.

Kirk, Andrew G. "Rereading the Nature of Atomic Doom Towns." *Environmental History* 17, no. 3 (July 2012): 634–47.

Kirk, Andrew G., and Kristian Purcell. *Doom Towns: The People and Landscapes of Atomic Testing, a Graphic History.* Oxford: Oxford University Press, 2016.

Kirsch, Robert. "You Can't Handicraft the Apocalypse: The Invidious Consequences of 'Opting Out.'" *New Political Science* 41, no. 4 (2019): 529–43.

Klein, Naomi. *The Shock Doctrine: The Rise of Disaster Capitalism.* New York: Picador USA, 2008.

Klinger, Julie Michelle. *Rare Earth Frontiers.* Ithaca, NY: Cornell University Press, 2018.

Kotsko, Adam. *Neoliberalism's Demons.* Stanford, CA: Stanford University Press, 2018.

Lampkin, Jack A. "Mapping the Terrain of an Astro-Green Criminology: A Case for Extending the Green Criminological Lens Outside of Planet Earth." *International Journal of Space Politics & Policy* 18, no. 3 (2020): 238–59.

Lavigne, Carlen. "Making the End Times Great Again." In *The Routledge Companion to Gender and Science Fiction*, ed. Lisa Yaszek, Sonja Fritzsche, Keren Omry, and Wendy Gay Pearson, 79–86. London: Routledge, 2023.

Lawrence, Andy, Meredith L. Rawls, Moriba Jah, Aaron Boley, Federico Di Vruno, Simon Garrington, Michael Kramer, et al. "The Case for Space Environmentalism." *Nature Astronomy* 6 (April 2022): 228–35.

Lawson, Tony. "Process, Order and Stability in Veblen." *Cambridge Journal of Economics* 39, no. 4 (2015): 993–1030.

Lay, James S. "A Report to the National Security Council—NSC 68." Truman Papers. Charlottesville, VA: Miller Center, April 12, 1950. http://web1.millercenter.org/cpc /brownell/mod5-doc1-NSC-68.pdf.

Lécuyer, Christophe. *Making Silicon Valley Innovation and the Growth of High Tech, 1930–1970.* Cambridge, MA: MIT Press, 2007.

Lepore, Jill. "The Disruption Machine." *New Yorker*, June 16, 2014.

Levina, Maria. "Disrupt or Die: Mobile Health and Disruptive Innovation as Body Politics." *Television and New Media* 18, no. 6 (2017): 548–64.

Luke, Timothy W. *Anthropocene Alerts.* Candor, NY: Telos, 2020.

——. "Beyond Prepper Culture as Right-Wing Extremism: Selling Preparedness to Everyday Consumers as How to Survive the End of the World on a Budget." *Fast Capitalism* 18, no. 1 (2021): 50–62.

——. "The Climate Change Imaginary." *Current Sociology Monograph* 63, no. 2 (2015): 280–96.

——. *Ecocritique: Contesting the Politics of Nature, Economy, and Culture.* Minneapolis: University of Minnesota Press, 1997.

——. *Ideology and Soviet Industrialization.* Westport, CT: Greenwood, 1985.

——. "Kanban Capitalism: Power, Identity, and the Exchange in Cyberspace." 1998.

——. "One-Dimensional Man: A Systematic Critique of Human Domination and Nature-Society Relations." *Organization and Environment* 13, no. 1 (March 2000): 95–101.

——. "What Is Information? The Neoliberal Turn, Digitalization, and Interdisciplinarity." In *Transforming Higher Education: Economy, Democracy, and the University,* ed. Stephen J. Rosow and Thomas Kriger. Lanham, MD: Lexington, 2010.

Lynch, Casey R. " 'Vote with Your Feet': Neoliberalism, the Democratic Nation-State, and Utopian Enclave Libertarianism." *Political Geography* 59 (2017): 82–91.

Maalsen, Sophia, and Jathan Sadowski. "The Smart Home on FIRE: Amplifying and Accelerating Domestic Surveillance." *Surveillance & Society* 17, no. 1/2 (2019): 118–24.

MacDonald, Robert H. *Sons of the Empire: The Frontier and the Boy Scout Movement, 1890–1918.* Toronto, CA: University of Toronto Press, 1993.

Macleod, David. "Original Intent: Establishing the Creed and Control of Boy Scouting in the United States." In *Scouting Frontiers: Youth and the Scout Movement's First Century,* ed. Nelson R. Block and Tammy M. Proctor. Newcastle-upon-Tyne: Cambridge Scholars Publishing, 2009.

Marcuse, Herbert. *Eros and Civilization: Philosophical Inquiry Into Freud.* Boston: Beacon, 1992.

——. *One-Dimensional Man.* Boston: Beacon, 1968.

Marino, Alessandra, and Thomas Cheney. "Centering Environmentalism in Space Governance: Interrogating Dominance and Authority Through a Critical Legal Geography of Outer Space." *Space Policy* 63 (2023): 1–10.

Masco, Joseph. *The Future of Fallout, and Other Episodes in Radioactive World-Making.* Durham, NC: Duke University Press, 2021.

Matheson, Calum. "Enjoying the Heat: Anxiety, Fantasy, and Doomsday Prepping." In *Lacan and the Environment,* Palgrave Lacan Series, 135–53. Cham: Palgrave, 2021.

Mayhew, Anne. "Culture: Core Concept under Attack." *Journal of Economic Issues* 21, no. 2 (1987): 586–603.

McCarthy, Kevin. "Text—H.R.2262—114th Congress (2015–2016): U.S. Commercial Space Launch Competitiveness Act." Legislation, November 25, 2015. https://www.congress.gov/bill/114th-congress/house-bill/2262/text.

McEnaney, Laura. *Civil Defense Begins at Home: Militarization Meets Everyday Life in the Fifties.* Princeton, NJ: Princeton University Press, 2000.

McFarland, Floyd B. "Thorstein Veblen Versus the Institutionalists." *Review of Radical Political Economics* 17, no. 4 (1985): 95–105.

McHugh, Josh. "For the Love of Hacking." *Forbes.* August 10, 1998. https://www.forbes.com/forbes/1998/0810/6203094a.html.

Messeri, Lisa. "Gestures of Cosmic Relation and the Search for Another Earth." *Environmental Humanities* 9, no. 2 (November 2017).

Miller, Char. "In the Sweat of Our Brow: Citizenship in American Domestic Practice During WWII—Victory Gardens." *Journal of American Culture* 26, no. 3 (2003): 395–409.

Mills, Michael F. "Preparing for the Unknown . . . Unknowns: 'Doomsday' Prepping and Disaster Risk Anxiety in the United States." *Journal of Risk Research* 22, no. 10 (October 3, 2019): 1267–79.

Mills, Sarah. "'An Instruction in Good Citizenship': Scouting and the Historical Geographies of Citizenship Education." *Transactions—Institute of British Geographers (1965)* 38, no. 1 (2013): 120–34.

Mirowski, Philip, and Dieter Plehwe. *The Road from Mont Pèlerin*. Cambridge, MA: Harvard University Press, 2009.

Mirr, Nicholas A. "Defending the Right to Repair: An Argument for Federal Legislation Guaranteeing the Right to Repair." *Iowa Law Review* 105, no. 5 (July 2020): 2393–2424.

Mitchell, Ross E. "Learning from Veblen's Masterless Man for Grassroots Democratic Change." In *The Anthem Companion to Thorstein Veblen*, ed. Sidney Plotkin, 237–56. New York: Anthem, 2016.

Mitchell, Scott. "Narratives of Resistance and Repair in Consumer Society." *Third Text* 32, no. 1 (January 2, 2018): 55–67.

Morin, Jean-Frederic, and Benjamin Richard. "Astro-Environmentalism: Towards a Polycentric Governance of Space Debris." *Global Policy* 12, no. 4 (September 2021): 568–73.

Morozov, Evgeny. "Making It." *New Yorker*, January 13, 2014. https://www.newyorker.com/magazine/2014/01/13/making-it-2.

Nancy, Jean-Luc. *After Fukushima*. New York: Fordham University Press, 2014.

National War Garden Commission. "Home Canning & Drying of Vegetables & Fruits." Washington, DC: National War Garden Commission, 1919. https://archive.org/details/homecanningdryino1nati/page/n1/mode/2up.

Nixon, Rob. *Slow Violence and the Environmentalism of the Poor*. Cambridge, MA: Harvard University Press, 2013.

Oakes, Guy. *The Imaginary War: Civil Defense and American Cold War Culture*. London: Oxford University Press, 1995.

Oelschlaeger, Max. *The Idea of Wilderness from Prehistory to the Age of Ecology*. New Haven, CT: Yale University Press, 1991.

O'Hara, Phillip. "Veblen's Critique of Marx's Philosophical Preconceptions of Political Economy." *European Journal of the History of Economic Thought* 4, no. 1 (1997): 65–91.

Olson, Valerie, and Lisa Messeri. "Beyond the Anthropocene: Un-Earthing an Epoch." *Environment and Society* 6, no. 1 (January 1, 2015).

Park, Lisa Sun-Hee, and David Naguib Pellow. *The Silicon Valley of Dreams: Environmental Justice, Immigrant Workers, and the High-Tech Global Economy*. New York: New York University Press, 2002.

Patterson, J. M. "The Patriotic Garden: Somebody Has to Raise Everything You Eat." *Garden Magazine*, June 1917.

Peterson, Val. "Panic: The Ultimate Weapon?" *Colliers*, August 21, 1953.

Pike, David L. "Haunted Mountains, Supershelters, and the Afterlives of Cold War Infrastructure." *Journal for the Study of Religion, Nature, and Culture* 13, no. 2 (2019): 208–29.

Plotkin, Sidney. "The Critic as Quietist: Thorstein Veblen's Radical Realism." *Common Knowledge* 16, no. 1 (December 25, 2009): 79–94.

——. *Veblen's America: The Conspicuous Case of Donald J. Trump*. New York: Anthem, 2018.

Plotkin, Sidney, and Rick Tilman. *The Political Ideas of Thorstein Veblen*. New Haven, CT: Yale University Press, 2011.

Powell, Liam J. S. "America's Nuclear Wasteland: Conflict Landscape, Simulation, and 'Nonplace' at the Nevada Test Site." In *Beyond the Dead Horizon: Studies in Modern Conflict Archaeology*, 218–29. Oxford: Oxbow, 2012.

Rabinbach, Anson. *The Human Motor*. Berkeley: University of California Press, 1992.

Raymer, Emilie J. "A Man of His Time: Thorstein Veblen and the University of Chicago Darwinists." *Journal of the History of Biology* 46, no. 4 (2013): 669–98.

Reynolds, Glenn H., and Robert P. Merges. *Outer Space: Problems of Law and Policy*. 2nd ed. Boulder, CO: Westview, 1997.

Richardson, Mark. "Pre-Hacked: Open Design and the Democratisation of Product Development." *New Media & Society* 18, no. 4 (April 1, 2016): 653–66.

Robin, Corey. *Fear: The History of a Political Idea*. London: Oxford University Press, 2006.

Rose, Kenneth. *One Nation Underground: The Fallout Shelter in American Culture*. New York: New York University Press, 2004.

Roy, Eleanor Ainge. "New Zealand Gave Peter Thiel Citizenship After He Spent Just 12 Days There." *The Guardian*, June 29, 2017. https://www.theguardian.com/world/2017/jun/29/new-zealand-gave-peter-thiel-citizenship-after-spending-just-12-days-there.

Scheer, Robert. *With Enough Shovels: Reagan, Bush, and Nuclear War*. New York: Vintage, 1982.

Schmitt, Carl. *Political Theology*. Chicago: University of Chicago Press, 2005.

Schnuer, Jenna. "This Startup Is Making Stylish Earthquake Survival Kits." *Entrepreneur*, March 13, 2015. https://www.entrepreneur.com/article/242518.

Schulz, Joy. "Making Men Into Boys: How the Boy Scouts of America Put on the Uniform of U.S. Imperialism and Became the Face of Twentieth-Century Masculinity." *Diplomatic History* 43, no. 5 (2019): 956–58.

Smith, Adam. *An Inquiry Into the Nature and Causes of the Wealth of Nations*. Simon & Brown, 2012.

Smith, Harrison, and Roger Burrows. "Software, Sovereignty, and the Post-Neoliberal Politics of Exit." *Theory, Culture, and Society* 38, no. 6 (2021): 143–66.

Spencer, Brett. "From Atomic Shelters to Arms Control: Libraries, Civil Defense, and American Militarism During the Cold War." *Information & Culture* 49, no. 3 (2014): 351–85.

Stamp, Elizabeth. "Billionaire Bunkers: How the 1% Are Preparing for the Apocalypse." *CNN.* https://www.cnn.com/style/article/doomsday-luxury-bunkers/index .html.

Steer, Cassandra. "Global Commons, Cosmic Commons: Implications of Military and Security Uses of Outer Space." *Georgetown Journal of International Affairs* 18, no. 1 (2017): 9–16.

Strauss, Neil. "Elon Musk: Inventor's Plans for Outer Space, Cars, Finding Love." *Rolling Stone*, November 15, 2017. https://www.rollingstone.com/culture/culture-features /elon-musk-the-architect-of-tomorrow-120850/.

Suddaby, Roy. "Can Institutional Theory Be Critical?" *Journal of Management Inquiry* 24, no. 1 (January 1, 2015): 93–95.

SurvivalRealty.com. "Rural, Sustainable, Off-Grid Property and Agents." https://www .survivalrealty.com/.

Szasz, Andrew. *Shopping Our Way to Safety.* Minneapolis: University of Minnesota Press, 2009.

Takemura, Noriyoshi. "Astro-Green Criminology: A New Perspective Against Space Capitalism." *Toin University of Yokohama Research Bulletin* 40 (June 2019): 7–16.

Thiel, Peter. "The Education of a Libertarian." *Cato Unbound*, April 13, 2009. https:// www.cato-unbound.org/2009/04/13/peter-thiel/education-libertarian.

Tilman, Rick. "Some Recent Interpretations of Thorstein Veblen's Theory of Institutional Change." *Journal of Economic Issues* 21, no. 2 (1987): 683–90.

——. "Thorstein Veblen: Science, Revolution, and the Persistence of Atavistic Continuities." In *Institutional Economics and the Theory of Social Value: Essays in Honor of Marc R. Tool*, ed. Charles M. A. Clark, 241–48. Boston: Springer, 1995.

——. "Thorstein Veblen's Views on American 'Exceptionalism': An Interpretation." *Journal of Economic Issues* 39, no. 1 (2005): 177–204.

Tool, Marc R. *Evolutionary Economics: Foundations of Institutional Thought.* M. E. Sharpe, 1988.

Triggs, Oscar Lovell. *Chapters in the History of the Arts and Crafts Movement.* Bohemia Guild of the Industrial Art League, 1902.

Truman, Harry S. "Statement by the President Upon Signing the Federal Civil Defense Act of 1950." National Archives, Harry S. Truman Library and Museum, January 12, 1951. https://www.trumanlibrary.gov/library/public-papers/10/statement-president -upon-signing-federal-civil-defense-act-1950.

Turner, Fred. *From Counterculture to Cyberculture.* Chicago: University of Chicago Press, 2006.

United Nations Office for Outer Space Affairs. "RES 2222 (XXI)." 1996. https://www .unoosa.org/oosa/oosadoc/data/resolutions/1966/general_assembly_21st_session /res_2222_xxi.html.

Vanderbilt, Tom. *Survival City: Adventures Among the Ruins of Atomic America*. Chicago: University of Chicago Press, 2010.

Veblen, Thorstein. *Absentee Ownership: Business Enterprise in Recent Times—the Case of America*. New Brunswick, NJ: Routledge, 1996.

——. *The Engineers and the Price System*. B. W. Huebsch, Incorporated, 1921.

——. *Essays in Our Changing Order*. Transaction, 1997.

——. *The Higher Learning in America: A Memorandum on the Conduct of Universities by Business Men*. Baltimore, MD: Johns Hopkins University Press, 1926.

——. *Imperial Germany and the Industrial Revolution*. London: Macmillan, 1915.

——. *The Instinct of Workmanship: And the State of Industrial Arts*. Macmillan, 1914.

——. "The Socialist Economics of Karl Marx and His Followers." *Quarterly Journal of Economics* 21, no. 2 (1907): 299–322.

——. *The Theory of Business Enterprise*. New York: C. Scribner's Sons, 1915.

——. *The Theory of the Leisure Class*. Ed. Martha Banta. Oxford: Oxford University Press, 2009.

——. "Using the I.W.W. to Harvest Grain." *Journal of Political Economy* 40, no. 6 (1932): 797–807.

——. *The Vested Interests and the Common Man: The Modern Point of View and the New Order*. New York: B. W. Huebsch, 1920.

Virilio, Paul. *Bunker Archeology*. Hudson, NY: Princeton Architectural Press, 1994.

——. *Speed and Politics*. Semiotext(e) Foreign Agent Series. South Pasadena, CA: Semiotext(e), 2006.

Vitale, Patrick. "Wages of War: Manufacturing Nationalism During World War II." *Antipode* 43, no. 3 (2010): 783–819.

Vrooman, Carl. "The Patriotic Garden: Crop Conservation and Distribution." *Garden and Home Builder*, August 1917.

Waller, William. "Public Policy Adrift: Veblen's Blind Drift and Neoliberalism." *Forum for Social Economics* 46, no. 3 (2017): 223–33.

Waters, Colin N., James P. M. Syvitski, Agnieszka Gałuszka, Gary J. Hancock, Jan Zalasiewicz, Alejandro Cearreta, Jacques Grinevald, et al. "Can Nuclear Weapons Fallout Mark the Beginning of the Anthropocene Epoch?" *Bulletin of the Atomic Scientists* 71, no. 3 (May 1, 2015): 46–57.

Watson, Bruce. "We Couldn't Run, So We Hoped We Could Hide." *Smithsonian Magazine*, 1994.

Weber, Andrew. "Texas Winter Storm Death Toll Goes Up to 210, Including 43 Deaths in Harris County." *Houston Public Media*, July 14, 2021. https://www.houstonpub licmedia.org/articles/news/energy-environment/2021/07/14/403191/texas-winter -storm-death-toll-goes-up-to-210-including-43-deaths-in-harris-county/.

Weber, Max. *Max Weber on the Methodology of the Social Sciences*. Free Press, 1949.

Westberg Brostrom, Anna. " 'Wild Scouts': Swedish Scouting Preparing Responsible Citizens for the Twenty-First Century." *Child & Youth Services* 34, no. 1 (2013): 9–22.

Whyte, William H., Jr. *The Organization Man*. Doubleday Anchor, 1957.

Wiebe, Sarah Marie, and Jennifer Lawrence, eds. *Biopolitical Disaster*. New York: Routledge, 2017.

Wills, John. "Exploding the 1950s Consumer Dream." *Pacific Historical Review* 88, no. 3 (2019): 410–38.

Wilson, Woodrow. "The President to the People." *Garden and Home Builder*, 1917. https://babel.hathitrust.org/cgi/pt?id=coo.31924094248956&view=1up&seq=230&q1=woodrow%20wilson.

Wolin, Sheldon S. *Fugitive Democracy and Other Essays*. Princeton, NJ: Princeton University Press, 2016.

Wolschke-Bulmahn, Joachim. "From the War-Garden to the Victory Garden: Political Aspects of Garden Culture in the United States During World War I." *Landscape Journal* 11, no. 1 (Spring 1992): 51–57.

Wray, L. Randall. "Veblen's 'Theory of Business Enterprise' and Keynes's Monetary Theory of Production." *Journal of Economic Issues* 41, no. 2 (2007): 617–24.

Wunder, Timothy, and Thomas Kemp. "Institutionalism and the State: Founding Views Reexamined." *Forum for Social Economics* 37, no. 1 (2008): 27–42.

Zalaslewlcz, Jan, Colin N. Waters, Mark Williams, Anthony D. Barnosky, Alejandro Cearreta, Paul Crutzen, Erle Ellis, et al. "When Did the Anthropocene Begin? A Mid-Twentieth Century Boundary Level Is Stratigraphically Optimal." *Quaternary International* 383 (October 5, 2015): 196–203.

Zaveri, Mihir, Matthew Haag, Adam Playford, and Nate Schweber. "How the Storm Turned Basement Apartments Into Death Traps." *New York Times*, September 2, 2021. https://www.nytimes.com/2021/09/02/nyregion/basement-apartment-floods-deaths.html.

INDEX